POSSESSED
BY THE
DEVIL

POSSESSED BY THE DEVIL

THE HISTORY OF THE ISLANDMAGEE WITCH TRIALS 1711

ANDREW SNEDDON

The History Press

In memory of Andrew Sneddon (1948–2015)

First published 2013
This edition published 2024

The History Press
97 St George's Place, Cheltenham,
Gloucestershire, GL50 3QB
www.thehistorypress.co.uk

British Library Cataloguing in Publication Data.
A catalogue record for this book is available from the British Library.

ISBN 978 1 80399 270 9

Typesetting and origination by The History Press
Printed and bound in Great Britain by TJ Books Limited, Padstow, Cornwall.

Trees for Life

Contents

For if any wicked person affirms, or any crack'd brain girl imagines, or any lying spirit makes her believe, that she sees any old woman, or other person pursuing her in her visions, the defenders of the vulgar witchcraft tack an imaginary, unprov'd compact to the deposition, and hang the accus'd parties for things that were doing, when they were perhaps, asleep upon their beds, or saying their prayers; or, perhaps, in the accusers own possession, with double irons upon them.

Bishop of Down and Connor (1721-39), Francis Hutchinson, *An Historical Essay Concerning Witchcraft* ... (London, 1st ed., 1718), vii.

Acknowledgements
(First Edition)

Without the help and support (academic and otherwise) of my wife, Dr Leanne McCormick, this book would not have been possible and this is why it is dedicated to her. I must also thank my mum and dad, sister Sharon and her husband Steve, as well as my friend Peter Moore. I thank Dr Neal Garnham, for reading early drafts, sharing his expertise on Irish crime and law, and providing me with references and documents he has collected over the years in relation to Carrickfergus, County Antrim. I am also indebted to Brenda Collins for providing archival material and references to the Dunbars of Lisburn, and to Professor David Hayton for reading draft chapters at very short notice just before Christmas 2012. Dr Nerys Young also looked over drafts of early chapters for me, and her dad, David, tracked down a rare book for me on a well-known auction site! I would also like to thank the staff at the library of the University of Ulster at Coleraine, and those of the Public Record Office of Northern Ireland (PRONI), who are not only erstwhile colleagues but friends, namely Iain Fleming, Wesley Geddis, Carrie Green, Janet Hancock, Graham Jackson, Ian Montgomery and Stephen Scarth.

I must also thank postgraduate, MRes and PhD students in history at the University of Ulster, Coleraine, who have completed (or are currently completing) theses relating to British and Irish witchcraft under my supervision (John Fulton, Cara Hanley, Robert Rock and Jodie Shevlin), as well as successive undergraduate dissertation students, and those who have taken my Witchcraft and Magic module (HIS304) – I have learned much about Irish witchcraft from teaching you.

Acknowledgements
(Second Edition)

Eleven years is a long time in History and it has been that long since the publication of the first edition of this book. The wonderful reception it received from readers (for which I am truly grateful) gave me the encouragement to continue researching the case in the intervening years. Thanks also to those who invited me to talk about the trial in person, and on television, radio and in podcasts. Without this support, I would not have attempted a new edition.

I have accumulated more debts to individuals and institutions than it is possible to mention here. In addition to those already cited in the first edition, however, special thanks to the following people. Firstly, I owe a large debt for help and advice given by archival and library staff at PRONI; Queen's University Library, Belfast; Ulster University Library, Coleraine; The Presbyterian Historical Society, Belfast; Belfast Central Library; The Royal Irish Academy, Dublin; The National Library of Ireland, Dublin; and The British Library, London. A big thanks to Adam Turkington (Seedhead Arts) for organising public talks in Belfast for me between 2016 and 2022. Thanks also to Elizabeth Shaw at The History Press, and to Dr Conor Reidy, for their editorial expertise.

At Ulster University, I have benefited greatly from the guidance and support of the Head of School of Arts and Humanities, Prof. Tom Maguire and the Research and Impact Team, especially Karen Reid, Prof. Ian Thatcher and Maria Prince. In 2023, two university prizes provided the resources and time to complete this book: the Ulster University Sabbatical Award, and the Distinguished Researcher Award. Thanks also to my friends and colleagues in the School of Arts and Humanities for the innumerable times they helped me with my research and provided stimulating conversation about shared interests and projects: Dr Lauren Bell, Dr Katherine Byrne, Brian Coyle, Dr Frank Ferguson, Prof. Justin Magee, Sabrina Minter, Dr James Ward and Dr Nerys Young. I would also like to thank David Campbell, Dr Shannon Devlin, Dr Helen Jackson, Dr Elizabeth Kiely (University College, Cork) and Dr Victoria McCollum for reinvigorating my interest in the trials and cementing my belief in their historical importance through our work on the 'Islandmagee Witches, 1711 Creative and Digital Project'. This project aims to bring the story of the Islandmagee witches to wider audiences by producing a range of creative and digital outputs, including a video game, a virtual reality application, an animated film, an interactive website and a graphic novel (see project website, w1711.org).

I would also like to thank Prof. Guy Beiner (Boston College), Dr Ciara Breathnach (University of Limerick), Dr Leanne Calvert (University of Hertfordshire), Prof. Owen Davies (University of Hertfordshire), Prof. Marion Gibson (University of Exeter), Dr Jan Machielsen (Cardiff University), Prof. Diane Purkiss (University of Oxford), Dr Clodagh Tait (Mary Immaculate College), Dr Lisa Tallis (Cardiff University) and Dr Thomas Waters (Imperial College, London) for involving me in projects, workshops and conferences that widened my knowledge of the family, folklore, gender and the supernatural beyond the early modern world and into the nineteenth and twentieth centuries. I also want to thank Adrian Rice, whose poetry and conversation made a deep impression on my work on cultural representations of the Islandmagee trials.

I would also like to thank my friends for their continuing support, many of whom are also colleagues and have already been mentioned, including Graham Jackson, Jonathan Hinder and Peter Moore. Special thanks to Stephen Scarth who has, from the very start of research into the Islandmagee witches, accompanied me on many field trips to places associated with the uncanny in Northern Ireland. Thanks again to my mother, to my in-laws, Jim and Vivian McCormick, and to the Reids (Pippa, Sharon and Steve) for their support. Once again, I owe the greatest debt of gratitude to my wife Prof. Leanne McCormick and my two children, Andrew and James. I have dedicated this new edition to my father, Andrew Sneddon, who died in 2015. He was a plumber who left school at 15 and I learned more from him than anyone else about politics, history and art.

Preface
(First Edition)

In early April 1711, a Dublin newspaper reported that the previous week, '8 witches were try'd at the Assizes of Carrickfergus, for bewitching a young gentlewoman, were found guilty, and ... imprisoned for a year and a day, and 4 times pilloried.'[1] This was, of course, the infamous trial of the Islandmagee witches, who were convicted of bewitching a teenage girl, Mary Dunbar. Although countless witchcraft trials were held in early modern Europe during the 'witch-hunts', a period that witnessed the execution of around 50,000 people, the Islandmagee case was one of only a handful held in Ireland under the Irish Witchcraft Act of 1586. More importantly, it involved the mysterious death of a minister's wife, demonic haunting and possession, spectral visitations, beneficial magic, and bewitched bonnets. It was also intimately related to infamous witchcraft cases in late seventeenth-century England, Scotland and Salem, New England.

The Islandmagee witches have long intrigued writers, with the nineteenth century seeing the first flurry of narrative accounts of the trial, provided in books, parish surveys, newspapers and periodicals.[2] The early twentieth century saw the publication of more narrative accounts, albeit ones more firmly rooted in local history[3] and the history of Irish witchcraft and demonology.[4] More recent treatments, however, have eschewed putting the case in its wider historical context,[5] with one going as far as fictionalising substantial portions of dialogue and events, as well as names, ages and professions of people involved: even period detail is 'imagined' rather than based on historical research.[6]

The approach taken in this book is different. It aims to be readable and intelligible to the interested reader by limiting the amount of footnotes and references, and the provision of supplementary explanatory material. However, it rests on solid historical research. The narrative presented, arguments made, and hypotheses posed, are all based on surviving documents from the early modern period, as well as being informed by an understanding of eighteenth-century Ireland and recent developments in the history of witchcraft trials and belief. This study has also been made possible by the fact that the Islandmagee case is one of the best-documented witchcraft trials in the British Isles, more so even than some infamous seventeenth-century English witch trials, to which whole books have been dedicated.[7] There are surviving pre-trial depositions or witness statements (taken by Mayor of Carrickfergus, Edward Clements in early 1711), a lengthy, anonymous, contemporary account,[8] and letters written by eyewitnesses present at the trial.[9]

I have also tried to bring the people involved in the case to life, which has proven to be one of the most challenging aspects of my research. It is extremely difficult to recover for eighteenth-century Ulster, due to incomplete record keeping and the destruction of archives, genealogical data of the type so readily available for other countries. As a result, some of the lives (and even names) of a minority of the protagonists remain hidden from view, probably forever. It has also been my aim to bring the story of the Islandmagee witches to a wider audience, as interest in, and knowledge of, it has undoubtedly waned in the last few years. So much so that, had I not released a press statement (via the University of Ulster's Media and Corporate Relations Office), the 300-year anniversary of the trial would have passed by unnoticed. This is in complete contrast to the commemorations in 2012 of the Lancaster witchcraft trial of 1612, when academic conferences were held, books and novels published, plays performed, and day trips to sites of historical interest organised. Although the human cost was far greater in the Lancaster case, in terms of adding to our understanding of witchcraft, the Islandmagee trial is surely just as important.

The book demonstrates that people living in Ireland, both among indigenous and settler populations, and in common with every other continent in the world at some time in their history, believed in witches, and that these beliefs had serious and lasting effects on the culture and society in Ireland. It also represents an exploration of Protestant *mentalities* in the north of Ireland at the beginning of the eighteenth century, revealing a place where belief in the moral, magical universe remained very strong, and where immaterial essences constantly interfered in the lives of humankind: from God and the Devil, to good and evil spirits. It also explains why Mary Dunbar's accusation was taken seriously by Antrim clergy, wealthy local elites and agents of law enforcement, when other similar cases were not. This in its turn throws light on how religious bodies and the criminal justice system handled witchcraft accusation at that time. Finally, the book demonstrates how a unique blend of local and national politics, religious beliefs, social tensions, and cultural persuasion came together to rob Ireland of any claim to have been a (witchcraft) trial-free island. Consequently, it follows in a tradition of recent case studies of individual trials (see the work of James Sharpe and Phillip Almond, among others) which add a layer of complexity to the 'one size fits all' approach to explaining patterns of accusation, prosecution and conviction favoured by some historians in the past.

Dr Andrew Sneddon
Ballymoney, County Antrim, December 2012

Preface
(Second Edition)

This expanded and revised edition walks a tightrope between bringing the book up to date by incorporating research completed over the last decade, and maintaining the characteristics that over the years readers have told me they liked about the original work. Some sections and chapters have been extensively rewritten while others have been extended or reworked. New primary material has been added, along with an extended discussion of the production and provenance of the original documents used in this book. I have included new research on Mary Dunbar and William Sellor, and how the trials were remembered in the local community and at a national level in newspapers and in historical and creative writing.

During the last decade or so, writing on witchcraft and magic in the early modern (c.1500–1800) and modern (post-1800) worlds has grown exponentially. I have added to this avalanche of words and paper in a small way by continuing to write monographs, articles, and edited book chapters on witchcraft and magic in Ireland. To include all or even most of the recent work on European witchcraft and magic would be tantamount to writing a new book. Additions to historiography in this edition have been made in the main body of the text where it has been necessary to explain, correct, augment, or expand upon specific arguments, themes or facts. Many chapters have been rewritten substantially as a result, specifically chapters 1, 2, 4, 6, 9, and 10. Two new chapters have been added. I have expanded the Author's Notes section to reflect these changes and some of the advances made in Irish witchcraft historiography more generally. The Further Reading section has been expanded to include important secondary work on the main themes of the book.

Since writing this book, micro-histories of individual trials have become even more important to our understanding of early modern witch trials and their social and cultural context. As I have said elsewhere, micro-studies of witch trials such as the one you are about to read provide a glimpse of how witchcraft trials were experienced by those caught up in them. They allow us to examine the limits and extent of human agency, 'demonstrating the freedoms individuals may have beyond constraining, normative and prescriptive systems'. I think this comes to the fore in the Islandmagee case, where agency and resistance 'is shown by the convicted witches in their everyday lives and in response to witchcraft accusations laid against them'.[1] However, this book was also consciously structured as a narrative rather than thematically arranged, with historical context and explanation being tightly woven into the fabric of the storytelling. This allowed me to carefully explore the lives, beliefs and environments of the individuals involved and provided space to discuss them in the detail they deserve, while at the same time saying something useful about Irish witchcraft and witch-hunts in understudied, peripheral parts of early modern Europe. Narrative history became devalued in mainstream, academic historical scholarship during the early part of the twentieth century and was rejected as part of the 'Great Men' histories that previously dominated history writing. This type of history was increasingly replaced with problem-orientated history, centring on specific research questions and wider use of primary material. In the latter half of the century, social history developed and used new theoretical tools and approaches taken from critical studies and the social sciences to study groups, topics and people marginalised in traditional histories. This included 'History from Below' focusing on ordinary people, Medical History, Gender History,

Queer History, and more recently, Emotional History. In common with these new historiographies, the narrative-driven micro-history this book represents provides a rare insight into the lives of marginalised groups. In County Antrim in the early eighteenth century this included women, religious minorities, people with disabilities, and the poor. That is not to say social and political elites, those with education, money and power, are neglected.

Dr Andrew Sneddon
Ballymoney, County Antrim, April 2024

Author's Notes

Notes on Sources and Referencing[1]

Internal evidence from our chief source for the Islandmagee witch trials, an anonymous, pamphlet account, suggests that it was written in late 1711. It presents such a detailed description of the case that its author was undoubtedly well acquainted with Islandmagee and its inhabitants, and was probably personally involved in the case. The manuscript of this account was edited and published in Belfast in 1822 by Carrickfergus grocer, antiquary and historian Samuel McSkimin (died 1843).[2]

This first edition was printed by Joseph Smyth, who was 'one of the giants of popular publishing in early nineteenth century Belfast'.[3] A unique copy of this pamphlet forms part of the papers of solicitor, antiquary and nationalist Francis Joseph Bigger, which are held in Belfast Central Library.[4] Before Bigger bought the pamphlet from an unknown party, it was in the possession of Revd Classon Emmett Porter (died 1885). Porter was the lifelong, non-subscribing Presbyterian minister for Larne, County Antrim, and a local historian and biographer. In this latter capacity, he 'wrote a series of articles on Ulster's ghosts and witchcraft trials for the *Northern Whig* newspaper which were reprinted in book form as *Witches, Warlocks and Ghosts* (Belfast, 1885)'. This book included a lengthy account of the first Islandmagee trial, which was based on a close reading of McSkimin's 1822 edition.[5] The inscription on the title page of the Porter/Bigger copy suggests that Porter received

it as a gift from historian of Belfast George Benn. Benn and Porter frequently corresponded on historical and antiquarian matters from the
late 1860s until the early 1880s.[6] Sometime between 'May 1875' and
his death in 1885, Porter wrote various notes on the Islandmagee trial
on its flyleaf, including the following: 'Mr Edward Blaine of Glenone
[County Londonderry] has the original Manuscript from which this
[pamphlet] is printed. I have seen what is left of this.' He confirmed the
manuscript's existence in *Witches, Warlocks and Ghosts*: 'This narrative
continued for many years in manuscript, in which form we have seen
its existing remains.'[7] Given the perilous condition of the manuscript
version at the end of the nineteenth century, it is unsurprising it did not
survive into the twenty-first century.

As an appendix to the 1822 edition, McSkimin added a detailed letter
about the day of the trial written in April 1711, by trial attendee Revd
William Tisdall (see chapter 8). This was a slightly shorter, edited version of the original letter first published in January 1775 in the literary
periodical, the *Hibernian Magazine*.[8] The original, manuscript version of
this letter is no longer extant. A privately printed second edition of the
pamphlet account appeared in the early twentieth century, which apart
from font size and pagination it is identical to the first edition. It also
bears a slightly different title.[9]

In 1896, Robert Magill Young, Belfast-based architect and antiquarian,
published the 'Depositions in the case of the Island Magee Witches'.[10]
These statements were taken before the trial, in early March 1711, from
key witnesses by Mayor Edward Clements. Young based his publication
on transcriptions made in the 1860s by Belfast-born antiquarian William
Pinkerton, from manuscripts held in Trinity College, Dublin (TCD),[11]
where they are still stored.[12] I have compared Young's version to the
original TCD manuscript and found it an exact copy. The depositions
played an important administrative role in the prosecution and
conviction of the Islandmagee witches (see chapter 8), but more than
that provide access to the voices of the main accusers and witnesses in
the case, including Mary Dunbar, albeit mediated through the men who
took down the statements. They are the sole surviving example of pre-
trial depositions for an Irish witchcraft case.[13]

Quotations and endnotes are used primarily to detail material written before 1900. Quotations from primary sources not referenced in endnotes have been taken from the second edition of the pamphlet account, *THE ISLANDMAGEE WITCHES*. The *Hibernian Magazine* copy of Tisdall's letter has been used in this book, as have the original manuscript depositions held in TCD. Modern secondary sources are detailed in an annotated bibliography contained in the Further Reading section, which is arranged by chapter. This reading list also provides an overview of witchcraft literature and a starting point for those new to the themes covered in this book.

Notes on Spelling and Terms Used

When quoting from primary source documents or publications, grammar, punctuation and spelling (as much as the maintenance of sense allows) have been kept as in the original. Capitalisation has been modernised and the abbreviation 'ye' has been replaced with 'the'. The terms 'fits' and 'fitting' are used imprecisely in surviving documents to refer to a variety of symptoms associated with demonic possession, but chiefly to contortions and convulsions involving writhing, shaking or trembling, and accompanied by shouting or screaming. Mary Dunbar also claimed that during some of her 'fits' she was attacked by the spectral or spirit forms of the accused 'witches'. 'Fits' and 'fitting' are used in this book to describe Dunbar's possession in contemporary sources but modern approximations, seizure and seizures, have also been employed.

Notes on Dates

The dates given in this book are given in the form related in the primary sources, but the new year is taken to begin on 1 January and not on 25 March as stipulated in the Julian Calendar. The official switch to the Gregorian calendar, where the new year begins on 1 January, occurred in 1752.

Who's Who?

A variety of spellings are used in contemporary sources for those involved in the Islandmagee witchcraft case. For example, the family name Hattridge is also spelled Hatterick, Hattrick and Haltridge. I have used one surname consistently, Haltridge, to avoid confusion and because it is the one used most frequently in surviving sources. I have adopted this approach for the rest of the surnames mentioned in the book.

THE HALTRIDGE FAMILY
The Haltridge residence, Knowehead House, stood in the townland of Kilcoan More in mid-west Islandmagee, County Antrim.

Revd John Haltridge (died 1697) – Scottish-born, Presbyterian minister of Islandmagee from 1674.

Mrs Ann Haltridge (died 1711) – widow to John, a pious and respected neighbour, she was believed to have been bewitched to death.

James Haltridge – son of John and Ann, he was absent from Islandmagee when a large part of the incidents described below took place. When he returned to Knowehead House in late March he gave a pre-trial deposition or statement to Mayor Edward Clements. He later appeared as witness for the prosecution at the first trial on 31 March 1711.

Miss Haltridge (forename unknown) – daughter of John and Ann and sister to James. She brought Mary Dunbar to Islandmagee for the first time in February 1711.

Young Mrs Haltridge (forename unknown) – wife of James Haltridge, she had two young children and was the only woman to give evidence at the trial.

Mary Dunbar – a 'victim' of demonic possession and witchcraft, she was eighteen years of age in February 1711. Educated and articulate, Dunbar came from a gentry family in Castlereagh, County Down, and was first cousin to James Haltridge and his sister.

Margaret Spear – a servant to the Haltridge family who witnessed much of the supernatural phenomena said to have occurred in the Haltridge house in Islandmagee.

THE ISLANDMAGEE WITCHES

Catherine McCalmond – was considered by her neighbours to be of 'an ill fame' and 'an ignorant irreligious woman'. She lived close to Revd Robert Sinclair in the townland of Balloo in mid-east Islandmagee.[14]

Janet Liston – from Islandmagee, was married to William Sellor and by 1711 had a long-standing reputation for dabbling in witchcraft. She was described by Mary Dunbar as wearing dirty clothes and having a dirty face. Mary referred to her as 'the lame woman'.

Elizabeth Sellor – from Islandmagee, she was the daughter of Janet and William Sellor. In 1711 she was 17 years of age and described as small, having a pretty face and being 'lame of leg'.

Janet Carson – from Islandmagee, maintained her innocence in the face of Dunbar's accusations both before and during the trial. Her daughter tried unsuccessfully to defend her against Dunbar's charges.

Janet Main – from Broadisland, County Antrim, was married to Andrew Ferguson, and considered locally as an irreligious woman with a bad temper. She had an unkempt appearance, had small brown eyes and a long face. She suffered from severe arthritis, her face was badly scarred with smallpox and she was said to have 'a mark upon her breast'. Main was considered by Dunbar to be one of the ringleaders of the Islandmagee witches.

Janet Millar – from Scotch Quarter, Carrickfergus, was blind in one eye and had survived smallpox and falling into a fire. This left her body scarred and badly burned. She ranted and cursed when interviewed about Dunbar's bewitchment.

Janet Latimer – from Irish Quarter, Carrickfergus, was tall with black hair, prone to temper tantrums and possessed a reputation for low morals in her local area.

Margaret Mitchell – from Kilroot, County Antrim, she was married to a man called 'Johnny'. Dunbar claimed Margaret was one of her 'greatest tormentors' and was known as 'Mistress Ann' or 'Mrs Ann' to the other suspects. She was described as having a red face, red hair, 'unevenly set' teeth, and was 'blind of an eye, which was sunk in her head'.[15]

William Sellor – husband to Janet Liston and father to Elizabeth, he was accused of and arrested for bewitching Mary Dunbar in spring 1711, just after his immediate family had been convicted of the same crime.

PROSECUTORS AND INVESTIGATORS

Edward Clements (died 1733) – Whig Mayor of Carrickfergus who inherited his brother's estate, Clements Hill. In early March 1711, he took effective control of the investigation into Dunbar's allegations.

Revd Robert Sinclair – lived in the townland of Ballymuldrogh, Islandmagee. He was Presbyterian minister there from 1704 until his death in 1731 and was involved in the case from the beginning.

Revd David Robb – Church of Ireland curate of St John's parish in the townland of Ballyharry in Islandmagee. He helped Revd Sinclair and Mayor Clements interview the accused witches and other witnesses.

Revd William Ogilvie (died September 1712) – Presbyterian minister of Larne and witness for the prosecution. He initially displayed caution when dealing with Dunbar's accusations.

James Blythe – from Bank-Head in Larne, he provided Clements with a deposition and appeared as a witness for the prosecution. Although there is no record of him holding an official legal position, he played a leading role in the investigation and apprehension of the suspected witches.

Bryce Blan – constable of Larne, County Antrim and a deponent. He discovered image magic in Janet Millar's house.

Randal Leathes – a Ruling Elder (in 1710) for Islandmagee Presbyterian Church, he gave farmland to his church so they could build a manse for Revd Sinclair.

John Man – a Ruling Elder in 1714, he stayed overnight in the Haltridge house and prayed for the release of Ann from the grips of the Devil.

William Fenton – deponent, prosecution witness, and Ruling Elder, he was landlord to Janet Sellor and helped search McCalmond's house for spells.

Robert Holmes (died 1724) – was a wealthy Ruling Elder and helped search McCalmond's house.

John Logan – a constable of Broadisland, he arrested Mitchell.

William Hatley – deponent, prosecution witness and participated in the search of McCalmond's house. His wife's cloak was found mysteriously stuffed with straw and was believed to be bewitched.

DEPONENTS, WITNESSES AND COMMENTATORS

Revd William Tisdall (1669–1735) – rabidly anti-Presbyterian, High Church Tory vicar of Belfast, he owned property in Carrickfergus. Convinced of the innocence of convicted women, he spoke with Dunbar immediately after the trial.

Revd William Skeffington (1659–1741) – Church of Ireland curate of Larne and witness for the prosecution.

Revd James Cobham (1678–1759) – prosecution witness and Presbyterian minister of Broadisland (Ballycarry) from 1700.

Revd Patrick Adair (died June 1717) – prosecution witness and Presbyterian minister of Carrickfergus from 1702.

James Stannus – he and his wife visited Dunbar in Islandmagee before allowing her to stay in their home in Larne until the day of the trial.

John Smith – while staying overnight in the Haltridge house, he witnessed the apparitions of two men. He helped Blythe interview Margaret Mitchell, gave depositions to Mayor Clements on two separate occasions, and was a witness for the prosecution.

James Hill – deponent and prosecution witness.

Sheela McGee – was assaulted in the Haltridge house by an invisible, demonic entity while staying overnight.

Hugh Donaldson – of Islandmagee, deponent and prosecution witness.

Charles Lennan – a member of the Islandmagee gentry, he was a deponent and prosecution witness.

John Wilson – from Islandmagee, deponent and prosecution witness.

Hugh Wilson – from Islandmagee, deponent and prosecution witness.

John Campbell – heard a bedroom door fly open of its own accord and ghostly cat noises while staying overnight at Knowehead House.

John Getty – a merchant from Larne, he witnessed Margaret Mitchell in her spider 'form'.

Anthony Upton – Tory Justice of the Common Pleas, and one of the judges who tried the Islandmagee witches. He directed the jury to acquit them.

James MacCartney – Whig Justice of the Queen's Bench, he also tried the women but directed the jury to convict them.

Timeline of Events

Witchcraft in Early Modern Ireland

1586 – first Irish Witchcraft Act passed, which was almost identical to its English counterpart passed thirteen years earlier. It made various magical practices, including harming or killing using witchcraft, a felony or serious crime.

1655 – Marion Fisher sentenced to death at Carrickfergus Assizes (overturned a year later) for bewitching to death Alexander Gilbert.

1661 – Florence Newton, of Youghal, tried at Cork Assizes for using witchcraft to kill her gaoler, David Jones, and demonically possess a local servant, Mary Longdon.

1672 – neighbours suspect that James Shaw, Scottish-born Presbyterian minister of Carnmoney, County Antrim, and his wife, had been killed by witchcraft.

1698 – in Antrim town, County Antrim, an elderly woman is strangled and burned by a local mob for bewitching a nine-year-old girl .

The Islandmagee Witches

SEPTEMBER 1710 – Ann Haltridge, while living with her son James and his wife at Knowehead House in Islandmagee, County Antrim, is 'haunted' by a demonic presence.

DECEMBER – Ann and her servant Margaret Spear are visited by a demonic 'boy'.

11–12 FEBRUARY 1711 – the demonic boy returns, smashes a kitchen window and threatens to kill everyone in the house. Stones and turf are hurled at the house by invisible forces.

15–16 FEBRUARY – bedclothes are stripped from beds and remade in the shape of a corpse. Revd Robert Sinclair contacted to investigate the matter and stays in the house with his church Elders. Ann Haltridge reports stabbing pains in her back.

16–22 FEBRUARY – too frightened to return to her bedroom, Ann retires to another room, where she remains bed-bound and in constant pain.

22 FEBRUARY – Ann dies at twelve o'clock midday and rumours quickly circulate that her death and demonic haunting were caused by (as yet) unnamed witches.

27 FEBRUARY – Dunbar arrives in Islandmagee from the hamlet of Castlereagh, County Down, now a townland lying south-east of Belfast, to keep young Mrs Haltridge company while her husband, James, was in Dublin. Almost immediately supernatural disturbances are felt in the house, as Dunbar unties a knotted apron containing Ann Haltridge's missing bonnet, which turns out to be the 'spell' used to bewitch her.

28 FEBRUARY – Dunbar becomes demonically possessed, is seized by intense pain, and falls into a series of fits. She sees the spectres of a number of women who threaten to kill her, among whom are Janet Main and Janet Carson.

1 MARCH – Dunbar accuses Janet Carson of her possession, and is then visited spectrally by more witches, Janet Liston and her daughter, Elizabeth Sellor.

2 MARCH – Liston and Sellor are brought to Knowehead House, identity paraded, and tested by Revd David Robb and Revd Sinclair on their Christian faith. A smell of brimstone appears in the house and Dunbar's body is wracked with pain.

3 MARCH – Dunbar moves to first floor of the house and experiences a catatonic trance. Mayor of Carrickfergus, Edward Clements, takes over investigation of Dunbar's accusations and begins taking witness statements.

4 MARCH – Dunbar accuses another woman named Catherine McCalmond and picks her from a line-up. McCalmond's house is then searched for charms.

5 MARCH – Mayor Clements issues a warrant for the arrest of Janet Carson, Catherine McCalmond, Janet Liston and Elizabeth Sellor. They are brought before Dunbar who immediately has a fit. The women are then arrested and remanded in custody at County Antrim gaol at Carrickfergus. Dunbar then describes two more of her spectral attackers, Janet Main and Janet Latimer.

6 MARCH – Main and Latimer are arrested, brought before Dunbar and interviewed by Mayor Clements, who remands them in custody. Dunbar's health improves as a result.

7 MARCH – the demonic boy reappears to Margaret Spear and a bewitched cloak of one of the Haltridges' house guests is found stuffed with straw. Dunbar relapses.

8 MARCH – Dunbar experiences more fits and accuses two more witches of attacking her: a woman with one eye and one called Mistress or Mrs Ann.

10 MARCH – Revd Sinclair and various local elites interview Dunbar and she reveals that the witches in their spirit forms have promised to bewitch other members of the Haltridge family.

11 MARCH – Dunbar goes to the local Presbyterian church but during the sermon has several fits and is taken back to Knowehead. A number of women are brought to the house who fit the descriptions of the suspected witches who are still at large: the one-eyed woman and Mrs Ann. No positive identification is made and demonic activity continues to cause havoc in the house.

12 MARCH – Mayor Clements takes Dunbar's statement or deposition, during which she repeats the descriptions of the witches still at large.

13 MARCH – Dunbar travels to Larne by boat and by road to the house of James Stannus. Dunbar has numerous fits and experiences bodily contortions, and a renewed search of the countryside is made for those responsible. A number of women who match Mistress Ann's physical description are brought before Dunbar but are released soon afterwards. James Blythe, by chance, sees a woman in a Carrickfergus street fitting Dunbar's description of the one-eyed woman; she is called Janet Millar.

14 MARCH – Janet Millar is arrested and transported to Carrickfergus gaol. Bryce Blan, constable for Larne, finds image magic in Millar's house. Janet Main is chained and bolted in her cell when it is discovered she has been spectrally attacking Dunbar. Local schoolchildren are brought to Knowehead by young Mrs Haltridge but are attacked by the demonic presence in the house.

15 MARCH – Mrs Ann appears to Dunbar in spirit form before leaving in the shape of an insect.

17 MARCH – Mrs Ann visits Dunbar several times in spectral form and threatens to kill her. Dunbar uses (albeit unsuccessfully) a 'charm' to fight the effects of the witch's harmful magic.

19/20 MARCH – Margaret Mitchell from the parish of Kilroot is suspected of being Mrs Ann, and is brought to Larne to confront Dunbar.

21 MARCH – Mitchell is arrested by the constable of Broadisland, John Logan, before being chained, bolted, and gaoled. Dunbar's overall health improves.

24 MARCH – Dunbar is attacked by Main and Liston in spirit form after they are released from their bolts and chains in Carrickfergus gaol. Dunbar is witnessed levitating above her bed in Larne.

25 MARCH – Dunbar loses the power of speech, which is returned to her upon reading the Bible.

28 MARCH – Margaret Spear, the family servant, feels a demonic presence crawl slowly over her body, and pillows are thrown at her by an invisible perpetrator.

29 MARCH – Dunbar travels to Carrickfergus for the trial but is confronted on the road by the spectres of a mysterious man (William Sellor) and two women, who tell her that they will magically remove her ability to speak in court. She loses the power of speech and is forced to stay the night on the road as her fits worsen.

30 MARCH – Dunbar loses the power of speech in late afternoon until early the next morning, when she is told by the witches from the previous day that she will not be able to testify at the trial.

31 MARCH – the eight women are convicted, at the spring session of County Antrim Assizes in Carrickfergus, of bewitching Mary Dunbar under the 1586 Irish Witchcraft Act. The trial lasts eight hours, from six o'clock in the morning until two in the afternoon. At five o'clock Dunbar leaves for her mother's house in Castlereagh.

1 APRIL – Dunbar faints several times and vomits feathers and pins.

4 APRIL – Revd William Tisdall writes a letter to an unknown recipient detailing the trial.

2–7 APRIL – Dunbar has regular fits and vomits pins and feathers.

8 APRIL – Dunbar claims William Sellor visited her in spirit form and threatened to kill her.

10 APRIL – a warrant is issued for William Sellor, who is subsequently arrested trying to flee Islandmagee. He is brought before Dunbar who fails to identify him. Dunbar later claims that she 'did not accuse him for fear of his threatening'. He is set free.

12 APRIL – Sellor appears before Dunbar in spectral form and stabs her with a butcher's knife below the right shoulder. It leaves a visible wound.

13 APRIL – locals arrest Sellor for a second time and put him in gaol to await trial.

14 APRIL – a Dublin newspaper, *The Dublin Intelligence*, reports that the '8 witches' were found guilty and are to be imprisoned and pilloried for their crimes.

24 APRIL – the same newspaper reports that Mary Dunbar 'is dead'.

11 SEPTEMBER – at the spring session of County Antrim Assizes held in Carrickfergus, William Sellor is tried and convicted of killing Mary Dunbar using witchcraft.

6 APRIL 1821 – the 1586 Irish Witchcraft Act is repealed by the Westminster parliament in London.

A Well-Respected Woman

In the early seventeenth century, Sir Arthur Chichester (died 1625) gained the freehold for Islandmagee, County Antrim, and leased the land there to successive generations of absentee landlords from the Hill family. Chichester was a politician and soldier who led the English crown's violent military campaign (which included a scorched-earth policy) during the Nine Years War against Hugh O'Neill, 2nd Earl of Tyrone, and his allies. After the war settlement of 1603, Chichester acquired extensive estates in Ulster including a castle and lands in Belfast. In 1604, he was appointed Lord Deputy, the head of the English Administration in Ireland.

By the end of the seventeenth century, the peninsula of Islandmagee was a small, rural Presbyterian-Scots community containing around 300 people. Its inhabitants were employed in farming, spinning and fishing. Ships regularly landed at Port Davey from Portpatrick in Scotland, a journey that took just over four hours (see fig. 1).[1] In 1683, Richard Dobbs, of Castle Dobbs, Carrickfergus, and later mayor of the town, surveyed County Antrim for a report for an ultimately unpublished atlas of Ireland commissioned by London bookseller, Moses Pitt, and overseen by Dublin-based political writer and scientist William Molyneux. In his survey, Dobbs stated that 'Island Magee' is 'encompassed by the sea and Loughlarn', and contained 5,000 acres 'fit for fork and scythe ... nor did I ever see better ground for so much together, whether for grain or cattle'. Dobbs noted that the peninsula was named after 'the Magees that lived here in former times'. The Magees were a Catholic family who came from Islay in Scotland in the mid-1500s. They were increasingly displaced by English Protestants during the late sixteenth and early seventeenth centuries. In January 1642, during the conflict that followed the Irish rebellion that began on 22 October 1641, a considerable number of remaining Catholics, around thirty families, were murdered in reprisals by Protestants. Ominously, and perhaps an omen of events to come, Dobbs also reported, 'I have heard surveyors say "they could never get their compasses to answer their expectations here, and thought it was bewitched".'[2]

In September 1710, Ann Haltridge, an elderly widow, was living with her son, James Haltridge, his wife, their two children and their servants in Islandmagee. Ann epitomised Presbyterian matriarchy as a respected, God-fearing gentlewoman and neighbour. She was described in surviving sources in terms that would not have been out of place in a eulogy:

> During her marriage and widowhood she behaved herself Christianly, prudently, and exemplary, so that she, as much as any in her station, deserved the name of a mother of Israel, by engaging, both by advice and example, those she conversed with to fear and serve God. She was a constant attendee upon public ordinances, a frequent and devout communicant, charitable, and tender in her walk and conversation.

As the widow of Revd John Haltridge, late Presbyterian minister of Islandmagee, she would have enjoyed an elevated social position within the community and commanded a high level of respect in an era when Presbyterian clergy played leading roles within their communities and were looked to for leadership and direction.

Revd John Haltridge was ordained by the Presbytery of Antrim on 8 May 1672 in a building rented by the congregation in the nearby village of Ballycarry, in the parish of Broadisland (also known as Templecorran), as there was no Presbyterian meetinghouse in Islandmagee.[3] Haltridge's congregation eventually built one in 1674 in the townland of Kilcoan More, which lay midway up the peninsula on the western side.[4] Although the meetinghouse building underwent considerable alterations in subsequent years, it stood until 1900 (see fig. 2) when it was replaced by the current First Presbyterian Church. The congregation also built for

Haltridge a thick-walled, two-storey, thatched manse, which local historian Dixon Donaldson referred to as Knowehead House (see figs 3, 4). Knowehead House was constructed around the same time as the meetinghouse, in a similar architectural style, complete with heavy buttresses at the angles of the walls (see fig. 4). The manse stood adjacent to the meetinghouse and *THE ISLANDMAGEE WITCHES* suggests the church was 'within musket shot of the house', which in eighteenth-century terms meant around 100 yards.[5] After John Haltridge's death in 1697, his family continued to live at Knowehead House.[6]

Death ultimately ended Haltridge's ministry in Islandmagee, but in 1689 he had fled to Scotland, along with other Ulster Scots, including many clergymen, to escape the escalating conflict between supporters of Catholic James II and those of Protestant William of Orange. In common with many refugees, Haltridge returned to Ulster and was back preaching in Islandmagee by November 1690. This decision was possibly arrived at after failing to find a position within the Church of Scotland in Galloway.[7]

Most Presbyterian ministers officiating in Ulster before 1680 were Scots. However, between 1680 and 1730, 56 per cent of Ireland's Presbyterian ministers were born in Ulster, with around 29 per cent, in common with John Haltridge, being of Scottish birth. The majority of Scottish-born ministers, as well as merchants and gentry, came from the south-west of the country. Presbyterian ministers were highly educated, through school attendance, private study and later university training. Trinity College, Dublin was the only university in Ireland at that time, and because of its strong Church of Ireland ethos many Presbyterians (including would-be ministers) made the journey to the pleasingly cheaper Scottish universities for their higher education, especially the University of Glasgow. Haltridge graduated from Glasgow University as MA in 1654 and was later chaplain to Sir William Cunningham. He first came to Ireland when he was deprived of his clerical living for non-conformity by the Court of High Commission in Glasgow in 1664. Haltridge had three brothers who had done well for themselves in Ulster: Alexander, merchant from Newry, County Down, died in 1679; Matthew, graduated from Glasgow University in 1669 and ministered at Ahoghill, County Antrim, from 1676 until his death in 1705; and William (died 1691), a successful merchant in Dromore, County Down, who owned estates in Scotland and in counties Down and Armagh. The Irish economy in the late seventeenth and early eighteenth century was largely agricultural, and Presbyterian merchants in Ulster were engaged in the overseas provisions trade, exporting goods mainly from the ports of Belfast and Derry. Presbyterian merchants were largely of Scottish birth or heritage, provided leadership within their congregations, and formed part of the urban elite of most Ulster towns. Until the Test Act of 1704 was passed prohibiting it (see chapter 9), they were also active members of local and municipal government. Some leading merchants like William Haltridge were also landowners, and as a result moved easily within the ranks of the Presbyterian gentry.[8]

An Unwelcome Visitor

While sitting by the kitchen fire in Knowehead one night in early September 1710, Ann Haltridge was hit by a number of stones on her back and shoulders, presumably coming through the open window behind her. Unhurt but frightened, Ann retreated to her bedroom on the first floor, where she was barraged with stones and turf, hurled with so much force they caused the curtains to move. Ann also felt a presence crawl slowly over her body, moving 'from one side of the bed to the other'. With the windows and door now firmly closed, she searched the pitch-black room but 'nothing could be found which might in the least occasion any disturbance'. Two nights later, Ann's pillow was pulled from her head and her bedcovers and blankets mysteriously removed. Frightened, she made her young granddaughter 'lie beside her in the room, yet notwithstanding, the clothes were often pulled off her at night time'. Still seeking a natural explanation, Ann 'apprehended that it might be a cat which pulled off the clothes and desired the girl to light a candle and search the room, which she did but nothing was found'. However, when a candle was lit, quietness descended, but when extinguished the disturbances started once more. As night was widely believed to belong to supernatural entities such as ghosts, it must have occurred to Ann that what she was dealing with was not of the natural world. A few days later a cat was found in the house. This would have explained the night-time disturbances if it had not vanished into thin air after it had been killed and slung into the garden.

The cat was not the only thing to mysteriously vanish: Ann's cane regularly disappeared only to return days later. Thankfully for the family, this was the only uncanny event to trouble the house for the next two months. This all changed on 11 December. Ann was once more sitting at the kitchen fire when a boy appeared before her and one of the servants, Margaret Spear, who was known as Meg by the family. The expansion of domestic service in Ireland during the eighteenth century meant that even relatively small households would probably have employed a male and a female servant, either on a temporary or permanent basis. We know that Spear was a young adult, and from what we know about others in service at that time we can speculate that she was also unmarried and from a poorer, rural background. Her job would have entailed a wide range of demanding domestic chores, from cleaning to serving food and working in the dairy.

Spear described the boy as being 10 or 12 years of age and wearing an old black bonnet over short black hair, with 'a half-worn blanket about him, trailing on the ground behind him, and a torn black vest under it'. Given his ragged appearance, Ann assumed the boy was a 'strolling' beggar looking for something to eat. Beggars were not an uncommon sight in early eighteenth-century Ulster, especially at times of harvest failure, high unemployment, and economic downturn. More unusual was the fact that the boy covered his face with his hand, despite Ann's repeated requests for him to remove it, name himself, and tell her where he came from or where he was going to. Instead, he became agitated and danced frantically and menacingly around the kitchen, before leaping out of an open window and running to the end of the garden and into the cow house. Ann's servants gave chase but soon lost sight of him, only to discover later, when they returned to the house, that he was waiting for them. This charade was repeated around a dozen times before Spear confronted the boy and warned him that, 'now my master [James Haltridge] is coming; he will take a course with this troublesome creature'. The boy then left Knowehead and the house remained free from supernatural disturbance for the next two months.

On the evening of Sunday, 11 February 1711, Ann was reading a hefty book of sermons on the covenant by Scottish Presbyterian minister Alexander Wedderburn, to compensate for the lack of a sermon that morning in the meetinghouse in Islandmagee.[9] In Presbyterian religious culture the sermon was regarded as the high point of the service, and ministers often encouraged literate women in their congregation to engage in private reading of the Bible and devotional texts. After reading for a time, Ann laid the book down, but when she went back to collect it, it had disappeared. She searched the room thoroughly but could not find it. At seven o'clock the next morning, 12 February, the ragged boy returned to Knowehead and smashed the kitchen window with his hand while clutching Ann's missing book. He also spoke for the first time, to Spear, a conversation that *THE ISLANDMAGEE WITCHES* records word for word:

Boy: 'Do you want a book?'
Spear: 'No.'
Boy: 'How came you to lie? For this is the book the old gentlewoman wanted yesterday.'
Spear: 'How came you by it?'
Boy: 'I went down quietly to the parlour when you were all in the kitchen, and found it lying upon a shelf with a Bible and a pair of spectacles.'
Spear: 'How came it that you did not take the Bible too?'
Boy: 'It was too heavy to carry.'
Spear: 'Will you give it back? For my Mistress can't want [for] it any longer.'
Boy: 'No, she shall never get it again.'
Spear: 'Can you read it?'
Boy: 'Yes.'
Spear: 'Who taught you?'
Boy: 'The Devil taught me.'
Spear: 'The Lord bless me from thee? Thou hast got ill lear [learning].'
Boy: 'Aye, bless yourself twenty times, but that shall not save you.'
Spear: 'What will you do to us?'

The boy answered Spear's final question by pulling out a sword and threatening to kill everyone in the house. Spear then bolted the door and took her charge, Ann's 8-year-old grandson, to the parlour. Undeterred, the boy followed them, jeering, 'Now you think you are safe enough but I will get in yet.' Spear shouted back, 'What way? For we have the street door shut,' to which the boy replied, 'I can come in by the least hole in the house, like a cat or a mouse, for the Devil can make me anything I please.' 'God bless me from thee,' Spear then stated, 'for thou art no earthly creature if you can do that.' The boy responded by hurling a large stone at the parlour window and vanishing once more.

Animal Sacrifice

The boy reappeared later that day with one of the family's male turkeys hung over his shoulder. Although he gripped the turkey's feet tightly, it kicked him so hard that he dropped the stolen book he was carrying. With the turkey still on his back, he ran up the side of the house and leapt over a wall at the west end of the garden. Spear, Ann, and her grandson observed all of this and quickly moved to recover the book. A short time later, when Spear peered out the parlour window, she saw the boy lay the turkey down on its back, but as he raised his sword to kill it, the bird made its escape. With the valuable book and turkey gone, the boy entered on a new course of action, and with a club he proceeded to break 'the glass in the side window of the parlour'. He then went 'to the end window through which the girl was looking' and removed every pane of glass. Not finished, he went to the bottom of the garden and frantically dug a hole with his sword. When Spear asked him what he was doing, he replied that he was digging a grave for her master, James Haltridge, whom he claimed had died fourteen days previously. James was still alive and well and in Dublin, but would not return to Knowehead until the following month. When the grave was finished the boy vaulted over a garden hedge, as if he had 'been a bird flying'. During this episode Spear was described as being 'the whole time in a terror'.

Son of Satan

The Presbyterian Scots diaspora in Ulster still had strong familial, economic and cultural ties with Scotland, where, in the early modern period, people at all levels of society, from the wealthy to the rural poor, were well aware of the image and the power of the Devil and were constantly reminded of such from the pulpit. Satan, after all, occupied an important position within the theology of Calvinist Presbyterianism in Scotland and Ulster. The Devil was a master of disguise and could appear in any form he chose, but was often witnessed as a mixture of man and animal. His subordinate demons also appeared in the shape of animals as well as black men and children. In seventeenth-century Scottish confessions of witchcraft, the Devil was commonly described as a man dressed in black or with black hair or wearing a black hat or shawl. Alexander Hamilton, who was executed in Scotland in 1630 for witchcraft, described Satan as a man in black clothes who carried a wand. It is unsurprising that the Devil's preferred colour was black because it was widely associated with sin.

It is therefore understandable that members of the Haltridge family were now convinced the strange little 'beggar boy' with black hair and dressed in black clothes, who disappeared for months only to suddenly reappear, was a demon in child form. He is even referred to as an 'apparition' in the pamphlet account to reflect his true nature: the Devil and demons were believed to be entirely spirit in form even if they appeared to be made of flesh and blood. Furthermore, the boy's clothes were not only black but ruined, which further confirmed his demonic status: the torn fabric reflected the inner decay and corruption of an emissary of the Devil (see chapter 6). In common with all satanic creatures, he displayed an aversion to the revealed word of God, the Bible. This was implied by his weak explanation that he was unable to pick up the Bible because it was too heavy, even though he was able to lift a turkey cock and several panes of glass. He also admitted to Spear that the Devil had taught him to read and given him the power to turn into any animal he wished. With this admission, any questions raised the previous September about the true nature of the vanishing cat would have been answered: it was the demon in cat form.

By the twelfth century, cats were the preferred animal form Satan and his demons took when visualised as presiding over heretical rites and rituals, and would later form a key part of heresy accusations. In Kilkenny in 1324, Dame Alice Kyteler and her associates were accused of heresy and demonic conspiracy by Richard de Ledrede, the English, Franciscan Bishop of Ossory. Kyteler was accused of consorting with a demon called Robin Artison who variously appeared to her in the form of a black man, a black dog, and a cat. In the succeeding four centuries, cats became closely associated with witchcraft in European culture as one of the guises demons took when they carried witches to nocturnal gatherings. They were also one of the insect or animal forms that familiar spirits in England took when doing the evil work of their witch masters, including sneaking into houses. Demons in the shape of men, children and animals, including cats, were often witnessed during episodes of demonic possession.[10]

Satan was able to spare the demon boy in order to haunt the Haltridge family because it was believed that Hell was literally crawling with demons. They were, for the most part, fallen angels, and although the New Testament of the Bible suggested they were legion, it did not detail their numbers, allowing demonologists to speculate wildly. The fifteenth-century Spanish theologian Alfonso De Spina argued there were 133,306,668 demons in Hell, while others suggested that six or seven million was nearer the mark. Chief demons were often ranked according to their magical attributes or gifts and how many legions of lesser demons they controlled (each legion containing 666 lesser demons). They were even given names such as Beelzebub, Leviathan, Belial, and Behemoth, some of which were derived from the Bible. It was believed that humans were able to invoke demons and bring them to earth.

Early modern, male, learned, ritual magicians performed complex rituals to summon and command demons to reveal secret or hidden knowledge. Witches, on the other hand, were thought to conjure demons to harm or to kill. To the annoyance of learned magicians, Church authorities and mainstream Christian theology sometimes made little distinction between the two: both involved sinful (heretical, even) dealings with demons.[11] Those lucky and youthful enough to be considered foolish and sinful rather than evil could be looked upon more favourably by authorities. In Carnmoney, County Antrim, in 1672, a young servant, George Russell, was lightly disciplined by Presbyterian ministers and Elders for 'conversing and conferring with that spirit which appeared to him ... and conjuring it by drawing circles and other circumstances att the demand and direct[io]ne of the s[ai]d spirits.'[12] The demon who had tricked Russell into doing its bidding was also responsible for haunting his master, James Shaw, the Scottish-born Presbyterian minister of Carnmoney. Shaw later died after a prolonged illness and his neighbours suspected both he and his wife had been murdered by this demon, which had been initially conjured up and subsequently controlled by the 'sorcery of some witches in the parish'.[13]

Searching the House

After the demonic boy had stolen the glass, dug the grave and disappeared, Ann Haltridge and Margaret Spear alerted people in neighbouring farms, who immediately combed the house for evidence of him. Having discovered nothing untoward, they left Ann and the children alone in the house. Soon afterwards the women and children heard a 'great many stones [and] turf' hitting the walls and windows. Terrified and cut off from their neighbours, because they 'durst not go out', they huddled in one room until the attack ceased eight hours later.

The short period of calm which followed ended on 15 February, when Ann's bedclothes were stripped off the bed and thrown in a heap on the floor. The servants remade the bed but discovered later that they had been taken off again, folded and placed under a large table which stood in the room. On top of the bedclothes was placed a box belonging to Ann. The bed was made a third time, but when members of the family returned to the room, Ann's bolster pillow had been placed vertically on the bed with sheets stretched over it so it resembled a corpse lying in its winding sheet.[14] Even though 'the digging of the grave and making [of] the bed clothes in the shape of a corpse was looked upon as a presage of death', Ann displayed remarkable fortitude, never neglecting 'her hours of devotion' and refusing to sleep in another room, stating that it was 'not good to give place to the Devil'.

The Local Community Gets Involved

As almost invariably happened in cases of demonic possession and witch-craft in the British Isles, rumours of the disturbances at Knowehead spread very quickly and people flocked to the house. Interested and sympathetic they may have been, but early modern people, especially the educated elite, did not take supernatural events at face value. This explains why the Haltridges' neighbours 'took particular notice' to investigate the corpse shape in the bed, 'lest there might be a trick in it'. Despite close investigation, 'they were obliged to own that it was done by some invisible agent'. As was customary in Presbyterian communities, they asked for the opinion of the local minister, Revd Robert Sinclair. Revd Sinclair had been called to the ministry of Islandmagee in May 1704, the position having lain vacant since Revd Haltridge's death seven years previously. Sinclair ministered in Islandmagee for almost twenty-seven years until his death in January 1731.[15]

It did not take Sinclair, his two Elders (Randal Leathes and John Man)[16] and 'some other pious Christians and neighbours' long to decide to stay the night in Knowehead to engage in 'prayer and other religious' duties. The use of prayer and fasting to drive a demonic entity from a house or a person had Biblical precedent in the New Testament and was considered acceptable by Protestant non-conformist gentry and dissenting clergy, if not their Church of Ireland counterparts. For example, in Dublin in the 1650s, Sir Jerome (or Hierome) Sankey, a lay preacher and prominent Irish Baptist, suggested his dispossession ceremony conducted on behalf of demoniac Mr Wadman had failed because the demon he was attempting to expel 'was of the sort that required fasting as well as prayer'.[17]

Despite the best efforts of Sinclair and his helpers, as soon as night fell the bedclothes were rearranged into a corpse on Ann's bed. In defiance, Ann retired to her room in the early evening, but woke at midnight screaming and moaning. When Sinclair rushed to the room he found Ann convulsed by an unbearable pain, so intense it felt like 'something was stuck into her back like a knife'. Finally defeated, in the morning Ann informed those present she was now 'too afraid to stay' in the room 'any longer'.

Tragedy Strikes

Driven from her bedroom by fear, Ann spent the last seven days of her life tormented by the agonising pain in her back. During her illness, every time Ann's old bed was remade, the corpse shape would reappear in the bedclothes, even when a chair or table was put on top of them. During her final sickness, however, she often enquired after 'her grandchildren and others in the family, and when she heard they were well, would say it was a great mercy [the] Devil's got no power over them.' Confined to a spare room, she periodically sat up in bed, gazed into the middle distance, sighed, and lay back down again. This bizarre ritual 'gave some ground to suspect she had seen some apparitions or witches, though she did not discover it for fear of affrighting the family'. The end came at twelve o'clock on 22 February 1711, as Ann Haltridge slipped out of life.

Islandmagee: A Possessed Community

The inhabitants of Islandmagee lived in a county and a country in the grips of political and religious turmoil, a hang-over from the previous century. By the early eighteenth century, a Protestant Ascendancy, peopled with communicants of the Church of Ireland, had emerged in the years after the defeat in the early 1690s of Catholic James II and his Jacobite supporters. Concentrated in county towns, the metropolis of Dublin, and the north of Ireland, Anglicans controlled much national and local government and held the majority of the country's landed wealth. Despite this privileged position, many feared the Catholic majority were intent on slitting Protestant throats at their first opportunity, just as they were perceived to have done during the 1641 rebellion. It was suspected that Irish Catholics would rebel during a French-backed, Jacobite invasion. Britain and her allies, after all, had been in almost continuous, total war with the military might of Louis XIV's Catholic France since 1689, with the War of Spanish Succession (1702–13) proving extremely bloody, hugely expensive and domestically unsettling. Fear of the Catholic Gaelic-Irish was rooted in their majority status as the biggest religious and ethnic group everywhere but Protestant Ulster. By the 1730s, Roman Catholics made up around 80 per cent of the estimated 2.5 million people in Ireland, a population that had grown by around 25 per cent in the previous fifty years.[18]

Many members of this Anglican Ascendancy, especially the rank and file of the parish clergy, also fretted over the rising influence of Irish non-conformists. These were Protestant dissenters who worshipped or took communion outside of the Episcopalian state Church, the Church of Ireland. Among non-conformists, which included Baptists, Quakers, Independents and English Presbyterians, Scottish Presbyterians in Ulster were deemed the biggest threat to the grip the Anglican Church and state had on social, economic and political power (see chapter 9). The main cause of this anxiety was the sheer scale of migration from Scotland to Ulster in the later seventeenth century. In the plantation period (before 1641) between 20–30,000 Scots came to the province. Between 1690 and 1715, the Scottish population in Ulster doubled to 200,000, with 50,000 of these migrants arriving in the 1690s from south-west Scotland: 20,000 arrived in the famine years of 1696–98 alone. Migration slowed down substantially after 1698 but along with Anglican migrant fearmongering it did not stop completely. By the 1710s, when emigration had tailed off, Presbyterians made up around a third of the total population of Ulster. They were found in greatest number in counties Antrim, Donegal, Down and Londonderry, but also in Armagh, Monaghan and Tyrone. There were also small pockets of Presbyterians further south in towns such as Cork, Limerick and Dublin. The Ulster Scots migration story turned to an emigration one with the mass migration of Ulster Presbyterians to North America after 1718. Poverty caused by a subsistence crisis was not the only reason Scottish migrants came to Ulster in the decades after 1690. They crossed the Irish Sea to join the Presbyterian ministry, to live with family already settled there, and to avail themselves of low rents and economic opportunities in trade and manufacturing. It was not only the clergy, gentry, tradesmen and merchants that came to Ulster; medical professionals also made the journey, along with the labouring and wandering poor, and criminals and moral offenders hoping to escape the retribution of Scottish secular courts and Kirk Sessions.

Although by political necessity loyal to the British Crown as Protestants, Ulster Presbyterians at that time viewed themselves not as Irish or English but as the Scottish in Ireland. This identity was tied up in their culture and language, which had its roots in Scotland. James Boyle, a collector for the Ordnance Survey Memoirs of Ireland, noted that the 'dialect, idioms and phraseology' of Islandmagee residents in the mid-nineteenth century were 'purely Scottish and resemble those of inhabitants of Ayrshire, Scotland, but they have little accent'.[19] More importantly, their identity was shaped by their Presbyterian religion. The Presbyterian Church emerged distinct from the Church of Ireland after the rebellion of 1641. Between 1689 and 1707 numbers of Presbyterian congregations and minsters doubled. This figure grew by a further 30 per cent during the next decade. By this time Ulster Presbyterianism was, in the words of historian S.J. Connolly, 'an autonomous and highly organised ecclesiastical polity',[20] consisting of the Synod (which first met in 1691, and yearly afterwards) and various Presbyteries and Sessions. The Presbyterian Church structure was hierarchical, with the annual synod representing its top layer. As Leanne Calvert has suggested, the synod was 'made up from the ministers and representative elders from all the congregations under its care' and 'was responsible for the oversight of the whole work of the church, from the discipline of ministers and the laity, to the management of funds for the widows and families of ministers.' Next came presbyteries, which were held on a regular basis, usually monthly, and comprised ministers and representative Elders within its boundaries. They dealt with complaints regarding individual minsters, calls for new ministers to serve congregations with vacancies, and complex disciplinary cases referred to it by the Sessions. The principal concern of the Sessions was the spiritual and moral discipline of their congregation, and the cases it heard 'usually fell into one of three categories: sexual offences, such as fornication and adultery; breaches of social and religious norms, such as drunkenness, sabbath-breaking and slander; and marital offences, such as bigamy.' It also, occasionally, heard cases concerning the use or practice of beneficial and harmful magic. As Sessions had no legal power to enforce moral discipline, the extent to which it was able to do so was dependent on the personalities, attitudes and agendas of the minister, the Elders, and the local community.[21]

Protestant dissent in Ulster was thus distinct from that in England, where non-conformity was more sectarian and geographically spread throughout the country. Shared public worship and other religious observances, along with the enforcement of discipline through the use of Church courts (Sessions and Presbyteries), helped foster a sense of community among Ulster Presbyterians. It was a community that often felt detached and excluded from the eighteenth-century Anglican State, haunted by the collective memory of the latter half of the seventeenth century as a time of injustice and persecution. This sense of persecution and isolation from the established Church and state worsened in the two decades after the defeat of James II in the early 1690s, when their religion would be denied state recognition and Presbyterian schooling and marriage heavily criticised by elements within the Church of Ireland (see chapter 9).

Early modern culture was not one 'in which seeing spirits or hearing voices was entirely normal and everyday, but one in which within certain limits and at certain points, it was explicable as a phenomenon of the real world.'[22] In Calvinist, Presbyterian Ulster, where the earthly power of the Devil was a theological necessity, and the social, religious and political order was crumbling before their eyes, it was easy to believe that Satan was singling out Presbyterians for persecution as the true upholders of Christianity. In other words, politically, theologically and culturally, the demonic attacks on the Haltridge family made perfect sense to Islandmagee Presbyterians (see also chapter 5).

Witchcraft Belief

When a community such as Islandmagee feared the works of the Devil even more than was normally the case, its inhabitants were more likely to attribute inexplicable illness or misfortune to witchcraft. By the sixteenth century, belief in witchcraft was deeply embedded at all levels of society almost everywhere in Protestant and Catholic Europe. Early modern witchcraft belief is often divided by historians into elite and popular models: elite beliefs were held by the educated, the powerful, the wealthy, and the well connected, while popular beliefs were those of the peasants, wage labourers, smallholders and artisans. In educated culture, witches were more likely to be regarded as the agents of Satan, men and women who had renounced their covenant with God to make a pact with the Devil. All of their magical power and knowledge of the dark arts came from Satan and their attacks on Christendom were inspired or facilitated by him. Witches were thus pawns in an eternal, cosmic war between good and evil, dark and light, God and the Devil. However, it must be recognised that, paradoxically, it was considered unorthodox by the learned to regard Satan as equal to God: in other words, to regard the Devil as an eternal being, able to overturn the natural laws of the universe at will. Writers on witchcraft, lawyers, theologians and philosophers (especially in continental Europe) also endlessly debated the more outlandish aspects of witchcraft theory, such as night-flying, sex with demons, and the witches' Sabbat, where witches received their orders from Satan and danced, drank and debauched (see fig. 5).

If the culture of elites was more concerned with the theory of witch-craft, popular culture centred on its effects, or in early modern language, *maleficium*. The mass of the population was more concerned about the consequences of what witches did rather than how they did it or where their power came from. They also worried about how to best prevent, detect and counter potentially fatal magical attacks on their property, livestock families and persons, and how to punish those responsible; not only to break a witch's spell, but to obtain closure, revenge and/or retri-bution. Witchcraft was for most people personal in nature. It was viewed as an attack on their family, health and livelihood and was practised by people they knew and probably had argued with. Popular witchcraft was therefore far removed from the idea of an international threat of a Satanic cult.

Although this model is useful, it is important to remember that belief in witchcraft varied between individuals, religious denominations, regions and countries. It also changed over time. As the seventeenth century wore on in England, elite culture absorbed facets of popular thinking about witches, and popular culture likewise adopted concepts originating in elite culture such as demonic sex, infanticide, the demonic pact and the Sabbat, often changing them in the process. There was also a small minority of men who challenged witch-hunting in print, namely sceptics. Almost all sceptics believed in witchcraft (at least in public) but gave biblical, legal and medical reasons for not killing people for allegedly practising it. Their arguments, as we shall see, became more mainstream as the seventeenth and eighteenth centuries wore on.

At all levels of Presbyterian society in Ulster there was a very real and sincere belief in the power of witchcraft. This is perhaps unsurprising since many of them were born in, or had recently come from, Scotland, a country which in the late sixteenth and seventeenth centuries witnessed some of the worst witch-hunting in Europe. Given the demonic disturbances at Knowehead, Ann's spectral visitations, and the fact that people in Islandmagee were of Scottish heritage or birth, it was almost inevitable that the events surrounding her death would be linked by some to witchcraft.

Noisy Ghosts and Demonic Obsession

Another prominent characteristic of the episode was the mysterious stone-throwing, or in contemporary language, Lithobolia. In the early modern world, Lithobolia was commonly associated with evil spirits and witchcraft. In colonial America, in the summer of 1682, George and Alice Walton's tavern in Great Island (now New Castle, New Hampshire) was terrorised for months on end when hundreds of stones were hurled by unseen hands, mysterious demonic voices and noises were heard and objects seemingly moved of their own accord. The Waltons accused their elderly, widowed neighbour, Hannah Jones, of using witchcraft to orchestrate the attacks. Jones responded by counter-accusing George Walton of being a witch. The attacks ended abruptly in autumn 1682 and all charges of witchcraft were dropped by the courts.[23]

By the later nineteenth century, Lithobolia, along with many of the other incidents at Knowehead House, was no longer widely attributed to demons or witches but to poltergeists: noisy ghosts drawn to specific individuals, especially adolescents, who moved or threw inanimate objects, and physically attacked people. In early modern England, ghosts (the spirits of the dead appearing to the living) formed an important part of the supernatural beliefs of ordinary Protestants, but differed from their nineteenth-century counterparts in that they were more likely to be heard or smelled than seen, and did not haunt buildings, hurt people, or radiate physical power. They rarely slammed doors, smashed windows, moved furniture, threw objects, or knocked on or walked through walls. They did, however, form part of a mental world where the supernatural was perceived and organised in moral terms. Ghosts did what they did for a reason: to right a wrong, to punish a criminal (including murderers) and to warn the living, especially those falling into spiritually tumultuous waters. Their clergy, especially the higher-ups, disapproved (in public at least) of popular ghost beliefs largely on theological grounds. Ghosts, after all, implied belief in the Catholic doctrine of Purgatory, the intermediate state between Heaven and Hell which Protestant reformers had rejected as either fraud or fable.

In his seminal book on popular religion in Ireland, the late Raymond Gillespie demonstrated that ghosts in seventeenth- and early eighteenth-century Protestant culture followed much the same pattern as in England: as apparitions that materialised to deal with unfinished business or to right a wrong.[24] In the later eighteenth century, Irish ghost narratives also functioned to reinforce accepted gender roles and as a way for Protestant, evangelical religious groups such as Methodists (an eighteenth-century religious movement with its origins in the teachings of John Wesley) to fuse conversion narratives with popular beliefs to attract new converts. In 1788, after numerous ghostly visitations and years of getting drunk, having extramarital affairs, and attacking his wife (Mary Creed, daughter of a local merchant), Cork candlemaker Cadwallader Acteson was driven by the spirits to repent and abandon a plan to poison her and run off with the maid. His ghostly visitors included his deceased mistress, Sarah Harris, whom he met in a porterhouse (she had died in 1786 shortly after ending and repenting their affair), a red, fiery monster (almost certainly Satan) with menacing claws, and a disembodied voice that promised redemption if he gave up his dissolute ways. In the narrative, the wife is portrayed as the epitome of a pious and virtuous Methodist woman, the deceased mistress as redeemable having repented, and the maid as everything a woman should not be: grasping, vindictive and morally reprehensible.[25] By that time, however, poltergeist-type hauntings were beginning to be reported. In November 1786, in Strabane, County Tyrone, a local newspaper reported that a nearby house was being tormented by a ghost that moved objects and rained blows upon its occupants. Almost like a bad joke, a Presbyterian minister, an Anglican parson, and a Roman Catholic priest tried to rid the home of this spectral nuisance. All but the priest failed, but when locals accused him of orchestrating the haunting in the first place, he reversed the rite of exorcism he had just performed and the spirit apparently returned.[26]

If not linked to haunting or poltergeist activity at the time, events at Knowehead House did fit the pattern of another early modern phenomenon distinct from (especially in demonological writing), but linked to, demonic possession and witchcraft: demonic obsession. If demonic possession occurred when a demonic spirit entered the human to control their organs and faculties, demonic obsession was when a demon attacked them externally. The obsessing demon or even the Devil himself appeared to victims and struck and generally harassed them. It could also work on victims on a psychological level, in the hope of finally possessing them, or to make them think and do things ordinarily inconceivable. In common with possession, obsession was not necessarily linked to the presence of witchcraft, neither was it restricted to Ulster. In 1678, a young niece of 'Alderman Arundel in Dublin' was pursued by 'very terrible noises' in the 'chambers she frequented', becoming 'enfeebled' in both body and mind until the demon was driven away by the prayer and fasting of some local non-conformist ministers.[27] In the summer of 1702, Thomas and David Bell asked the Session of Carnmoney, County Antrim, to investigate their house in Monkstown which they believed was 'haunted with some evil spirit'. The Session considered that this was 'probable' and on two separate occasions sent Elders to the house. They later reported to the Session that they had heard noises in the middle of the night that 'were more than ordinary'. It was then resolved that the case would be referred to a higher Church authority, the Presbytery. In the meantime, the minister was to visit the Bell brothers and offer them spiritual support.[28]

Natural Explanation

It has already been suggested that early modern people did not attribute every inexplicable occurrence to witchcraft because there were other, alternative explanations available, such as the direct intervention of God, or the trickery and mischief of Satan and his demons. It was also accepted that bewitchment may have been caused by a natural wonder, something at work in the universe which, although at present inexplicable, might be fully explained in natural terms in the future. There was also the possibility that the victim had faked their symptoms, of which there were numerous cases in Britain, and which had been publicised in popular literature by the early eighteenth century. Physical and mental illnesses were also used as explanatory mechanisms by contemporary doctors (see chapter 6).

Apart from the possibility that the un-making of the bed had been faked and that the demonic boy was a real person, there is no evidence that other explanations were debated by Ann's neighbours. It is highly probable they were considered, even if only briefly. The believability of the victim, compelling contemporary evidence to suspect demonic, harmful magic was at work, and a general heightened fear of the Devil and his works was nevertheless enough to overturn any doubts those involved may have had. Six days after the funeral of Ann Haltridge, events took a dramatically darker and more sinister turn, and Islandmagee would become infamous in the history of County Antrim.

2

Arrival in Islandmagee, County Antrim

Five days after the death of Ann Haltridge, on 27 February, James's sister arrived in Islandmagee to keep his wife company while he was in Dublin. Accompanying her was her first cousin, Mary Dunbar.[1] A resident of Castlereagh, County Down, where she lived with her mother, Dunbar is described in the pamphlet account as 'an absolute stranger' to Islandmagee, who had never been within 'fifteen miles of the place before'. She is described by contemporaries as educated, intelligent and articulate, while Church of Ireland clergyman William Tisdall described her as a 'girl, aged about eighteen years, with an open and innocent countenance … a very intelligent young … gentlewoman.'[2] Having 'discoursed with her after the trial', Tisdall further remarked that he 'had received very satisfactory and reasonable answers' from Dunbar.[3] Landowner, scientist, and later secretary to the Prince of Wales, Samuel Molyneux also attested to the 'good character and education and sense of the young woman and her family'.[4] Given where she lived and her high social status, it could be that Dunbar was related to gentry of that (rather uncommon) surname who lived in the greater Lisburn area from the mid-seventeenth century onwards.[5]

On the night of her arrival, Dunbar and her fellow guest were preparing for bed when they noticed 'some head clothes' and a new mantua were 'taken out of a trunk and scattered through the house'. Their 'head

dresses' were also found 'thrown out of doors, and the sleeves of the ...
mant[ua] ... they were making, were suddenly snatched from them,
and found out of doors besmeared with dirt'. From this description, it
is clear that Dunbar and her companion wore homemade clothes of the
type common among Scottish women. In Scotland, the basic item of
female clothing was a mantua, which 'consisted of a close fitting bodice
and loose skirt', 'with a loose shift or petticoats underneath, the latter
sometimes quilted for warmth'. More likely to go un-shod than men,
Scottish women often wore aprons and scarves over their clothes and
covered their heads with cloth.[6]

During her search for the mantua, Dunbar found an apron lying
on the parlour floor, which was 'rolled close together and tied hard
with the string of the same with five strange kind of knots upon them'.
It was immediately recognised as a foreign object because the doors and
windows of the parlour had been locked for the previous two days.
Well versed in the early modern culture of witchcraft, and probably
particularly sensitive to the supernatural after the mysterious death of
Ann Haltridge, no one in the house was brave enough to 'loose[n] the
knots' of the apron, fearing there 'was a charm' in it, 'designed for some
in the family'. The knotted apron was in fact a form of image magic,
which in England was usually produced by fashioning a waxen picture
of an intended victim before melting it or sticking it with pins. Through
a process of sympathetic magic,[7] the victim was subsequently harmed or
even killed. One of the most famous examples of this involved Queen
Elizabeth I, when in August 1578 three wax images, believed to represent
the queen and her advisors, were found under a dunghill. However,
it was in early modern New England that image magic in the form
of knotted strips of material, known to contemporaries as 'poppets',
was to be found. 'Poppets' are mentioned in the witness testimonies
given during the infamous witch-hunt in Congregationalist Salem,
Massachusetts, in 1692, where the accusations of a number of female
demoniacs led to over 100 formal accusations and nineteen executions.

There were, of course, ways other than image magic to bewitch
someone. Some witches intentionally used magical powers located in
their eyes to harm humans, livestock and property, sometimes referred
to as the 'evil-eye'. In Derbyshire in 1650, a widow named Ann Wagg

was accused of bewitching a servant named Elizabeth Parkinson, having 'frowned upon the said maide' as she entered her parish church.[8] Other witches were believed to harm using words, by cursing their victims. This form of bewitchment was particularly prevalent in early modern England. In sixteenth- and seventeenth-century Ireland, witches were believed to use the 'evil-eye' to bewitch cattle or to steal milk and butter (see chapter 4). The touching of a victim was a method employed by one of Ireland's most infamous witches, Florence Newton, in the English settler port town of Youghal, County Cork. Newton was arrested and committed to prison in late March 1661 for bewitching (by cursing and kissing) Mary Longdon, a young servant to local gentleman and future mayor, John Pyne. The accusation soon changed from a relatively straightforward bewitching to a case of demonic possession, and ended in the death of Newton's gaoler, David Jones. Newton pleaded not guilty at the Cork Assize Court, on 11 September 1661.[9] The outcome of the trial is not recorded and we do not know what happened to Florence Newton. She may have been convicted and executed under the provisions of the 1586 Act, or she may have even died during the trial. Witches also used spells and potions to harm, and some did so by giving victims food or drink. In the small Presbyterian town of Antrim in May 1698, a 9-year-old girl became demonically possessed after eating a bewitched sorrel leaf given to her by an elderly beggar woman.[10] The fact that the herb entered the victim through the mouth is also significant because it was widely believed, from the late sixteenth century onwards, that demons entered the body through its various orifices: the anus, vagina, mouth and nose.

From Obsession to Possession

Although the other women in the house were too frightened to touch the magical apron, Mary Dunbar carefully undid the knots, 'without the least fear or suspicion of witchcraft'.[11] Inside, she found old Mrs Haltridge's cap, which had been missing for over a week before her death. When she 'saw the cap she was frightened, and threw it, with the apron, to Mrs Haltridge'. It was too late, as her actions had unleashed a second spate of demonic activity in a household that had lain in silence since the funeral.

At nine the next morning, 28 February, bedclothes were stripped from the deceased woman's bed. An hour later, Dunbar crept upstairs to see if anything else had been disturbed in the room, but she only got within three stairs of the top landing before being 'suddenly seized with a pain in the thigh which made her fall down and cry out very violently'. She was quickly brought downstairs, and although she recovered within a few minutes, her body was wracked once more by stabbing pains in her head, breasts and back. Confined to bed, she experienced a series of convulsions lasting eight hours. As the ninth hour of her ordeal approached, she 'struggled very much, shouting violently'. She then fell into 'a swoon' while softly repeating to herself, 'so and so'. When recovered, the Haltridge women asked her what her words meant and to whom they were spoken, as there was no one else in the room. Dunbar replied that a woman with 'a dirty biggy' (the head clothes that farmer's wives wear in Scotland) and 'a dirty face' came to her bedside and asked, 'How do you do, Mary Dunbar?' Falling into the first of a series of fits, Dunbar cried out, 'Fie, fie upon you for a wicked woman. I trust in God you shall never get advantage against me. Your master afflicted Job, but God preserved him. I believe that God who preserved him, and the children of Israel in the Red Sea, is able to deliver me from thee. I trust in Christ you will get your reward.'

Dunbar later explained that she had been speaking to 'the woman in the dirty biggy and several others' who gathered by her bedside and 'threatened to kill her'. When asked if she knew the spectral women, who were invisible to everyone but herself, she replied that 'she had never seen any of them in all her life except what she saw in her fits'. However, her attackers had mentioned two names, Janet Main and Janet Carson. As her fits steadily increased in frequency and intensity, Dunbar continued to talk to the spectres and was heard repeatedly 'putting up petitions to God for her safety'.

Demonic Possession

Mary Dunbar articulated her ordeal using Biblical language and imagery immediately recognisable to her Presbyterian audience. It is probable that, as a daughter of the gentry, she would have been 'home-schooled' by a private tutor in matters of religion and possibly classical languages and literature. Private religious study would have also provided the Biblical knowledge needed to compare her situation with that of Job. In the Bible, Job was tested by Satan through a serious of trials and torments and was ultimately rewarded by God for his unrelenting faith. This self-made comparison to Job enabled Dunbar to cast herself in the role of a martyr: a pious, virtuous victim, pitted against the forces of darkness. This pose was often adopted by demoniacs (a contemporary term for a demonically possessed person) in early modern Europe. With her mysterious bodily pains, violent fits, and reports of spectral visitors, Dunbar was already ticking many of the boxes to be categorised as a demoniac. As this episode, and subsequent chapters in this book, demonstrate, possession was central to the Islandmagee trial, which makes the fact that historians overlooked this aspect of the case all the more surprising.

Demonic possession also played an important part in the language of the supernatural in the early modern world and had secured roots in educated Catholic and Protestant culture as well as in the popular mind. Classical Greek and Roman texts demonstrate that possession had been a part of the mental landscape of Western Europe for centuries. The Bible, especially the New Testament, was full of examples of Jesus Christ using his divine authority to cast demons from human bodies.[12] The symptoms of possession were stereotyped and changed very little during the early modern period. This characteristic, along with its frequency and the publicity that high-profile cases created, meant people in Britain and its colonies knew by the seventeenth century what the signs and symptoms of possession were and how to identify a demoniac. These signs were described in the Bible, debated in learned witchcraft and demonological tracts, and publicised in ballads and popular pamphlets about well-known witch trials and possession cases.

The range and degree of severity of symptoms of possession differed from demoniac to demoniac, but some were more common than others. The vomiting of household objects, particularly needles and pins but also coal, feathers, pottery, nails, glass, dung, hair and thread, was widely reported. As were violent fits, in which victims variously writhed, thrashed about, shook, trembled, or shuddered. Many demoniacs also experienced physical pain, ranging in severity from pinpricks, to feeling living things moving beneath the skin, to unbearable torments. Their eyes bulged, their faces, throats and stomachs became swollen, or they demonstrated preternatural levels of strength inconsistent with their age or physique. Other demoniacs were deprived of bodily function: they fell into trances, were insensible to pain, or temporarily lost their hearing, sight, speech or (occasionally) the ability to eat or drink (often because their jaws became tightly clenched). Paralysis, in which muscles and limbs stiffened and straightened, was also reported, as was exceptional flexibility. The demonically possessed often screamed, shouted, cursed, hurled obscenities, and blasphemed, or acted in ways that violated contemporary codes of morality. Some spoke in languages they had no prior knowledge of. Other symptoms included demonic ventriloquism, where the incumbent demon(s) spoke using the body of the 'host', and clairvoyance, where they foretold the future, or knew about things beyond their years and experience. The possessed also encountered strange smells and noises and displayed an adverse reaction to anything associated with God or religion, including prayer, the Bible, sacred objects, or the presence of clergymen. As it was common for bewitched people to see the otherwise invisible spectres of their human tormentors, this became a prominent proof in English witchcraft trials in the mid-seventeenth century, especially in those involving possession. It was even used, albeit controversially, in Salem in 1692, when victims complained that witches had frequently attacked them in spectral form (see chapter 9). Levitation, in which the demoniac floated above the floor or a bed, was rare in possession cases.

Demonic possession was believed to have two causes. The first was direct possession by Satan himself or one of his lesser demons. This was a characteristic of most continental demonic possessions. Direct demonic possession was associated with sin, as it was assumed Satan specifically targeted the sinful. In early modern Christian orthodoxy, the Devil was paradoxically God's greatest foe but also under his complete control, and was sometimes used by the Creator to punish the sinful. In other words, as sinners, demoniacs were at least partly to blame for their afflictions. The second type of possession predominated in the British Isles and in Protestant Ireland and was linked to the activities of witches. In this reading, witches were believed to have chosen a victim, conjured up evil spirits and commanded them to enter their bodies. As acts of witchcraft these actions were punishable by law and were often followed by the prosecution of those deemed responsible. Contemporaries, however, failed to point out that no connection was made in the Bible between possession and witchcraft. Demonic possession was nevertheless associated with victimhood, as a demoniac was regarded as the helpless victim of a witch's malice.

Possession cases reached almost epidemic proportions in both Protestant and Catholic countries in sixteenth- and seventeenth-century Europe. Brian Levack suggests that 'the number of people reputedly possessed by demons in early modern Europe certainly reached into the thousands',[13] while Philip Almond has called 'the period from 1550 to 1700 … the golden age of the demoniac'.[14] In England alone, he found over a hundred cases of possession in which the majority of demoniacs were under the age of 20 and a slight majority were girls or women.[15] For example, in 1593, the five daughters (ranging from 9 years of age to 15) of Huntingdonshire gentleman Robert Throckmorton accused elderly Alice Samuel, her husband John, and daughter Agnes of conjuring and commanding evil demons to enter their bodies. For this crime, and the murder of Lady Cromwell (second wife of Sir Henry Cromwell of Hinchinbrook), these 'witches of Warboys' were convicted and hanged (see fig. 6).[16]

The educated may have believed in possession in early modern Britain but they often had very different views on how to tackle it. Before the end of the sixteenth century, the Catholic rite of exorcism, which used 'verbal formulae and liturgical actions' to command evil spirits to leave the human body, 'was very much a matter of improvisation'.[17] The rise in possession cases throughout Europe after 1550 saw the publication of numerous semi-official and unofficial, do-it-yourself, Catholic exorcism

manuals. These manuals led the Catholic Church to issue an author-
ised and standardised (in terms of form and content) rite of exorcism,
the *Rituale Romanum* of Pope Paul V (1614). It stipulated that exorcism
should be conducted only by priests in churches. How rigorously these
rules were followed is, however, open to debate. Certainly, laymen and
priests acting without Church permission continued to conduct exorcisms, and unofficial exorcism manuals remained popular. Exorcists who
followed the *Rituale Romanum* were expected to command the Devil
to depart in God's name, say prayers, read from stipulated parts of the
New Testament, and mark the demoniac's breast with the sign of the
cross. Both before and after the issue of the official rite, Catholic priests
in England were performing exorcisms. Between the springs of 1585
and 1586, twelve Catholic priests in Denham, Buckinghamshire, drove
spirits from six individuals, and during the next century members of
their order continued to perform exorcisms in secret. Reformation-era
Protestantism, however, shunned this rite, seeing it variously as pagan,
magical, or another way in which Catholic priests ensnared the gullible
and propagandised the old faith.

There was no direct discussion of demonic possession in the English
Witchcraft Acts of 1563 and 1604. However, Canon 72, passed in 1604
by the Convocation of Canterbury of the Church of England (an
assembly of bishops and clergy), prohibited all unlicensed exorcisms.
It also stipulated that the Protestant version of exorcism, dispossession,
was to be only performed by minsters licensed by an Anglican bishop.
Rather than an elaborate ritual concerned with commanding a demon to
depart a victim's body, dispossession used prayer and fasting, interspersed
with preaching and the reading of the Bible, to ask God to send the
possessing, evil spirits back to Hell. The hostility to dispossession
enshrined in the 1604 Canon lay in the increasing concern from the
late 1590s onwards that stricter Protestant Puritan factions were using
it to strengthen their cause and threaten the unity of the Church of
England. Canon 72 effectively banned Anglican exorcism, as no bishop's
licences were issued after 1604. Dispossessions nevertheless continued
to be performed in private during the seventeenth century by English
Protestant non-conformists.[18] In Ireland, dispossessions were carried out
by Presbyterian Robert Blair in Larne, County Antrim, in 1630, and

by Baptist Sir Jerome Sankey in Dublin in the 1650s (see chapters 1 and 7). It was also used by Presbyterian minsters and Elders in Islandmagee during the demonic obsession of Ann Haltridge, and in Salem village in 1692 by Samuel Parris, a local Puritan minister and father of one of the afflicted girls, against the advice of his fellow clergymen.

Irish Catholic priests also performed exorcisms in seventeenth-century Ireland, but the 1614 standardised form was not closely followed. Consequently, exorcism was 'carried out in haphazard way[s]' using 'whatever manifestation of the power of God was locally accepted and available, adapting their methods to suit local customs'. The ritual was for the most part conducted in English rather than in Latin. Some priests used prayer and the sign of the cross, while others employed religious relics or the host (the bread used during Holy Communion).[19] In 1609, at the Cistercian Abbey of the Holy Cross in County Tipperary, Abbot Richard Foulow used a belt that had touched the relic of the True Cross of Christ in an exorcism of a woman from County Kilkenny. Francis Young has noted that early seventeenth-century Ireland exorcism 'had the potential to re-establish the restored monasteries at the centre of their communities, as well as boosting the prestige of relics they claimed to possess and challenging Protestant claims to authority.' In the later seventeenth century, however exorcism worked specifically as a 'force for the conversion of Protestants', as a spectacle to convince onlookers of the power of the Catholic Church.[20] As agents of Counter-Reformation Catholicism, Jesuit missionaries working in seventeenth-century Ireland regularly used exorcism to spread orthodox religious practice among ordinary people and combat the spread of Protestantism. The demoniacs Jesuits encountered were mostly victims of direct demonic possession, which, as we have said, carried with it the implication of personal or community sin. In Meath in 1613, a pious 14-year-old girl, the daughter of a man 'born of very honourable rank', was struck by an obsessing demon in the form of an old woman while making her way to Mass with her mother. She became possessed soon afterwards: her 'eyeballs rolled around', she was 'rendered mute', was attacked by the spectral forms of demons and suffered extreme pains in her stomach. After weeks of torment, she was cured by a Jesuit exorcism.[21]

The first case of demonic possession using witchcraft to come before the courts in Ireland occurred in Youghal in 1661. Florence Newton's victim, Mary Longdon, displayed paranormal strength and suffered from recurrent fits and trances, during which she claimed to have been attacked by the spectral forms of Newton and the Devil himself. Longdon also experienced physical pain, vomited household objects such as pins, needles, wool and straw, and displayed an adverse reaction to the Bible.[22] In the Antrim case of 1698, the young victim was 'tortured in her bowels' and began to 'tremble all over, and then to be convulst' and 'swo[o]n away and fall as one dead'.[23] It was reported that the Presbyterian minister of Antrim, Revd William Adair, had 'scarce laid' his 'hands on her when the child was transformed by a daemon into such shape ... [that] a man that hath not beheld it with his [own] eyes, would hardly be brought to imagine.' The demon then 'began first to rowl itself about, and nixt to vomit horse dung, needles, pins, hairs, feathers, bottoms of thread, pieces of glass, window nails draven out of a cart or coach wheels, an iron knife above a span long, egg and fish shells.' The old woman believed responsible was eventually apprehended, made to confess, and then strangled by her neighbours and burned after the Scottish method of witch execution. This case was not in fact a witchcraft trial carried out by legal authorities using the law of the land, but a lynching carried out by a mob.[24]

In contrast to England and Protestant Ireland, possession in Scotland before the 1690s was blamed by the educated elite on Satan directly and interpreted as a consequence of sin and moral failure on the part of the victim. This made people less willing to expose themselves to ridicule by accusing others of their possession. It was only a decade or so before the Islandmagee case that the Godly elite of the Presbyterian Church of Scotland began to recognise the English type of possession and take accusations involving it seriously. This was because they now regarded it as a useful tool in their campaign against atheism, as it helped explain the universe in spiritual rather than in the new 'scientific', materialist terms. As a result, between 1696 and 1704, Presbyterian lowland Scotland experienced its first wave of possessions and trials, including the widely publicised case of 11-year-old Christian Shaw, a pious laird's daughter from Bargarran, Renfrewshire. In late 1696,

Shaw began having fits, was unable to eat, experienced bodily pains, and vomited hot embers, pins, hair, and hay mixed with dung. She was also temporarily unable to speak, hear or see, and on occasion became stiff and lifeless. After local ministers, neighbours and family members fasted and prayed for her, and physicians and apothecaries failed to cure her by medical means, seven people were eventually tried, convicted and executed for her possession.[25]

Putting a Name to a Face

On the morning of 1 March 1711, when Dunbar had recovered from 'three different fits', she 'named Janet Carson' as one of her attackers. Dunbar was able to identify Carson by name because it had been used by her spectral accomplices the previous day.[26] Janet Carson's daughter, who was in the house when the accusation was made, was understandably 'concerned to hear her mother named ... for a witch' and immediately sought the intervention of Revd Sinclair. This was not an uncommon response in that period as witchcraft suspects, or their friends and family, often put up spirited defences to witchcraft accusations. This was especially important because, as Alison Rowlands has put it, 'in many regions, women, especially if they were poor, might simply have ... lacked the social, financial and educational resources to mount effective strategies in their own defence'.[27] In any case, possession was a phenomenon confirmed by professionals such as physicians or clergymen, not by amateurs.

Revd Sinclair advised Janet Carson's daughter 'to go and tell her mother' about Dunbar's accusation. He further resolved to 'go and speak to' Janet himself to ask her to accompany him to nearby Knowehead House to 'make trial whether she [Dunbar] would know her or not'. Carson initially refused his request 'by saying she was weak, and not able', but after 'being earnestly desired' to do so by Sinclair she 'went accordingly'. On Carson's approach to Knowehead, however, 'a great terror ... and a great heat' came upon Dunbar, who 'began to stare and look about her after an unusual manner'. Furthermore, just as Carson reached Dunbar's bedroom door, unannounced, the girl cried out, 'There's Janet Carson!' When Carson entered the room, Dunbar was struck by 'the greatest agony imaginable', with 'three strong men being scarcely able to hold her in the bed'. Revd Sinclair quickly moved Carson to another room, where he asked her to pray for Dunbar's recovery, which she initially refused to do on account that she had done the girl 'no wrong'.

Dunbar's fits continued unabated, and she claimed that Carson and several accomplices visited her in her bed and when she was in 'greatest pain would lie laughing at her, and diverting themselves at her expence'. These visits had the unexpected benefit of providing Dunbar with physical descriptions of her attackers (whom she claimed to have never seen before), and locals with the means to identify and track them down. Dunbar correctly described Carson as a 'low set woman, well favoured' (small and stocky), while another suspect, Janet Liston (Sellor), was said to have been wearing a 'dirty biggy upon her head, her face swarthy', with 'a large rolling eye, [and] very thick lips'. Liston was also said to be 'lame of foot, pretty thick, and of a low stature'. A final suspect (Liston's daughter, Elizabeth Sellor) was described as being 'much handsomer', but of 'the same stature, and also lame of a leg'. Revd Tisdall described her in a similar manner, as 'a young girl of about seventeen, who … had a fair complexion and a very good face'.[28] Tisdall also remarked that 'the description the afflicted gave of them, together with some of their names, were so very particular, that several of them were guessed at'.[29]

It was at this point that 'some in the neighbourhood being present, thought it proper to send for' Janet Liston at the home she shared in Islandmagee with her husband, William Sellor. A local woman, Mary Twinam, was given the task of fetching Liston. Liston, however, informed Twinam that 'she would not goe for all Island Magee' to 'see Mary Dunbar', except if 'Mr Sinclair wou'd come for her'. Liston went on to state that if:

> the plague of God was on … Mary Dunbar, the plague of God be on them altogether: the Devil be with them, if he was among them. If God had taken her health from her, God give her health. If the Devil had taken it from her, the Devil give her it.[30]

This may have been a loose paraphrasing by Liston of Job 1:21, which in the Bible states: 'the LORD gave, and the LORD hath taken away'. It may also demonstrate Liston's awareness of mechanisms other than witchcraft to explain Dunbar's fits and trances, in that God or the Devil could have caused the girl's malady without the agency of a witch. Revd Sinclair nevertheless interpreted Liston's 'horrible expression' that 'the devil be with them' as a witch's curse. The reputation of Liston may have further convinced Sinclair to side with Dunbar (see chapter 6).

Evening brought more demonically inspired disturbances. When no one was in the parlour, 'clothes were taken off the bed, and thrust into the grate, and a great part of them burned before any notice was taken of their being in the fire'. Soon afterwards one of the servants, presumably Spear, was hit with 'great force' with 'a stone of a pound and a half weight'. This made such a noise that everyone in the rooms downstairs heard it. The servant thought it had been 'thrown from a corner of the room, which was immediately searched very narrowly, as they did also below stairs, yet nothing could be seen that might have occasioned it'. That night stones and turf were thrown into the kitchen.

After her refusal to accompany Twinam to Knowhead House, it was agreed the next day, Monday, 2 March, that Liston's landlord, William Fenton,[31] would 'use his interest with her [Liston] to bring her to see' Dunbar, along with her daughter, Elizabeth, which 'he and a few others did with some difficulty'. Liston's initial resistance to the investigation process was therefore even stronger than Carson's. As spectacles promising the sight of the Devil (or his demons) in action, possession cases often drew large crowds. As these cases were shared public experiences, validated by witnesses, spectators were often called up later to give evidence to magistrates or in court. Among the throng at Knowehead House was David Robb,[32] Church of Ireland minister of St John's parish church, located in the townland of Ballyharry in Islandmagee.[33] Assisted by Robb, Revd Sinclair arranged for over thirty female members of the crowd to be brought before Dunbar, 'to see if they could deceive her either in the name or description of the accused person'.[34] In other words, the men had organised a crude identity parade to safeguard against a deliberate attempt by Dunbar to accuse innocent people of witchcraft: if she could not identify her spectral attacker from a line-up, her testimony would be invalidated. This 'test' had legal precedent in England, having been used by Sir Matthew Hale during the infamous trial of Rose Cullender and Amy Denny at Norwich Assizes in Lowestoft in March 1662. As the women were led 'one by one' into the girl's bedroom and paraded past her bed, Dunbar was observed to have been 'not the least moved' by their presence, 'declaring she saw none there who were her tormentors'. As soon as Liston appeared, however, she screamed, 'that was she!' before falling into a fit and crying out loudly in pain. Dunbar's reaction was so severe that it took three men a great deal of effort to put her back into bed, despite her being thin and light in weight. It is interesting to note that fluctuations in weight and even height were often witnessed in demoniacs in early modern England.

Although the sexual element was not as obvious here as it was in some Catholic possession cases on the Continent, where simulated copulation by demoniacs was reported, it was nevertheless tangible. In the situation they found themselves in – three strange men restraining a young woman convulsing in her bed – the parties concerned were able to act in a socially unacceptable manner, laden with sexual overtones, without any damage to their reputations. Similarly, when 20-year-old demoniac Anne Gunter, in the country parish of North Morton, near Oxford, writhed and screamed on her bed during possession fits, local young men were reported to have taken a keen interest in her.[35] As this battle of wills between the men and the demon in Dunbar was being fought, it was reported that the assembled 'company ... trembled and ... cried out with fear to see the miserable condition' the girl was in. English possession narratives often describe how crowds at possessions were both repelled and captivated by what they saw. It is probable that the reaction of the crowd reminded Janet Liston of the potential danger she was in due to Dunbar's allegations, and she began praying 'to God' to send the girl 'her health'.

Robb and Sinclair then cleared Knowehead of spectators and took Liston and her daughter Elizabeth to the parlour to examine them on 'the articles of the Christian religion' and make them recite the Lord's Prayer and Apostles' Creed. Both women were unable to carry out these tasks 'distinctly, nor give any satisfactory answer to the questions put to them'. Founded on the belief that a witch was an agent of the Devil and thus averse to the word of God, the inability to say the Lord's Prayer was taken by authorities (from 1590 onwards) as a 'proof' of witchcraft. In Youghal, Cork, in 1661, 'Newton's inability to say the Lord's Prayer and Longdon's adverse reaction to her approach was regarded as enough evidence for her to be arrested and imprisoned to await trial at the next assizes ... while imprisoned, Newton was tested again.'[36] In Hertfordshire in 1712, this test was administered by local clergy and Justices of the Peace (JPs) to suspected witch Jane Wenham, who failed it on at least two occasions. Francis Hutchinson, later Bishop of Down and Connor, visited Wenham a few years after her trial, at her house on the estate of a local landowner, and discovered that, in the intervening years, she had learnt both the 'Lord's Prayer and Creed', albeit 'with such little errors of expression, as those that cannot read are subject to'.[37]

Robb and Sinclair, however, were still not completely at ease with attributing the girl's possession to witchcraft and so brought Elizabeth Sellor into Dunbar's room. Almost on cue, Dunbar had a seizure and did not recover until Sellor left the room. The minsters then made Dunbar face the wall and placed three men at the foot of her bed to ensure she could not see who entered the room. Sellor was then brought quietly and secretly into the room, but still Dunbar convulsed. A little later, both mother and daughter were brought into the room and made to touch Dunbar, with exactly the same results as before. The 'touching test' was administered in the expectation that if the suspect was guilty their victim would react adversely. It became a relatively common feature of English witchcraft and possession cases, most notably in the Lowestoft trial of Denny and Cullender in 1662. After they had administered the test, Sinclair and Robb questioned the women again and once more received 'no satisfactory answers'. Amongst other questions they asked of Sellor was why she thought Dunbar was 'seized after so extraordinary a manner upon their going into the room, more than when any other went in'. Sellor replied that 'perhaps God was at that time punishing the girl for the sins more than at another time', a sentiment repeated by her mother. In short, Sellor was suggesting that Dunbar's possession was God's punishment for some type of sinful behaviour. A similar argument was used in relation to victims of witchcraft by non-conformist clergyman and sceptical witchcraft writer George Gifford in late sixteenth-century Essex.[38] Unfortunately for the women, their attempts to demonstrate religious orthodoxy and present an alternative explanation for the girl's malady went unheeded.

Dunbar's Condition Worsens

That night, 2 March, Dunbar's 'fits' alternated between the 'violent' seizures she had experienced previously, in which her body jerked and shook, and a new type, 'fainting fits', in which she fell to the floor where she would 'lay a considerable time without any motion'. During these episodes, Dunbar complained of being pricked with pins and felt 'a burning heat at her breast, as if she were a-roasting'. Onlookers noted that 'through the violence of the pain she struggled with her hands and feet, as if she had been in the pangs of one strangling, and was not able to make the least noise.' Furthermore, when Dunbar was 'taken out or into the room where she lay, that exactly upon the door threshold she fell down in the posture of one that had been dead for some time; all the parts of her body being frigid and stiff, and of three times greater weight than at other times when not in a fit.' Before the onset of her fits, Dunbar noticed 'a heavy sulphurous smell' which was so strong it caused 'a woman in the neighbourhood' to faint. Brimstone, or sulphur, was associated in the Bible with Hell and eternal punishment for the damned,[39] but rarely recorded in possession cases. However, in Nottingham in 1597, William Sommers claimed that when he had 'fits, strange smells were in the place where he lay'.[40] In 1564, the wife of Edmund Kingsfield believed she became possessed while praying in church, a development marked by the sudden appearance of smoke and the smell of brimstone.[41]

Thirsty from the exertion of her fits and trances, Dunbar drank a glass of water, but when asked if she would like anything else to drink or eat, 'her throat … contracted, and her teeth set, and appeared in danger of being choked'. In the early modern period, it was widely believed that possession cut off the body from all sensation, a state revealed by being ice cold to the touch, having tightly clenched jaws, or the onset of temporary blindness. This closure of the body from the outside world was reinforced by the inability to eat. The teeth of Elizabeth Throckmorton, one of the child accusers of 'the witches of Warboys', were so tightly clenched that she could not even be forced to drink milk through a quill.

In a matter of days, Mary Dunbar had displayed such a range of recognisable symptoms as to convince the local community in Islandmagee that she was demonically possessed. The evidence she provided to link her possession to the witchcraft of local women was largely of the spectral variety. She claimed to have never met the women in the real world and was only able to provide descriptions of them (or their names) after they attacked and threatened her in spirit form. In doing so, she set in motion a sequence of events that she was quickly losing control over, leaving her little option but to carry on a drama in which her body became a battleground for good and evil, God and the Devil.

To Catch a Witch

Mayor of Carrickfergus, Edward Clements, Takes Charge, 3 March 1711

Days and nights of fits, trances, praying, crowds and commotion must have taken their toll on the grieving Haltridge family, which was still without a head as James was still in Dublin. Consequently, by 3 March 1711 they were understandably anxious for respite. It was decided to move Mary Dunbar from the ground to the first floor, 'where there was less disturbance'. On approach to the third stair from the top landing, she fell once more 'down as dead', her body becoming so heavy that it took 'three strong men' to move her. When she was taken back downstairs, she recovered enough to drink 'two draughts of beer'. Although probably not as potent as today's equivalent tipple, it nevertheless had a soporific effect on Dunbar, who fell into a deep sleep lasting five hours. This was the first sustenance, except for water, she had taken in three days, which, along with clenched jaws, cationic trances, and fluctuations in weight, must have provided onlookers with further evidence that she was a genuine demoniac.

In the early eighteenth century, it was not the state who initiated prosecutions for criminal offences but private individuals, usually the victim, their relatives or acquaintances. Proceedings usually began when prosecutors took their complaint to a JP, who decided whether or not to take things any further. Irish JPs were male, Protestant and drawn from the gentry class, but their ranks also included members of the clergy, lawyers and aristocracy. They represented the bottom level of the judiciary, and JPs were expected to screen initial accusations, gather evidence and witness statements, and examine and commit suspects to gaol. Dunbar's prosecution of the suspects was facilitated by Sinclair and Robb and some important, wealthy local men. It began on 3 March, when Edward Clements, Mayor of Carrickfergus, acting in his role as ex-officio magistrate or JP, took statements from witnesses and delegated investigative responsibilities to Islandmagee grandees. Clement's decision to become personally involved in the case was probably due to the fact that up until the nineteenth century there was no magistrate based in Islandmagee, with those wishing to engage of their services having to travel to Carrickfergus, which was 5 miles away from the most southerly point of the peninsula.[1] It may have been that the relatively small population there, along with its close proximity to Carrickfergus, negated the need for a resident magistrate. In any case, in the context of the early eighteenth century, it would have been difficult to locate anyone in Presbyterian Islandmagee able to take up the position of JP: the 1704 Test Act (see chapter 9) excluded members of that denomination from office.

Edward Clements (died 1733) was married to Eleanor (died 1696), the daughter of Alexander Dalway of Ballyhill townland, 3 miles north-east of Carrickfergus, who bore him seven sons and two daughters. He inherited the estate of Clements Hill, Straid, County Antrim, also a few miles from Carrickfergus, from his brother Henry, who died in November 1696 at the age of 52 while still mayor of the town. Edward and Henry joined the Antrim Association to put up armed resistance to Catholic James II and were later attainted (found guilty of treason) by the Dublin Parliament in 1689. Another brother, Andrew (died c.1718), was Mayor of Carrickfergus in 1692, 1702, 1703 and 1715. Mayors of Carrickfergus were elected annually, heading a corporation of a recorder, seventeen aldermen (including the mayor), and twenty-four burgesses, and were afforded the captainship of the militia and the position of first JP for County Antrim.[2] Clements was a Whig in politics and friendly to Presbyterians, which may have motivated him to investigate Dunbar's accusation fully.

Hunting Catherine McCalmond, 4 March

The next morning, Dunbar, reinvigorated by a good night's sleep, named 'Catherine to be one of her tormentors, saying she was a large dark coloured woman.' In this context, 'dark' likely meant Catherine had black hair or a sallow complexion. Possibly acting on the orders of Mayor Clements, an identity parade comprising every woman called Catherine in Islandmagee was hastily organised by James Blythe of Bank-Head in Larne, and Islandmagee locals Mrs Wilson, James McAlexander and Janet Martin. As the selected women passed one by one before her, Dunbar was observed to be 'not in the least disturbed till one Catherine McCalmond came'. Blythe later provided sworn testimony that as soon as McCalmond entered 'Mary's roome', Dunbar 'fell into such violent fitt of pains that three persons were not able to hold her'. He also deposed that after Dunbar recovered, she was able to formally identify McCalmond as one of her spectral attackers.[3] When McCalmond was in the room Dunbar 'grasped at her with great eagerness', but was suddenly 'pulled back as it were by some external power, though invisible'. She then screamed for the 'wicked woman' to leave the house, which McCalmond initially refused to do.

McCalmond's reluctance to leave is surprising since she had been brought unwillingly to the Haltridge house by neighbours, on the instructions of Revd Sinclair, who lived only a short distance from her. It is probable she wanted to stay on to try and clear her name. Sinclair's house was built for him in the townland of Ballymuldrogh by the congregation of Islandmagee on the farm of Church Elder, Randal Leathes.[4] McCalmond's reaction to Dunbar's allegations undoubtedly threw more suspicion on her, which, as we shall see, was a dangerous position to be in for a woman who already enjoyed a bad reputation locally as 'an ignorant irreligious woman', who was 'of an ill fame'. It was intensified by the testimony of Revd Sinclair, who claimed that when he was making his way to the Haltridge house he heard a loud noise moving through the air above his head. Stopping to listen, he realised it sounded 'like a horse, but more dull and melancholy'. Another local man, and wealthy Ruling Elder of the congregation of Islandmagee, William Brown,[5] swore he had heard the same noise at the same time, precisely fifteen minutes before McCalmond was brought before Dunbar – the implication being that the noise the men heard was made by an invisible, demonic entity hastening on horseback to attack Dunbar and protect its mistress, McCalmond. Janet McAlexander (presumably the wife of James) also witnessed a supernatural phenomenon in the house on that day, claiming she 'saw a cloth, like the lower end of a petticoat, turning round in the middle of the floor, about a foot high from the ground, which frightened her very much, seeing nothing that could cause it.'

Seeking Justice

A few hours later, around three o'clock in the afternoon, four men, Fenton, Blythe, Robert Holmes[6] and William Hatley, proceeded to McCalmond's house 'to search for charms or pictures'. Although there is no evidence they were acting in an official legal capacity, it is more than likely they were acting on the orders of Mayor Clements.[7] The decision to search for this particular type of image magic may have been based on instructions contained in English-born politician and lawyer Sir Richard Bolton's *A Justice of the Peace for Ireland …* (Dublin, 2nd ed., 1638). Bolton's book was an essential guide for otherwise untrained agents of local law enforcement, as well as a handy tool for those investigating witchcraft accusations. It contained a straightforward summary of the 1586 Irish Witchcraft Act and a list of acceptable legal 'proofs' taken from a pamphlet account of the Lancaster witch trial of 1612, written by Thomas Potts, *The Wonderfull Discoverie of Witches in the Countie of Lancaster …* (1613). Bolton justified the inclusion of a list of 'proofs' because in witchcraft cases, he reasoned, a JP 'may not altogether expect direct evidence, seeing all their workes are the workes of darknesse and not witnesses present with them to accuse them'. He went on to state that witches 'often have pictures of clay, or waxe (like a man, etc.) found in their house', and instructed JPs to secure the 'voluntary confession' of the suspect because it exceeded 'all other evidence'. Failing this, they were to gain sworn testimony from victims and the children or servants of the accused.[8] They were also told to search the house of the accused for ownership of a familiar and to search their body for a Devil's mark. Ronald Hutton has suggested that 'the idea of attendant demons, which had special relationships with individual witches and took animal shape, was actually built into the new stereotype of satanic witchcraft from the very beginning'. On the Continent, where the concept of the witches' Sabbat held sway, the 'main purpose of the servitor demonic animal was to transport the witch thither'. In England, where this was 'not central to images of witchcraft, the relationship ended up as being conceived differently'.[9] In England, from the sixteenth century onward, the main contact witches were thought to have with the Devil was through their familiar spirits, which took a variety of animal forms, from fleas, ferrets, mice, and rats to turkey cocks and dogs. For doing the witch's bidding, familiars received sustenance from blood sucked from the Devil's mark on the bodies of their masters. These marks usually took the form of teats on or near the suspect's 'secret parts' and were regarded to be legal proof of practising satanic witchcraft.[10] In sixteenth- and seventeenth-century Scotland, witches who travelled on demonic animal spirits rarely appeared in witch trials and the concept of a familiar spirit almost never. Although Satan and his minions were said to have appeared to humans in animal form, 'none seems to have settled into a domestic or nurturing relationship with a witch as was believed to happen in England'.[11]

Searching McCalmond's House

While the men carried out the search, two other (unnamed) men were sent to examine the walls of a nearby ruined house for hidden charms or spells. Revd Sinclair witnessed this from the window of his house, noting that after a short time one of the men went back to McCalmond's house, while the other remained to conduct a further examination. Using a 'perspective glass' or telescope, Sinclair then saw a woman dart from the dilapidated building and enter McCalmond's house. The two searchers found nothing suspicious in the building and reported that they had not seen the woman. Reading between the lines, Sinclair was suggesting that to avoid detection McCalmond had assumed invisible spirit form and removed any trace of her charm-making from the ruined house. In this way, Sinclair provided a convincing explanation for the lack of material evidence linking McCalmond to her supposed crimes.

More Names, More Suspects, 4 March

Dunbar's fits worsened as the day progressed and she was heard 'reasoning with her tormentors, and desiring them to let her alone'. She also prayed to God for her deliverance, while Revd Sinclair sang the 142nd Psalm. This, however, only served to cause her to have another fit, during which her teeth were so tightly clenched they could only be opened using a key 'forced in betwixt them'. When her mouth was opened, Sinclair discovered her tongue had doubled in two and been forced down the back of her throat, 'in such a manner', wrote Revd Tisdall later, that she was likely 'to choke'.[12] When she recovered, Dunbar told Sinclair she had seen McCalmond, 'lame woman, Janet Liston' and another woman named Janet Main jump onto the bed beside her, accompanied by a woman they called 'Latimer'. It was Main, however, who had 'twisted her tongue ... tore her throat, and tortured her violently by reason of her crooked fingers and swelled knuckles'. It was revealed later during her trial that Janet Main did indeed suffer from arthritis, with all the joints in her hand 'distorted, and the tendons shrivelled up'.[13] Pain, illness and disease were undoubtedly more a part of everyday experience in this period than they are today, but some afflictions, such as severe arthritis, were more likely to affect those who had undertaken years of hard manual labour. For example, the poorer sort.

During the next few hours, Sinclair forced open Dunbar's mouth around twenty times and forced down her tongue, and every time he did so the girl 'sighed, and gave a sudden start, and immediately recovered'. Realising his singing and praying were provoking the demon inside to cause the girl to fit, Sinclair stopped immediately. From this point on, Dunbar experienced only 'light fainting fits' until midnight, after which she fell asleep. Upon awakening at 'the break of day' on 5 March, she took a draught of beer, having fasted the whole of the previous day.

Revd Robert Sinclair, an Exception to a Rule

Although Revd Sinclair may have been in broad agreement with much of his congregation (including its religious leaders, the Elders) that Mary Dunbar was a genuine demoniac, his involvement as prosecutor in the case which he helped bring before the legal authorities was an odd choice for a Presbyterian minister at that time. Sinclair's credulity could be explained in much the same way as his Islandmagee congregation, in that he had a heightened fear of the Devil and demonic obsession and possession, during a period of social, religious and political instability, both in Ulster and elsewhere in the Calvinist network. Dunbar's social status and association with a respected clerical family, along with the fact she was able to repeatedly pick out suspects from an identity parade, may have persuaded him further. But Sinclair was bucking a general trend in which instances of magic and witchcraft were referred by ministers to Presbyterian Church courts (Sessions, Presbyteries, and Meetings), which usually dealt with them in a manner acceptable to both parties, avoiding the need for litigation.

It is arguable that the Presbyterian Church in Ireland could never have played such a central role in witch-hunting as it did in Scotland due to the fact the countries possessed different legal traditions, administrations and court procedures. Legally speaking, Ireland resembled England more than it did Scotland (see chapters 4 and 8). In sixteenth- and seventeenth-century Scotland, Kirk Sessions and Presbyteries took a leading role in identifying witches, investigating accusations and taking down suspects' confessions prior to indictment and trial. By the early eighteenth century, prosecutions for witchcraft were becoming rare in Scotland and the Sessions and Presbyteries largely lost their traditional witch-hunting role. Nevertheless, they occasionally handled witchcraft accusations and suspicions in the form of defamation, cursing and counter-witchcraft cases up until the mid-eighteenth century.

From the outset, the Presbyterian Church in Ulster dealt with witchcraft accusations themselves rather than passing them on to the judicial and court system. Presbyterian Church courts usually handed out very light punishments to malefactors and often condemned accusers for making false accusations. In July 1647, the suspension of the crown court system in the midst of war compelled the Session of the South Antrim parish of Templepatrick, followed by the Presbytery of Antrim, to handle an accusation of witchcraft made against Janet Wilson themselves. Wilson denied the accusation and the Presbytery eventually ruled in her favour.[14] In February 1656, Elizabeth Kennedy of Islandmagee complained to the Antrim Meeting that 'one Thomas Etkin in the same place ... called her an witch and Said he wold prove the same'. The matter was referred back to the Islandmagee Session to 'try the woman and censure the slanderer, or returne the proven process to the next meeting'.[15] The Antrim Meeting was led by Elders and ministers and functioned as Church court and 'a sort of halfway house, an intermediate body between the local ministers and sessions, and the Presbytery that covered all of Ulster'.[16] The case was not mentioned again in the minutes and the Session book for Islandmagee has been lost.

In the early eighteenth century, when the Presbyterian Church became more organised and structured, and the Presbyterian community increasingly cut-off from the Anglican (Church of Ireland) Ascendency at a local and national level, 'this impulse to handle its own moral discipline within its own ecclesiastical structure became stronger'. As a result, 'Sessions and Presbyteries in Ulster continued to deliberate over witchcraft cases in a diligent and even-handed manner', either finding a way to mend relations between accuser and accused, or by censuring the accuser for slander thereby dissuading them from making similar, unfounded allegations in the future. In doing so, they 'may have been taking their lead from religious counterparts in Scotland, and in demanding even stronger evidence of guilt may have been influenced by an increasingly sceptical Irish judiciary'.[17]

In May 1701, William Lockert complained to the Session of Connor Presbyterian Church that a local woman, Agnes Woodburn, had wrongly accused him of witchcraft. The Session called Woodburn and interviewed her, but she denied all charges.[18] The next day they called Lockert and 'rebuked both parties' for un-neighbourliness and they apparently 'parted friends'.[19] In April 1721, at Carnmoney Session in County Antrim, Margaret Williamson stated that 'Mary Coruth had branded her with witchcraft and that she can prove that she said so'.

Aware that the would-be slanderer was of 'good report', the Session agreed to let an Elder, John McMahon, interview her and inform the Session of his findings at the next meeting.[20] The meeting must have reported in Coruth's favour, for the matter was later dropped by the Session.

Sarah Moor, in November 1723, complained to the Aghadowey Session in east Londonderry in Ulster that Timothy Knox, Mary Asking and Robert White had 'defam'd her, [by] saying she is a witch'. The Session ordered Moor to 'bring all her evidences to prove the charges against them next Session', while Elder John Givan ordered the defendants to accompany her.[21] Knox, White and Asking obeyed this request and in April 1724 informed the Session that 'they were rash in calling Sarah Moor a witch and promised to refrain such reproaches hereafter'. Moor accepted this apology and that the ruling was 'satisfactory and was made friends with all of them'.[22]

An Ill Wind?

Mary Dunbar had only been in Islandmagee for a few days but had turned a house which should have been shrouded in grief after the death of its matriarch into the site of a supernatural drama that enthralled and repelled the local community in equal measure. More importantly, she had formally accused five women of the serious crime of witchcraft and cast the shadow of suspicion on another. The interrogations and identity parades conducted by the great and the good of Islandmagee, including local minster Robert Sinclair, only served to confirm Dunbar's allegations. The girl herself made for a very convincing victim by displaying all the symptoms expected of a demoniac and portraying herself as a model of piety and morality, cruelly struck down by the reckless actions of witches. It was Revd Sinclair's involvement, possibly encouraged by Anglican curate Revd Robb, which ensured normal procedure was not followed and the case turned over to civil magistrates instead of Church authorities. As Dunbar's possession was now a legal matter, it is necessary to explore in the next chapter what the crime of witchcraft was in early modern Ireland and how it was handled by the judicial system.

4

Witchcraft

Out of an estimated 100,000 formal accusations of witchcraft made in both Catholic and Protestant European countries between the mid-fifteenth and later eighteenth centuries, around 50,000 people, mainly women, were executed. Most victims of the witch-hunts lost their lives between 1560 and 1640. Of the 50,000 people formally accused but not executed, some were given non-capital sentences such as imprisonment or banishment, while others were acquitted, had their cases dropped, managed to escape, or died in prison awaiting trial. There were many more who suffered because of accusations although they were not prosecuted for witchcraft or officially labelled as witches. This number included those lynched by accusers after authorities failed or refused to prosecute them. Notable cases can be found in France, Italy, Poland and Hungary. In England, around 500 men and women were put to death for witchcraft by the courts between the passing of the Elizabethan Witchcraft Act in 1563 and the last trial in 1717. The last execution, however, took place in 1685, and the last conviction in 1712. Taking into consideration that early modern Scotland held roughly a quarter of the population of England during this period, Scottish witch-hunting was twelve times more intense that its English counterpart: of the 3,837 people tried for witchcraft offences, an estimated 1,500–2000 were executed by manual strangulation followed by burning at the stake.[1]

The figures for prosecution and execution for witchcraft are so low in Ireland they make any statistical analysis or comparison impossible. We know of only three trials for witchcraft held under the 1586 Irish Witchcraft Act, those of: Marion Fisher, Carrickfergus, County Antrim, 1655 (conviction overturned in 1656); Florence Newton, Youghal, County Cork, 1661 (outcome unknown); and the trial of the nine Islandmagee witches (1711). Precisely why the Islandmagee trials occurred in a country with little thirst for hunting witches during a time of general European decline in witchcraft prosecution is one of the main themes of this book. In order to put this discussion in context, it is necessary to explore the reasons why Ireland avoided large-scale witch-hunting. For witch-hunting to take place it was essential for a country or state to possess belief in harmful witches (at all levels of society), a steady flow of witchcraft accusations, laws making it a serious crime, and a legal system and judiciary willing and able to prosecute and convict people.[2] The question to be answered, then, is how far did Ireland possess the intellectual and structural pre-conditions for witch-hunting?

Belief in Witchcraft in Irish Protestant Culture

As we saw in chapter 1, Presbyterians in Islandmagee and Ulster believed in, and were genuinely frightened of, harmful witches. Bringing their religion, culture and beliefs with them from Scotland, they were certain that witches were hell-bent on the destruction of man, beast and property. More so in the elite culture of wealthier or socially and politically influential Presbyterians, witches were believed to attack Christians and Christendom with the help of Satan. Communicants of the Church of Ireland at that time, at all levels of society, also believed in and feared malefic witchcraft, which explains the frosty reception Francis Hutchinson received when made Bishop of Down and Connor in late 1720: two years previously Hutchinson had published *An Historical Essay Concerning Witchcraft* (1718) in which he suggested that traditional witchcraft belief and the prosecution of witches was philosophically, legally and theologically unsound. In December 1720, the Anglican (Church of Ireland) Bishop of Kilmore, Timothy Godwin, informed the head of the Church of England, the Archbishop of Canterbury, William Wake, that Hutchinson's *Historical Essay* had angered his superior, Archbishop William King of Dublin:

> I know Dr Hutchinson a little, and I think he has always maintained a good character, but he must expect to be attacked by his Grace of St Sepultures [Archbishop King] for his book about witchcraft, but I suppose he will keep as much he can out of his way.[3]

Archbishop King was a firm believer in witchcraft and had written anonymously to Congregationalist minister Cotton Mather in 1693 to convince him that the best way for New Englanders, in the aftermath of the Salem witch-hunts, to protect themselves against 'Satan or any of his imps' was to turn their backs on non-conformity and be baptised and confirmed according to the liturgy of the Church of Ireland.[4] Hutchinson was further mocked about his scepticism concerning witchcraft in an anonymous ballad published in Dublin in 1726:

> Least witches and spirits our children should fright,
> He [Hutchinson] on that occasion did learnedly write,
> And at tea told her Grace [his wife] t'was no breach of the law,
> Tho' men should spew pins and old women spit straws.[5]

Mockery did not stop Hutchinson from being immensely proud of his *Historical Essay* and later that year he took copies with him to Dublin to show to acquaintances.[6] He also continued to take a scholarly interest in the supernatural in the 1720s. In a notebook he kept close to him, he tracked the activities of magical practitioners in his diocese along with fairy sightings and cases of witchcraft and demonic possession.[7]

Irish Protestants' belief in witchcraft and Satan inhabited a mental world that portrayed the universe in magical and moral terms: one where spiritual or supernatural essences constantly interfered in the natural world and in the lives of humans. Ghosts were widely believed in by Scottish Presbyterians in Ulster, who also used popular magic to protect themselves from the forces of evil. This magic was often provided by professional or semi-professional fortune-tellers, magical healers and cunning-folk (commercial magical practitioners who provided a range of magical services, see chapters 1 and 7). Irish Protestants differentiated between the unintentional evil-eye, often referred to in popular culture as 'overlooking', and the intentional evil-eye, which was firmly linked to witchcraft. In common with references to fairies, belief in the evil-eye is not widely detectable in surviving Protestant sources. A rare instance of Protestants falling prey to excitable, unpredictable fairies was reported in a pamphlet published in the late 1670s for the English book market. It stated that Dr John Moore, a retired London schoolmaster and now Irish landowner, claimed that when he was a child in County Wicklow in the 1640s he was abducted by a group of fairies on horseback and taken to a fairy fort and then to a feast in the woods. He was returned unharmed the next morning. He believed he had been abducted for breaking a cardinal rule of the fairies by speaking about an earlier abduction.[8]

It was a Biblical necessity for early modern Protestants and Catholics to believe in angels, which were conceived as immaterial, superhuman servants of God who worked for the good of all people. Protestant orthodoxy taught that humans should not expect to see or contact angels and worshipping or praying to them was regarded as idolatrous and Catholic. For this reason, Protestants were expected by their spiritual leaders to reject outright the notion of guardian angels. Human history was regarded as a record of God's providence working in the world. Economic crises, political events and wars were consequently often interpreted according to the following script: we won because God was on our side; or we lost because we sinned and offended God who then punished us. Protestant elites also regarded belief in modern miracles and prophecy as unorthodox at best. It was for this reason, along with political and social concerns about their malign influence on the populace, that both Protestant dissenters and Anglicans took a strong dislike to missionaries (and their handful of converts) of the cultish, millenarian group, the French Prophets. The Prophets arrived on Irish shores at various times between 1709 and 1711, and had first appeared among persecuted Protestant Huguenot communities in Catholic France during the late seventeenth and early eighteenth century. Outlawed after some of their number (the Camisards) led an armed revolt against Louis XIV's troops, the Prophets fled all over Europe.

They arrived in England in 1706, where they prophesised about the coming of the end of the world, worked an array of dubious miracles and exhibited the outward signs of divine possession (the belief that the Holy Spirit was inhabiting their bodies): heaving chests, gasping, trances, fits and emission of strange noises.[9]

Witchcraft Belief in Gaelic-Irish Culture

No demonological treatises or books were written or published in early modern Ireland in either English or Irish, and only one witchcraft pamphlet was produced, by a Protestant, Daniel Higgs, concerning the 1698 lynching: *The Wonderfull and True Relation of the Bewitching a Young Girle in Ireland* ... (1699). From the late sixteenth century onwards, Catholic clergy who were influenced by Counter-Reformation demonology condemned witchcraft and conceived witches similar in terms to Protestants: as debauched demonic agents out to destroy Christian bodies and property who had to be resisted at all costs. Catholic elites, from the wives of Gaelic-Irish noblemen to Old English aristocrats, also perceived witches as inherently threatening and were prepared to use legal means to counter them. In 1542, Charles Fitz Arthur ('Cahir mac Art, chief of the Kavanaghs, created 3rd Baron of Ballyan by Queen Mary')[10] sent an unnamed 'witche' in 1542 'to the Lord Deputie [Sir Anthony St. Leger] to be examined'.[11] In September 1640, the extremely wealthy and well-connected Katherine Manners, the English, Catholic widow of George Villiers, Duke of Buckingham, and new wife to the 2nd Earl of Antrim, Randal McDonnel, declared she had been bewitched by several poor Presbyterian women living in the pre-plantation town that lay outside of her Irish residence of Dunluce Castle, County Antrim. Despite taking her accusation to the heart of the government in Dublin, Katherine's case was dropped a few months later as political crisis engulfed Ireland.[12]

There is no evidence, however, that the mass of the Irish population, the largely Gaelic-speaking, Catholic Irish, made formal accusations of witchcraft or initiated legal proceedings against suspected witches. There may have been some witchcraft accusations hidden in the legal and official records destroyed in the fire at the Public Record Office in Dublin in 1922 during the Irish Civil War, but this seems unlikely as historians working there before the conflict failed to find any new cases. It also seems doubtful that the native Irish avoided bringing formal witchcraft complaints to seventeenth-century Irish common law courts as a form of passive resistance to a colonial judicial system imported from England. As Raymond Gillespie points out, in the mid-seventeenth century the native Irish were 'deeply involved in the workings of the common law system ... and eagerly prosecuted theft, assault, and murder through these courts, so it is difficult to see why witchcraft should have been excluded in such a way.'[13] A more persuasive answer as to why the mass of the Gaelic-Irish made few formal allegations lies in their culturally specific witchcraft beliefs. This approach poses its own problems, as early modern Gaelic scholarship and literature, including poetry and song, had little to say on matters of witchcraft and popular magic. Instead, they were chiefly concerned with specific families, patronage, religion, politics, war, history and historical memory. We therefore rely on evidence written in English by (mostly but not always) Protestants. These historical sources suggest that while the Gaelic-Irish undoubtedly lived in a moral, magical universe and believed in witchcraft, their witches posed far less of a threat than the malefic, demonic witches of their Protestant counterparts. This left little reason to resort to the costly and cumbersome process of having suspected witches prosecuted in Irish common-law courts.

Always female, Gaelic-Irish witches were not seen as demonically inspired, did not make pacts with the Devil, and did not fly, have sex with demons, or attend Sabbats. More importantly, they did not normally kill or injure livestock or people and certainly did not cause them to be demonically possessed. They were primarily thought to use magic to transfer the goodness or 'profit' from the milk of neighbouring cows to their own, resulting in an increase in their own butter production and a subsequent depletion in their neighbour's supply. To transfer fecundity in this way, the malefactor had to bewitch a symbolically significant substance or object taken from the owner of the targeted cow: life-giving moisture from dew skimmed from their long grass or crops; warmth-giving thatch taken from their roof; foodstuffs; or recently worn items of clothing. Gaelic-Irish witches were occasionally reported to use the intentional evil-eye or the 'taking eye' to steal butter as well, a practice detailed in Irish folklore up until the mid-twentieth century. They were also believed to transmogrify or shape-shift into hares to steal milk directly from cows. The belief in butter and milk stealing witches in Gaelic Ireland was old, certainly centuries older than the cumulative concept of demonic, harmful witchcraft formulated in Europe in the fifteenth and sixteenth centuries.

The harm and threat level that Gaelic-Irish witches posed was lessened by the fact that their attacks on butter and milk were easily prevented, deflected or countered. Gaelic-Irish witches were not nearly as dangerous as malefic, demonic witches, but as Ireland was a largely pastoral economy and 'dairy was undoubtedly a critical staple in the Irish diet', which included 'milk, cheese, butter, curds, and other fermented milk products',[14] it was important to protect dairy animals and produce. Fortunately, there was an unusually wide range of magical options available to do so in comparison with Irish Protestant culture. Bewitched or fairy-stricken cows could be magically protected or cured by availing of the services of a magical specialist, or by persuading a less reform-minded parish priest to use a holy relic or holy water on them. Ordinary people also had a range of magical protections and countermeasures at their disposal. The butter churn, milk and cattle could be protected with simple magical rituals, incantations, or amulets, or by killing hares found wandering near cows. May Eve drives were organised to protect cattle by hurrying them through the ashes or smoke of bonfires. This was believed effective because May Eve and May Day were an important part of the traditional ritual year and a time when the power of fairies and butter witches were believed to be at their height. As seasonal supernatural creatures, the appearance of butter witches could be predicted and thus prepared for by taking extra precautions such as ensuring no food or ashes left the house. Visitors were also kept from entering the house and farmland and from going near cattle or the butter churn.

In early modern Gaelic Ireland, fairy attack and the unintentional evil-eye was used to explain misfortunes (especially sickness, death and disease) that other cultures blamed on the activities of demonic witches. Although Gaelic-Irish witches used the evil-eye intentionally, it was more often used unintentionally by those who had inherited an innate magical power to harm by sight. Although fairies occasionally performed good deeds for humans, they could be very bad indeed when provoked, especially when their roads were blocked or the trees, hills or mounds they lived in were disturbed or destroyed. Fairies struck down or 'blasted' humans and children, shot cattle with 'fairy darts' (surviving examples have been revealed as neolithic arrowheads) and stole infants and replaced them with sickly changelings. In Ireland, up until the twentieth century, fear of fairies often influenced, to a greater or lesser extent, what people in rural areas ate, where they lived, how they raised and treated their children, where they travelled and how they tended their livestock and worked their land. It follows that if in the sixteenth and seventeenth centuries fairies and the unintentional evil-eye were already providing explanations for otherwise inexplicable misfortune to humans, there was little need for ordinary people to take up notions of demonic witchcraft to perform much the same function. There are plenty of examples, up until the twentieth century, of the Irish Catholic populace carrying on with magical beliefs and practices (including cursing, improper use of Holy Wells, magical healing, and divination) that the Catholic Church disapproved of or instructed against. There is no evidence, however, that the Catholic clerical hierarchy specifically targeted popular witch belief as part of wider cultural reform. The fact that not all instances of milk and butter theft were blamed on butter witches, but also on fairies and the evil-eye, further reduced the threat they posed to butter and milk.

Belief in witches that were not inherently evil or demonic and posed a low threat level by primarily targeted milk and butter can also be found in Gaelic-speaking regions of the British Isles. Critically, this is also where witchcraft prosecution remained relatively low, such as the Hebrides, the Central and Western Scottish Highlands, and the Isle of Man. In these communities, witches were also countered by a range of blessings and counter magic, and death, disease and destruction of property and crops was blamed primarily on fairies, the unintentional evil-eye, and cursing. Cursing was different from witchcraft as it was not necessarily seen as evil and was justifiable if directed at a person deemed to have deserved it. Places geographically and culturally closer to witch-hunting areas were also more likely to be influenced by ideas of ferocious, demonic witchcraft, resulting in more witch trials. These places included the Gaelic regions of Scotland that lay closest to the witch-hunting Scottish lowlands, and the Orkney and Shetlands islands, where a largely Scandinavian culture prevailed similar to that of Iceland, Norway, Denmark, Finland and Sweden. It was in these Scandinavian countries that significant witch-hunting took place in the early modern period: together they executed around 1,200 witches.

Witch trials also increased in Wales in the seventeenth century as English witch beliefs increasingly took hold of Welsh popular culture. The demonic element nevertheless remained relatively low in Welsh witchcraft, and misfortune continued to be explained by cursing and fairy attack. Consequently, witches were not considered a clear and present danger to their communities and therefore not widely feared or hunted. Wales held only thirty-four trials and executed five people for witchcraft. In the huge and diverse Polish-Lithuanian Commonwealth, which in the early modern period comprised much of what is now present-day Lithuania, Poland, Ukraine and Belarus, common people considered milk a precious household commodity and the milk cow a symbol of its prosperity and wellbeing. Magical milk theft was thus taken seriously and there were many ways in which ordinary people could restore milk supply to cows that had dried up. It was when these common folk practices were not followed to the letter or were secretive that the people involved were suspected of trying to magically steal milk rather than return it. Crucially, accusations of milk witchcraft did not translate into large numbers of trials and executions until the later seventeenth and early eighteenth century. At that time local and urban town elites, amid various wars and increasing environmental and economic crisis, and under the influence of continental demonology, began to see witches as Satanic agents and as threats to individuals and the country at large. Due to a series of cultural, economic, societal and language changes, it was not until the nineteenth century that Irish witches were regarded in both Protestant and Catholic rural culture as a threat to families and communities. It was at that point that people turned increasingly to the lower courts to bring those deemed responsible to justice (see chapter 11).

Laws to Prosecute Witches By

Witchcraft became a secular crime in the British Isles in the mid-sixteenth and early seventeenth centuries by virtue of several laws passed by the Scottish and English parliaments.[15] The Irish Witchcraft Act was passed in 1586 and was almost identical to the English Witchcraft Act enacted twenty-three years earlier in 1563.[16] The implementation by the Irish parliament of an essentially English witchcraft law (as opposed to the drastically different Scottish witchcraft law also passed in 1563) was part of a development, starting in the late fifteenth century and lasting up until the late eighteenth century, by which English laws were incorporated into Ireland's law books.

The Irish Witchcraft Act stated that anyone (man or woman) who caused illness or injury or destroyed goods or livestock by magic, or those who abetted them, were to be imprisoned for a year and made to stand four times a year 'upon the market day ... upon the pillorie by the space of six hours' where they were to 'confesse ... their errour and offence'. If a second offence was committed or the victim died as a result, the perpetrator was to be executed, or as the Act put it, to 'suffer death as a felon'. The Act also made the invocation or 'conjurations of evil and wicked spirites' for 'any purpose' a felony punishable by death. This clause targeted learned ritual magicians who used complex rites to conjure and control demons and force them to reveal hidden or secret knowledge. If accused of any of these crimes, lords or peers of the realm were to be tried in the House of Lords 'as it is used in cases of felonie or treason'. For practising 'beneficial', popular magic, such as love magic, finding hidden treasure or lost or stolen goods using charms, symbols or incantations, the punishment was the same as for harmful witchcraft, for a first offence. A second offence of practising popular magic promised life imprisonment and forfeiture of all property to the Crown. In this way, the Irish Act (and the English Acts they were based on) reflected attitudes of religious and political elites who drafted them and who, unlike ordinary people, considered beneficial magic as either fraudulent or demonically inspired to lure people away from true religion.[17]

The harsher English Witchcraft Act of 1604 passed by the Westminster parliament during the first year of the reign of James I did not extend to Ireland. James I was a demonologist in his own right and took a personal interest in the prosecution of Scottish witches in the 1590s as King James VI of Scotland. It is perhaps unsurprising that the 1604 Act was not enacted over the Irish Sea, as there was no real public concern about witchcraft in a country (especially Ulster) wracked by political and religious divisions in the immediate aftermath of the bloody Nine Years War and just before the flight to the Continent of the Ulster Gaelic earls in 1607. The 1604 Act was more concerned than its predecessor with the demonic aspects of witchcraft and specifically outlawed the use of body parts in magical rituals and the feeding of, or conversing with, familiar spirits. More importantly, it made it a capital offence to harm using witchcraft: you no longer needed to kill your victim.

Judicial and Legal System Able to Prosecute Witches

This copying of English laws, including the 1563 Witchcraft Act, occurred in a legal context which saw the gradual replacement by the mid-to-late seventeenth century of traditional Gaelic-Irish Brehon law and legal practices with English common law. As Neal Garnham points out, Ireland and England by this time shared 'near identical systems of legal administration, prosecution and law enforcement'.[18] By the early seventeenth century, and in the wake of Gaelic defeat, emigration and decline, Crown Courts had replaced Brehon legal structures for settling disputes. During the succeeding 100 years, despite periodic disruption due to conflict in the 1640s and between 1689 and 1691, County Assizes became Ireland's leading provincial criminal courts. The officers who ran Irish courts had trained or worked in England or were of English birth. As in England, witchcraft accusations were investigated by JPs and constables who, unlike those working in countries whose legal system operated according to Roman-Law principles (such as Scotland), could not torture suspects for confessions. Prosecutors also had to negotiate a final hurdle before a trial, in that a grand jury had to be convinced there was enough evidence to warrant one. Defendants of witchcraft prosecutions were not tried in local courts by amateur judges who often had a vested interest in bringing in a guilty verdict, as was the case in parts of Europe with high conviction rates, but in County Assizes before male petty juries of their peers and senior Justices. Justices of the Assize had legal training, often rigorously examined evidence brought before them, and were culturally and socially distanced from the cases they tried. In short, Ireland's legal infrastructure, in common with that of England, where acquittal rates were always high, made it harder to convict people of witchcraft than in most European countries.

A Ready Supply of Accusations: Europe

In most countries in Europe, including England, witch-hunting was endemic in that suspected witches were prosecuted either individually or in small groups. The idea that the medical profession or the clergy hunted down 'undesirables' such as female midwives or magical practitioners has not been borne out by decades of research by historians. Another misconception is that witches formed part of an organised sect of people attached to older, pagan religions who were systematically rooted out by Christian Churches and states. The vast majority of those accused of witchcraft did not call themselves witches, nor did they belong to self-defined groups who shared their beliefs. The label 'witch' was in most cases applied to them by others without their approval.

It is a sad truth that most European witches found their way to the gallows or the bonfire by the accusations of neighbours, and often by people they had known all their lives. Accusations arose after some sort of dispute or conflict had been followed by an otherwise inexplicable misfortune of the types referred to above. These conflicts came in a range of guises. The first is often referred to as the charity-refused model, first articulated by Alan Macfarlane and expanded upon by Keith Thomas. According to this model, an accusation began when an old, widowed woman was refused charity by the accuser who, feeling guilt for being uncharitable and un-Christian, attributed some type of subsequent misfortune to the women they had just turned down. Underlying this accusation were social tensions arising from conflict over traditional obligations of Christian charity between those in small rural communities who benefited from recent population growth and social and economic changes (the accuser), and those who found themselves in poverty because of them (the accused).

Accusations also arose as a way for those lower down the social scale to attack their social superiors after disputes or arguments, or stemmed from land disputes, inter-family rivalries, conflict over children, or perceived invasions of personal or shared living space. People at that time, after all, often lived in very close quarters to one another. The workplace, the church, or the washhouse were other shared spaces where personal animosity could develop and fester before erupting in an accusation of witchcraft. These personal tensions were magnified in times of religious, political or economic crisis such as during war, rebellion or times of religious persecution, subsistence crisis, or famine. In insular, close-knit communities the reputation of both individuals and households was extremely important, and when misfortune arose in which witchcraft was suspected, previous accusations and suspicions were recalled to inform the situation at hand (see chapter 6).

In practice, those with a reputation for witchcraft, or who belonged to a family of reputed witches, had a higher probability of facing prosecution. Witchcraft reputations could be transferred from one spouse to another, from a man to a woman, and vice versa. Some firmly believed that 'tainted blood' predisposed some to witchcraft and consequently 'the children and siblings of convicted witches were always in danger of being drawn in after them'.[19] Both demonological literature and English witchcraft pamphlets were particularly concerned in the late sixteenth and early seventeenth centuries about ungodly parents (both biological parents and those acting in quasi-parental roles) leading children into witchcraft and the clutches of Satan. Occasionally, confessing witches were put under pressure by authorities to incriminate children or spouses, and some husbands provided hostile legal testimony against wives accused of witchcraft. During a large witch-hunt in the Basque Country in 1609, around 60 per cent of those accused of witchcraft were related to one another, and in the 1730s in the Ukrainian, multi-ethnic and multi-confessional town of Vyzhva in the Polish-Lithuanian

Commonwealth, two sisters were repeatedly accused of witchcraft. In trials held in early modern German territories and the Dutch province of Drenthe, whole 'witch-families' were accused of witchcraft. Children could be drawn into witch trials as victims or as accusers, providing evidence (occasionally against their own family members) to legal officials investigating accusations or as trial witnesses in court. As we shall see, adolescents in demonic possession and witchcraft cases used accusations to attack elders and gain power in restrictive family settings. Children also confessed to practising witchcraft themselves, even when they had not been tortured for a confession first. In the early sixteenth century, self-confessing witch children were generally regarded by authorities as victims seduced by parents or other adults into attending Sabbats and performing demonic rituals. From the late sixteenth century onward, children were increasingly prosecuted for witchcraft and in some cases executed. Although the minimum age for execution was the age of majority (12 for girls and 14 for boys), guidelines were not always followed and children below that age were executed in seventeenth-century Germany, Spain and Austria.

Gender will always loom large in any discussion of witchcraft accusation because the sex-ratios of those executed for witchcraft are so striking: an average of 80 per cent were women. Percentages varied from place to place, and in some areas of Europe men formed the majority of those accused of witchcraft: Estonia (60 per cent); Iceland (90 per cent); Normandy (70 per cent); Finland (50 per cent).[20] These patterns are not easy to explain, as gender is one of the most debated and disputed issues in the history of witchcraft. Early modern Europe was undoubtedly a male-dominated society in which men held, or at least claimed, most social and political power. Social position could cut across this power structure in that a rich, well-connected, married woman had more agency and power than, say, a poor widow. Female agency can also be found within the family unit and some women actively resisted male dominance and power structures. It is nevertheless true that women played a subordinate role in society, politics, education, property ownership, and employment. More importantly, men controlled the machinery for the prosecution of witches: they wrote the laws witches were tried by, investigated witchcraft allegations, led the interrogation and torture of suspects, and ran the courts. This subordination of women was defended by doctors, lawyers, theologians, and as Christian and natural and justifiable because women were inferior in terms of mental faculties, emotional stability, rationality, and the control they were able to exert over their sexual urges. Drawing on these assumptions about women, demonologists did the most to create and maintain the stereotype of the female witch: that women were more likely to become witches because they were more susceptible to the deceptions and temptations of the Devil.

In early modern culture, women were linked to witchcraft in other ways. Witchcraft accusation was often closely related to households and the home, and those directed against women were often related to the worlds and roles they were closely connected with: childbirth, love, children, sickness and death. Female witches were also more likely to be suspected of poisoning, as women were responsible for preparing food and drink. The fact that childbirth and children loomed large in witchcraft accusations is partly explained by the vulnerability of children, especially infants, in an era of very high mortality rates. In some areas, such as Germany, young mothers were particularly likely to accuse those who helped with childcare and/or older women in their household. These witchcraft accusations have been seen by historians as fantasies constructed by young female accusers to cope with anxieties concerning housekeeping, infant sickness, and motherhood. For women who had recently given birth, the experience could reawaken tensions and insecurities they had with their own mothers growing up in strict, close-knit communities. For women who had lost children, removing a witch from a community guarded against future losses and relieved any residual feelings of guilt (however unwarranted) at being a bad parent.

Although often stereotyped that way in literature and in visual imagery, not all accused witches were older women, but in many places, including Germany, they were over-represented. Elderly women were particularly susceptible to accusation and conviction due to senility and physical frailty, which put them in a position of not being able to defend themselves when accused and interrogated. Older women may have even convinced themselves they were guilty due to mental illness. Claiming the power of the witch was something the sane did occasionally as it made them feared, and therefore more respected in their small communities. In other words, in some contexts fear of harmful witches provided power to the powerless. It is also true that it often took so long for suspicions of practising witchcraft to turn into a formal accusation that although suspected witches were often first accused as young women, by the time an accusation stuck they were middle-aged or older. Younger women who accused post-menopausal women of witchcraft believed the suspect was envious of their households, families, and children because they were no longer able to do God's work of bringing children into the world, and had instead turned to the Devil's work of poisoning and cursing.

Even if we reject on evidential grounds older studies that claimed witchcraft trials cost millions of lives in an outpouring of sexual violence directed at outspoken women by threatened male communities, or admit that witchcraft accusation and prosecution could have numerous interweaving and interconnected explanatory mechanisms, it is clear that women who did not fit the male ideal of child-bearing, nurturing, subservient womanhood were more likely to be accused of witchcraft than those who did. This included the argumentative, the post-menopausal, the widowed, those reliant on charity, the economically independent or competitive, the sexually promiscuous, or those who drank or swore. These were the type of women who had fallen headlong into sin and apostasy and were therefore the most likely to become prey for Satan and become witches. Witchcraft therefore acted as another way in which certain female behaviours, attitudes, and characteristics could be shaped and maintained by men. Linking what it meant to be a 'bad' woman with witchcraft reinforced male ideas of what it meant to be a 'good' woman. Witches were sexually licentious, uncontrolled, killed and harmed, and had spurned God, while good women were pious, chaste, silent, subservient, nurturing and caring.

The late sixteenth and early seventeenth centuries, when executions peaked, were marked by epidemic witch-hunts where tens or even hundreds of people were put to death in a short space of time. Men were more likely to be accused in areas where endemic or more moderate witch-hunting took place, while accusations directed at women were more likely in areas of intense witch-hunting. Although large witch-hunts were not started by clergymen, bishops, lawyers, princes and kings, some encouraged accusations made at a local level. These witch-finders used torture to force suspects to confess to Satanic witchcraft and to name accomplices. The people named as witches in this way were often known to the person being tortured, and as a result their accusation was also informed by interpersonal, gender and social tensions, or by local or familial reputation. Torture ranged from sleep, light and food deprivation to verbal abuse, branding, crushing, and cutting of flesh and removing limbs. By torturing suspects to name fellow witches, large numbers of people could find themselves accused, convicted and executed for witch-craft in what is often referred to as witch panics or chain trials. Lowland Scotland, parts of France, and central Germany were particularly prone to this type of witch-hunting. Even England was not immune to witch-hunters and large witch-hunts. In East Anglia between 1645 and 1647, Witchfinder General Matthew Hopkins and his assistant, John Stearne, tried 250 people for witchcraft and executed around 100. There were also some examples of rulers initiating and directing witch-hunts. In the late sixteenth century, James VI of Scotland aside, the Catholic Prince-Archbishop of Trier, Johann VII von Schonberg, and his vicar, Peter Binsfield, oversaw over 6,000 accusations and 300 executions along the Moselle Valley in Germany. Their determination to counter witchcraft was so intense that those who questioned their methods or authority were tortured until they confessed.

A Ready Supply of Accusations: Ireland

If a relatively non-threatening witch figure, combined with competing supernatural explanations for misfortune, kept witchcraft accusations low among the Gaelic-Irish, Irish Protestant settlers who did believe in and fear demonically inspired witchcraft did make accusations. These were, for the most part, grounded in the type of interpersonal, gender and social tensions and conflicts that underpinned witchcraft accusations elsewhere.

As was suggested in the previous chapter, Presbyterian ministers using their Church courts often found solutions to witchcraft disputes acceptable to both accuser and accused. This ensured that there was often little need to involve legal authorities in witchcraft accusations made in Presbyterian communities. Other, more mundane factors ensured that neither formal accusations nor prosecutions were made. Many people probably reacted to bewitchment with the stoicism and private prayer approved by mainstream Protestantism, but arguably this was most likely adopted by those higher up the social ladder. Those with the money to do so consulted physicians, while others opted for direct action by threatening and assaulting suspected witches or fighting them with the counter-magic of cunning-folk. Victims or their relatives may have found closure in this way, thereby avoiding the need for further legal involvement. Accusations were also not acted upon if the accuser, even one of high status, was believed to be mentally unstable. It was on these grounds that Michael Boyle, Church of Ireland Archbishop of Dublin, dismissed the elderly and rapidly declining Bishop of Ossory, Griffiths Williams's belief 'that he is bewitched, and that Captain [Thomas] Evans hath bin an Instrument in doeing it'.[21]

Some accusers died before a suspect could be named, examined and indicted. Sir James Ware noted that on 4 October 1630, John Cave of Dublin 'suddenly d'parted this life' after four days of 'being possessed with a conceit that he could not drink', stating before he died that 'hee was bewitched by a woman at Powerscourt'.[22] Victims of witchcraft were sometimes at a loss as to who was responsible. In March 1668, Thomas Jervis noted that 'there was never such a loss of cattle for many years, many dying fat and no one knowing their distemper. Tom Corbett's are all dead, cutting two inches of fat upon the brisket, so that no man can persuade him but that his were bewitched.'[23] Accusers could be persuaded to drop their charges by the accused, as was the case with Cork woman Barbara Blaugdon, a Quaker, who in the 1650s narrowly escaped being murdered with a butcher's knife after she was surrounded by an angry mob.[24] According to a petition lodged by the wife of William Ryan of Castletown County Tipperary at the Church of Ireland church court in Killaloe in 1704 for a maintenance allowance, 'and in due time … divorce', it was claimed that Ryan had got around (as opposed to remedying) his impotency (which ensured in the six months after their wedding that their stormy marriage was never consummated) by taking 'himself to the whore whom he declared formerly bewitched him'. Ryan's accusation is not unprecedented in early modern witchcraft. It was a widely held belief in seventeenth-century France that witches rendered grooms impotent through incantation and sympathetic magic in the form of knots tied in string.[25]

Judicial System Willing to Prosecute

Due to the almost total loss of Irish legal records during the Irish Civil War in 1922, including depositions taken by magistrates, presentments, indictments and gaol delivery books, it is extremely difficult to know how JPs, grand juries and judges handled felony cases before the mid-eighteenth century. Surviving evidence suggests there was never much enthusiasm for prosecuting witches among the Irish legal profession, mostly because they were made at a time of increasing judicial scepticism throughout Europe about the ability to legally prove guilt in witchcraft cases. As most accusations were made after 1660 with increased migration from Scotland to Ulster, judicial scepticism worked especially well at keeping prosecution rates low in Ireland.

In common with their English counterparts (in the later seventeenth century at least), some Irish JPs exercised summary jurisdiction to punish people for witchcraft. Summary jurisdiction was when a JP ruled, without the intercession of a trial jury, that perpetrators were to be whipped, fined or imprisoned for minor offences. This could satisfy popular demand for justice but at the same time avoid expensive trials. In March 1686, the demoniac Jack Crofts, son of Cork merchant Christopher Crofts, 'lay dying' having endured 'a convulsion for eight or nine hours'. While Crofts's wife and 'several others' were of 'the opinion that he was bewitched' by 'the old woman, the mother of Nell Welsh', Crofts believed Jack's possession was caused by 'the hand of God'. Despite his misgivings, Crofts had the old woman and her daughter committed to the local gaol, where the latter was to stay 'some time, because she is with child and therefore cannot be whipped'.[26] The use of such powers in Ireland was technically limited to religious infractions such as

Sabbath-breaking or swearing, but could be stretched to include witch-craft, for it was both a secular crime against society and a sin against God.

In different parts of Europe at different times during the seventeenth and eighteenth century, the legal profession became reluctant to convict on the strength of traditional proofs of witchcraft. Along with increased control of trials by central governments, and a reduction in the use of torture to extract confessions, this development saw a fall in numbers of trials and executions, a rise in acquittal rates, and an end to mass witch-hunts. In England, the decline in witchcraft prosecutions and convictions became marked in the second half of the seventeenth century when judiciaries increasingly regarded as vulgar and superstitious (and thus unconvincing) evidence brought before them by lower-class accusers they considered their intellectual, social, political and economic infe-riors. JPs were thus increasingly reluctant to indict suspects on these proofs, while Assize judges often tried to sway juries towards acquittal through their direction, method of summing-up, and overall attitude. If the JP who had prepared the evidence for the court was of a similar persuasion, the chances of acquittal were increased dramatically.

There is also evidence that Irish JPs in the later seventeenth century were reluctant to indict people on the evidence brought before them. And when they did issue them, Irish grand juries were not above rejecting them. In Charleville, County Cork, in early 1660, Patrick Fitzmaurice, Baron Kerry, petitioned Roger Boyle, 1st Earl of Orrery and Lord President of Munster, and a man with first-hand experience of and a scholarly interest in witchcraft, to issue a special warrant to have a woman recently acquitted of witchcraft by a grand jury re-arrested and placed in Cork gaol for bewitching his wife, Honora. Honora was a demoniac reported to have 'vomited pins and nails, wood and straw' and was 'every day in most horrid pains and tortures'. Fitzmaurice had accused the woman in question of his wife's bewitchment because her symptoms eased when the suspect was imprisoned, but returned imme-diately upon her release. As soon as Boyle's 'warrant was executed and the woman [placed] in custody', Honora 'was immediately at ease as upon observation of all circumstances they perceiv'd'.[27] In the early modern period, it was widely believed that symptoms of bewitchment either stopped or were at least alleviated when the witch responsible was imprisoned. As we shall see, a degree of judicial scepticism can be detected at every stage of the Islandmagee case: in the repeated attempts to test Mary Dunbar's claims; in the attitude of the grand jury to new evidence brought before them; and in the summing-up of one of the presiding judges.

Conclusion

In common with England, Ireland possessed the legal apparatus necessary for prosecuting and convicting witches. Ireland, however, lacked a ready supply of accusations coming from the mass of the population, the Catholic Gaelic-Irish. This fact goes most of the way towards explaining the low level of witchcraft prosecution in the country. Unlike the malefic, demonic witch of most European cultures, who posed a significant threat to person or property, Gaelic-Irish witches targeted milk and butter production only at certain times in the year. They were also successfully countered using religious and magical means by amateurs and professionals alike. Magical attacks that harmed or killed humans and livestock were more likely to be blamed on fairies, cursing, or the unintentional evil-eye. Not all magical milk and butter stealing was even blamed on witches, as fairies were also suspected of pilfering dairy produce. As Gaelic-Irish witches posed a minimal threat to individuals and their communities there was little need to go to the authorities to have them prosecuted, put in gaol, or executed to protect themselves, their families or property. However, the Protestant minority, found predominantly in Ulster, did believe that witches posed a significant threat to their communities, lives and livelihoods. Numerous factors ensured that Protestant witchcraft accusations never reached court, particularly the timely intervention and mediation of Presbyterian clergy. By the time ordinary Protestants were accusing each other of witchcraft in the second half of the seventeenth century, judiciaries were unwilling to convict people on the evidence brought before them; a trend common throughout Europe. These checks and balances spectacularly failed to operate in County Antrim in 1711.

The Wheels of Justice

From Accusation to Arrest, 5 March 1711

By early March 1711, Mary Dunbar had established herself as the victim of demonic obsession, possession, and witchcraft. All of this had been witnessed and verified by neighbours, including some pillars of Islandmagee's social and religious community. Although Mayor Edward Clements had taken witness statements on Saturday, 3 March, as part of his investigation into Dunbar's allegations, it was not until two days later, on Monday, 5 March, that he issued a warrant for the arrest of Janet Carson, Catherine McCalmond, Janet Liston and Elizabeth Sellor. This warrant was probably served by local high or petty constables, who, along with parish watchmen, were the first defence against crime in Irish localities. Constables were unpaid and elected every year at the Quarter Sessions[1] or Assizes, and although officially they were to serve for a year each, they were frequently reappointed. Although men of high social standing were exempt from sitting on the parish watch or acting as constables, Presbyterians and Roman Catholics were not, despite the passing in the late seventeenth and early eighteenth centuries of Penal Laws intended to limit their religious, economic and civil rights (see chapter 9).

Just as the warrant was being issued, Islandmagee man and later deponent Hugh Donaldson was 'lying on the bed taking care of the girl', and felt something running up his back and then 'pressing down his shoulder'. Revd Sinclair, who was sitting near the bed, then put his hand between Donaldson's shoulder and the bed and felt something moving. Dunbar did the same and, becoming frightened, was taken out of her bed, allowing the men to conduct a thorough search of her feather mattress and blankets. This revealed an unspecified creature, a little larger than a mouse, which immediately flew into the corner of a room and disappeared. Taking into account the Scottish influence on popular culture in Islandmagee, this creature was probably not seen as a nurturing/nurtured familiar spirit in the way it would have been in England but as a demon in animal form.

What is interesting about this incident is that just prior to it, Dunbar had been sharing an otherwise socially inappropriate, intimate moment with two men in her bedchamber, which involved the touching of each other's bodies. As has been noted, there had been numerous times in previous days when several local men struggled to hold her in bed during her 'fits'. Although Presbyteries and Sessions policed illicit sexual behaviour ('fornication') that took place outside of marriage, unmarried young Presbyterians did engage in sexual behaviour short of intercourse. As Leanne Calvert has pointed out, much of this was 'focused around the physical space of the bed': bundling (sleeping together fully clothed in bed), fondling, groping, and petting. This was only socially acceptable, or at the very least tolerated, if it took place during a courtship.[2] As Dunbar was not married nor courting, her behaviour could have landed her in clerical hot water if not for one mitigating circumstance: her demonic possession.

The four women were swiftly apprehended and brought before Mary Dunbar, who shook and sweated in their presence before falling 'into a violent fit', pleading for them to be taken away, 'for Christ's sake'. Once again, this outburst would have ordinarily been considered blasphemous and could have resulted in her being reprimanded by her ministers and Session rather than being supported by them. To her audience, however, it was not Dunbar swearing but the demon inside her, which meant she was not morally culpable. The positive reaction of Dunbar to the suspects was all the 'proof' the constables needed, and the women were formally arrested and sent to Carrickfergus gaol to await trial at the spring session of County Antrim Assizes. The suspects were refused bail as a matter of course, as this was usually only offered in non-violent cases constituting a first offence. Despite spells of light fainting, from the time the witches were committed to gaol, Dunbar claimed to no longer feel any searing pains in her chest. This improvement in her condition provided further proof to onlookers of the reality of Dunbar's bewitchment.

Carrickfergus County Gaol

In the early eighteenth century, Carrickfergus had two gaols: one for the Corporation of Carrickfergus Town (a right given in the Jacobean charter of 1610), and one for County Antrim. As suspected felons under the 1586 Witchcraft Act, the women would have been committed to await trial at County Antrim gaol and courthouse, which in 1711 stood at the head or western end of what was at that time Main Street. In 1779, County Antrim gaol and courthouse moved to new custom-built premises at the foot or eastern end of Main Street, on the site of Joymount, the manor house built by Sir Arthur Chichester in the years after 1610. The new county courthouse was apparently pleasing to the eye, complete with balustrades and water piped from a nearby stream. An inspection in 1787 by non-conformist English parliamentary inspector John Howard revealed that it contained five debtors and twenty-one felons, but the average number of prisoners was closer to 120 people. Typhus, dysentery, diarrhoea, rheumatism, fever and venereal disease were rife in the prison.[3]

If this was the new, modern, improved prison, conditions in the old County Antrim gaol in Carrickfergus must have been worse. It was built in 1613 (partly rebuilt in 1727) and had no running water.[4] The building itself was 'old [and] mean' and 'not worthy of notice' by the time it was demolished in the early nineteenth century.[5] Prisoners in the old county gaol were kept at the expense of the Antrim grand jury, who paid for men to staff it. These men were first mentioned in grand jury records in April 1715, when the 'master' of the gaol was listed as Matthew Wilson and the gaoler as Thomas Faulkner.[6] The grand jury also paid for the upkeep of the gaol, but most repairs were concerned with increasing security rather than improving prisoner conditions.[7]

Prisoners would not have spent much time in the gaol, as prisons in this period did not function in the modern sense as places of confinement and punishment for wrongdoing but rather as holding pens for those awaiting trial. If it was anything like its counterparts in early modern England, the prisoners would have received meagre rations, supplemented, if they were lucky, by friends and family. Malnutrition was common in English gaols, particularly true in times of subsistence crisis and famine, both of which early eighteenth-century Ireland, and Ulster in particular, were prone to.

Fire, Brimstone and More Suspects[8]

After the suspects were imprisoned, five unnamed people were bound over to prosecute at their trial. It is probable this group included William Fenton, James Hill, Hugh Donaldson, James Blythe and John Wilson as they all had given sworn evidence to Mayor Clements by that point. Shortly afterwards, three soldiers were sent from their garrison in Carrickfergus Castle[9] to investigate Dunbar's claim that 'there was a charm' on or near the threshold of the front door, which had once again 'made her fall dead upon her going over it'. Having found nothing untoward after an initial inspection, the soldiers then dug up the area around the threshold, releasing a strong sulphurous smell. This, it was believed, broke the charm that had been placed on the threshold by the witches, and Dunbar, for a short time at least, was able to leave the house without fainting.

Almost as if she were storing up energy for the evening's main events, Dunbar lay quietly in her room for the rest of the day. At six o'clock that evening, as Revd Sinclair said prayers, 'she fell into a violent fit ... with her teeth shut, and her tongue drawn back, which continued during prayer'. By this time Revd Sinclair was familiar with the pattern of the girl's seizures, and between episodes he took the opportunity to ask her if she had witnessed any visions, to which she replied that she had seen two women whom their accomplices had called Main and Latimer. Dunbar went on to claim that the women attacked her while she lay in bed, putting 'their hands to her mouth, upon which her teeth were closed and her tongue pulled back'. The women then informed her that they had restored the charm recently removed from the threshold, which was verified when Dunbar had a seizure just as she passed over it. Its position held special significance as this was where guardian charms were often placed to protect the family inside from unwanted supernatural influence. The threshold of a door was also significant in medieval and early modern Irish culture and family life, including in Ulster, because it was 'a place of coming and going, greetings and farewells, and can be considered a liminal area of a dwelling' which 'catches the first and last light of the day … again reflecting beginnings and endings of daily life.'[10]

During their attack, the witches had also whispered to her that she would no longer be able to 'hear Mr Sinclair's prayers' without convulsing, and that the minister's religious observances 'signified nothing' as 'they served a better master' who would cure her if she joined his Satanic Church. Dunbar's testimony further established that her attackers were indeed witches and servants of Satan, but also that she had enough moral rectitude to resist their temptations. This part of Dunbar's possession 'script' can also be seen to be particularly Presbyterian and was witnessed a decade or so earlier in Scotland, when Christian Shaw had resisted similar demonic temptations, thereby fulfilling an important part of the religious initiation of the Calvinist elect.[11]

Dunbar then provided Revd Sinclair with a description of her spectral visitors. She described Janet Latimer as a 'tall black woman, very ill coloured', meaning she had a sallow complexion with black hair. Janet Main was said to be 'a woman of a middle stature, something ill coloured, with very little eyes of a brown colour, short nosed, outmouthed, marked with smallpox, long visaged [having a long face], with a mark upon her breast.'[12] It is impossible to know what this 'mark' was or what it looked like but it was distinctive enough to be considered a distinguishing feature.

The effect on a person's appearance of smallpox scars could be dramatic. In 1731, the young widow Mary Pendarves noted of her acquaintance Letitia Bushe, the daughter of an office holder in the government in Dublin, that before she contracted the disease she 'never saw a prettier creature'. She thus lamented the loss of Letitia's 'fine complexion' and the damage she believed it would do to her attractiveness and thus her marriage prospects. Letitia herself remarked that one of the possible allures of the afterlife was that 'the smallpox won't stick to us in the other world, tho' hardly shook off in this'.[13]

These descriptions were, even by today's standards, fairly specific, and were promptly disseminated throughout the surrounding countryside. Reports soon came back that there was a woman named Janet Latimer living in the Irish Quarter of Carrickfergus who matched the victim's description and 'had been long under an ill fame'. Similarly, it was reported there was a woman called Janet Main who also fitted the girl's description and was widely regarded by neighbours as 'an ignorant woman with a malicious temper'. Although by the late seventeenth century Carrickfergus was largely Presbyterian, the town's most prominent citizens belonged to the Church of Ireland. It was home to around 1,800 people by 1700, and, once an important trading port, it had been eclipsed by Belfast. Nevertheless, as it retained many important legal, military and administrative functions, it was a place where local factions vied for power and office (see chapters 8 and 9). The walls around Carrickfergus, built in 1610, were still standing a century later, and were punctured by four gates: the Key, West, North and East (or Scotch) Gates. The Scotch Gate opened onto a suburb called the Scotch Quarter, which housed the town's fishermen, most of whom were of Scottish descent, while the Irish Quarter contained two streets of thatched houses.[14]

The Arrest of Janet Main and Janet Latimer,
6 March 1711

Dunbar's physical descriptions, along with reports given by neighbours of Janet Main and Janet Latimer, persuaded Mayor Clements to issue a warrant for their arrest on 6 March and to bring them to Islandmagee to test Dunbar's reaction. James Blythe 'and some others' were given the task of going to nearby Broadisland to apprehend Main. Blythe was chosen for the job because Islandmagee's constable and his guard were preoccupied with the arrest of Janet Latimer. Latimer was persuaded to go to Knowehead House of her own accord when it was pointed out the alternative was the shame of being taken there by force. She got there just before Blythe and Main, and although her arrival was not announced as soon as she 'entered the door … Mary Dunbar called out "There's Latimer" and fell into a violent fit'. This was enough to convince those gathered (including Hugh Wilson, Charles Lennan and William Hately) of her guilt.

Shortly afterwards, Blythe arrived from Broadisland with Janet Main, who was under warrant and accompanied by her husband, Andrew Ferguson. No marriage records survive for the couple and so we don't know whether their union was sanctioned by an Anglican clergyman (as required by law), by a Presbyterian minister, or represented a more 'common-law' arrangement. When Main was brought under warrant before Dunbar as part of an identity parade of local women, the girl fell immediately into a very ill fit and lost the power of speech. Once more Dunbar claimed to have never seen Main before except during her seizures, and she had not been warned of the suspect's arrival.

As soon as the parade ended, Revd Robb took Main and Latimer to another house, presumably his own, to examine their knowledge of the Bible.[15] Latimer and Main were unable to provide the expected answers to his religious questions, and more importantly, in terms of providing 'proof' of the crime of witchcraft, were only able to repeat the Lord's Prayer imperfectly, in much the same way as Elizabeth Sellor and Janet Liston had done a few days previously. Robb then presented 'a handsome discourse upon the danger of witchcraft, and the necessity of repentance, in order to obtain eternal life'. The fact he did so not only demonstrates he was convinced of the guilt of the women, but also provides one possible reason as to why a Church of Ireland clergyman was involved in what was, after all, a Presbyterian affair at a time when tensions between the denominations were running particularly high (see chapter 9). In short, he was a firm believer in witchcraft and witches and possessed a detailed knowledge of the subject. It may have been that, in common with other contemporary Anglican clergymen, Robb owned, or at the very least read, some demonological texts and witchcraft pamphlets, of either English or continental origin.[16] There may even have been a political motivation because, as one of the few representatives of the Established Church and state in Presbyterian Islandmagee, he, or indeed his clerical superiors, may have felt the need to keep a close watch on proceedings to ensure they were handled correctly.

Despite the zeal of Robb and his companions, Main's husband, Andrew Ferguson, expressed concern about the way the test had been undertaken. He was dissatisfied 'that the sick person [Dunbar] would anyway alter at the appearance of his wife'.[17] Revd Sinclair agreed to repeat the test, and this time Ferguson entered the room first. Onlookers noted his appearance did not affect Dunbar in any way. Main was then bid to enter the room, and when she did Dunbar fitted uncontrollably. Main was removed and Ferguson was told by Dunbar that 'Janet Main was one of her cruellest tormentors'. Ferguson's reaction to this visceral, face-to-face accusation that his wife was a witch unfortunately went unrecorded. His intervention lends further weight to an earlier assertion, based on the defence of Janet Casrson by her daughter, that women in eighteenth-century Ulster with limited educational, social, or financial backgrounds were particularly reliant on familial support to defend themselves against witchcraft allegations. Ferguson's defence of his wife was rare but not unheard of. There are scattered examples from across Europe where husbands prevented witchcraft accusations made against their wives from turning into prosecutions by getting accusers to withdraw their charges, either through persuasion or the threat of public humiliation or violence. There are even rarer cases where members of wider or immediate family tried to bribe officials, hangmen or gaolers to release their loved ones. In sixteenth- and seventeenth-century England, husbands defended the sullied reputations of wives accused of witchcraft and in some cases obtained pardons for them. Non-compliance with and resistance to the legal process was another option. As we have seen in the case of Carson, Latimer and Liston, this was hard to sustain when the community and clergy were fully behind their prosecution.

Once again, Dunbar's reaction to the blind approach of the suspects proved legally decisive for the arresting constables, and at four o'clock that afternoon the women were arrested and taken before Mayor Clements for a final examination. They were then committed to Carrickfergus county gaol and Charles Lennan and Hugh Wilson were bound over to prosecute at their trial, providing Clements with sworn testimonies four days later on 10 March.[18] As soon as the suspects were imprisoned there was perceptible improvement in Dunbar's health in much the same way as 'the confinement of Jannet Liston and her daughter, Cat[herine] McCamont, and Jannet Carson' had put an end to their spectral visits and attacks.[19] This publicly demonstrated that Dunbar had identified, and the authorities imprisoned, the right women.

The Obsession of Mary Dunbar, 7 March

Dunbar arose the next morning, 7 March, at 6 a.m. and ate some bread and beer. Although this was the first sustenance (apart from half an egg) she claimed to have eaten since 28 February, she was reported to have not complained 'of hunger during that time'. As has been mentioned, fasting was a common sign of possession, and it was often reported that although demoniacs refused or were unable to eat, they never seemed hungry or lost weight. As Phillip Almond has recently put it, the survival of demoniacs, 'in the face of their failure to eat, and their general well-being, pointed to God's special care of them'.[20] This all helped to increase the image of piety, morality and wholesomeness that many demoniacs sought to foster during their ordeal.

Later that day, the wife of William Hatley reported that she saw 'something fly in betwixt the hanging and the back of the bed where the girl lay', and when she opened the curtains to investigate she momentarily witnessed 'something the bigness of her two fists'. A little time after this, the bedclothes were taken from a bed upstairs and rearranged in the shape of a corpse, just as they had been during the demonic obsession of Ann Haltridge. Mrs Hatley put the covers back on the bed, but as she looked on an unseen hand pulled them off again. At ten o'clock the next morning the demonic boy reappeared to Margaret Spear and one of the Haltridge children, on the same step of the stairs where Mary Dunbar had first experienced a seizure. He came as before, clothed in elderly, ruined clothing, having a 'piece of an old covering about him, which was thrown by as useless'.

An immediate search of the stairs and top landing revealed nothing, although Mrs Hatley's cloak was later found by Spear on the parlour floor stuffed with straw, precipitating in Dunbar a series of fits that lasted until four in the afternoon. During these episodes she would 'swoon' and fall face first into her large bolster pillow, with her 'body as stiff as one some days dead'. On one occasion her head sunk so deep into the pillow it took an adult male neighbour all his effort to prevent suffocation.

The next day, 8 March, Dunbar fell into more catatonic fits and reported afterwards that two women had attacked her. The first was called Mistress Ann by her accomplices, while the other was 'blind of an eye' and wore 'a string of black beads about her neck'.[21] There were no more disturbances in the house that day and Dunbar was able to get a good night's sleep. She awoke the next morning, however, to find herself being pushed into the bolster pillow by a heavy weight on her back, so that an onlooker was 'obliged to lie in the bed with their arm under her to prevent her from being smothered'. After this point, every time Dunbar prayed it brought on a seizure during which her teeth became tightly clenched. Despite her continuing illness, Dunbar was able to point out that the incarceration of Main and Latimer had the positive effect of allowing her to eat and leave and enter the house freely, as the sulphurous smell that had permeated the threshold had vanished.

In quiet periods between Dunbar's seizures, stones were thrown at the house. These were believed to have been dug out of a lime wall, but it proved impossible to find 'from whence they could have been taken'. A search of the house further revealed seven knots placed at an equal distance apart on the children's gown laces and on Mrs Haltridge's apron strings. Three knots were also tied in a boy's cravat belonging to one of the Haltridge children. The clothing was promptly 'thrown into the fire' to destroy the 'charm in them'. At three o'clock that afternoon a box containing the papers of a houseguest, John Campbell,[22] mysteriously disappeared and one of the children's cloaks was seen rolling about on the parlour floor of its own accord. That night the household was awoken by a 'great noise' 'in the kitchen' and the screaming of young Mrs Haltridge, who had been assaulted with 'a pot lid' while she lay in bed.

The next day, 10 March, Revd Sinclair, James Stannus of Larne, and Robert and Hugh Donaldson came 'to bear her [Dunbar] and the [Haltridge] family company'. During their visit, the men asked Dunbar what the suspects had said to her when they had appeared to her in spectral form. She replied that they had not appeared to her since their imprisonment but before this they had regularly verbally abused her and 'dissuaded her from listening to any religious duty, prayers'. They also told her that the only way she could save her life was to join them in union with Satan and become a witch. The witches had also promised to bewitch members of the Haltridge family, and would continue their attacks on them until they left Knowehead House. Dunbar also told of how the women often discussed the types of magical objects they had left in their beds to make their husbands believe they were still sleeping when in fact they were attacking Dunbar. In what was almost a piece of pantomime, one of the women said she had left a broomstick or 'besom' in her bed, while another said she had 'left a little straw'. Dunbar was also at pains to point out that one of their number, Mistress Ann, spoke of her love of drinking wine with her husband 'Johnny'. By relating this particular tale, Dunbar was automatically casting aspersion on the character of the mysterious Mistress Ann, as this form of alcohol consumption (spirit drinking) would have, in Presbyterian society at least, been considered unbecoming for a woman. After Dunbar had been questioned, she rested for the remainder of the evening. The demonic presence did not leave the house, however, and Spear and the children were hit by turf, which had appeared out of nowhere.

All the World is a Stage

Explaining the Supernatural?

Previous chapters have shown that by 10 March 1711, Mary Dunbar had accused six people of witchcraft, but what is still to be discussed is what was really happening to her and the Haltridge family if we look beyond a supernatural explanation. The best way to do this is to be sensitive to the contexts in which the events took place and to relate them to what we know of similar cases in other countries – in particular, England and Scotland. It is acknowledged that the various social, cultural, medical, and gender explanations given below do not satisfactorily explain all the supernatural events related in surviving accounts recorded by seemingly reliable witnesses, often under oath. It is not for me to offer a conclusive judgement on what went on in 1710 and 1711 in Islandmagee. After all, the past has gone, history is what we write about it, and unfortunately both will always be distinct from one another. What is offered here is an examination of the case using surviving source material and informed by what we know about witchcraft and demonic possession in the western world in the early modern period.

Modern Medical Explanations

If we try to explain Dunbar's possession in natural terms, it is best to begin with possible medical explanations. Academic historians of medicine and witchcraft are wary of retrospective diagnosis because it involves the imposition onto the past of diagnostic labels taken from modern medicine. This can obscure the fact that such diagnoses are often at best educated guesses based on their own, time-bound views of disease: not only does the way in which diseases are described and defined change over time, symptoms are not often described accurately or in detail in surviving sources. Furthermore, diseases themselves may even change over time, so that symptoms from one era may not map directly onto their modern counterparts. Brian Levack's scepticism of the 'efforts of medical doctors and psychiatrists to link possession with illness', however, largely lies in the fact that it 'cannot be equated with, or attributed to, a single illness or disease' because its symptoms 'are too varied to support a comprehensive medical model'.[1] Taking into consideration these objections, it is difficult to explain all the events that happened in Islandmagee in modern medical terms. Nevertheless, some historians continue to apply modern psychological and medical theory to witchcraft and possession cases. It is therefore worthwhile considering some medical explanations for at least some of Dunbar's symptoms: from her screaming, shouting, fainting and convulsive fits, catatonic trances and inability to speak, to her locked jaws, mysterious bodily pains, fluctuations in weight, inability to eat, and her adverse reaction to prayers and the presence or touch of invisible, spectral attackers. As we shall see in later chapters, Dunbar would later void pins and other household objects from her mouth.

The inability or refusal to eat was more common in early modern female demoniacs than in their male counterparts, just as there is a similar gender bias today with regard to eating disorders such as anorexia nervosa. One of the seven people possessed in the Starchy household in 1594 in Cleworth, Lancashire, was 33-year-old Margaret Byrom, who alternated between long periods of fasting and binge-eating. If indeed she was also purging the food after consumption, she could have been suffering from bulimia nervosa. It has also been suggested that demoniacs who vomited pins or other objects or substances could have been suffering from pica (also called allotriophagy) where sufferers compulsively swallow a range of indigestible objects, from knives and thermometers to teaspoons. These objects usually work their way out of the body through the anus or mouth, but small pieces of glass or needles are sometimes exuded through the skin. In the late 1680s in Dorset, England, brass pins were taken from the shoulders, breast, arms, knees and legs of 18-year-old demoniac, Elizabeth Tillman.[2] Andrew Pickering has linked vomiting of pins by victims in witchcraft and possession cases to pica in his analysis of the unsuccessful prosecution of octogenarian beggar-woman Elizabeth Carrier at Taunton Assizes in Somerset in 1690 by two 18-year-olds, Mary Hill and William Spicer.[3]

According to Kathleen Sands, the fits and shouting and screaming episodes displayed by many demoniacs could have been the result of 'a disease, such as epilepsy, meningitis, encephalitis, Reye's syndrome, or some other illness characterised by convulsive episodes'.[4] These symptoms, along with blindness, numbness and paralysis, could be explained by reference to conversion disorder (referred to in the past as hysteria), where patients convert anxiety caused by difficulties experienced in life into physical symptoms. Furthermore, the trances, visions and apparitions experienced by demoniacs have been explained by James Sharpe: 'people who genuinely thought themselves to be bewitched and were consequently in a somewhat stressed state might easily convince themselves, in all honesty, that they could see the apparition of their tormentor as they suffered their fits.'[5] The demoniac displaying these symptoms could also be suffering from senile dementia, transient psychotic or trance disorder, paranoia, Parkinson's disease, diabetic coma, clinical depression, post-natal depression, schizophrenia, or compulsion neurosis. It would not be difficult to attribute a modern psychiatric condition to the man in 1624 who was convinced Satan had ordered him to murder Ayrshire-born minister Robert Blair. Luckily Blair was able to drive the 'devil' out of the man by fasting and prayer before he could carry out his demonic instructions.[6] Mild ergot poisoning caused by a fungus growing in cereals such as rye bread has been used (unconvincingly, according to most historians) to explain the convulsions and hallucinations of demoniacs in Salem village in 1692. People suffering from Munchausen's syndrome, a behavioural and psychological condition, exhibit symptoms remarkably similar to possession where sufferers hear voices, see things invisible to others, and experience mysterious chest and stomach pain. Young women between the ages of 20 and 40 are thought to be particularly prone to the disorder. Dissociative identity disorder (often referred to as multiple personality disorder) has also been employed to explain some of the symptoms experienced by demoniacs because 'during possession many apparently suffered temporary loss of their own personal identity as the Devil ... gained control over not only their bodies but also their mental faculties and their personalities.' This type of explanation is perhaps less applicable to Dunbar's case than it is to instances where demoniacs remained lucid, and their personalities coexisted with that of the possessing demon. Episodes such as these often led to verbal exchanges between the human host and the satanic interloper.[7]

Mass or group demonic possession, involving tens or even hundreds or people, occurred when symptoms of possession passed rapidly from individual to individual in close-knit communities such as convents, villages or orphanages. These cases represent most possessions in continental Europe but are rare in England. Relatively recently these 'psychic epidemics' have been explained using modern psychiatric categorisation such as mass delusion, collective psychoses and group psychopathology. This phenomenon was more likely to arise, and spread quickly from individual to individual, in communities containing large numbers of poor, uneducated people whose interconnected lives were highly regulated by social, cultural and religious norms and institutions, and therefore easily thrown into turmoil by periods of intense intellectual or political crisis or change. The function of mass possessions in this reading was to exert control over stressful situations or to express, in physical terms, opposition to them.

Early Modern Medical Intervention

In the early modern period, some illnesses were more likely than others to be attributed to witchcraft, and were subsequently referred to medical men for affirmation, such as mood swings or the 'wasting away' of a patient. On the other hand, gynaecological problems, venereal disease, skin outbreaks, or breathing difficulties rarely called for their attention. From the sixteenth century onwards, it was customary for English demoniacs to be examined by doctors in the early stages of possession. The medical professionals involved were aware of the range of possible explanations for the physical and mental symptoms displayed by possessed patients, from divine to demonic intervention. Although most of the conditions listed above were centuries away from a first diagnosis, illnesses such as epilepsy ('the falling sickness'), hysteria ('suffocation of the mother'), and mental illness ('melancholy') were known to contemporary doctors, clergy and lawmen. Melancholy in the sixteenth and seventeenth centuries was defined by physicians as a bodily disorder 'that affected the imagination and emotions, giving rise to anxiety, depression, fear, sorrow, sadness, and chronic fatigue'.[8] These illnesses were considered as alternative explanations for specific instances of possession. Prominent physician Sir Thomas Browne noted in his *Religio Medici* (1642) that, 'I hold that the devil doth really possess some men, the spirit of melancholy others, the spirit of delusion other.'[9] It was also recognised that both demoniacs and epileptics fell down suddenly, clenched their teeth, foamed at the mouth and struggled fiercely during their fits. Scattered evidence also suggests that in some Irish witchcraft cases medical explanation took precedent over diabolical diagnosis. In September 1655, Marion Fisher was convicted at Carrickfergus Assizes, County Antrim, for bewitching to death Alexander Gilbert, but the verdict was overturned a year later by Sir John Barry. Barry argued that Marion showed signs of mental instability (possibly throwing doubt on a previously obtained confession) and that Gilbert had died of natural causes.[10]

Although a diagnosis of witchcraft was usually the last resort for most English physicians, many continued to use it in the sixteenth and seventeenth centuries. Thomas Browne, who claimed that he had 'ever believed (and do now know) that there are witches',[11] testified at Lowestoft Assizes in March 1662 that the two young female victims were genuinely possessed. Physicians also were occasionally put under pressure by relatives or friends of the afflicted to attribute illness to witchcraft or possession. Towards the end of the seventeenth century, English physicians from mainstream Church of England backgrounds became increasingly reluctant to use it to explain illness. The picture in dissenting, non-conformist communities in England was somewhat different. Here witchcraft accusations continued to be made, and although few ended up in court, dissenting physicians played a leading role in establishing diabolism as the root cause of the patient's various maladies. Similarly, in Scotland in October 1696, demoniac Christian Shaw was examined by leading physician Matthew Brisbane, who concluded that Shaw was suffering from a 'malady' or mental illness called 'hypocondrick melancholy'. A few months later, in December, after a prolonged and careful examination of his patient, Brisbane provided written testimony that the objects he witnessed her void from her body were too 'contrary to humane nature' to be found 'in the catalogue of humane diseases'.[12]

There is no evidence, however, that Mary Dunbar was examined by a physician or any other medical practitioner, such as an apothecary or surgeon. This may be partly explained by the lack of supply and access to medical care in eighteenth-century Ireland. Many of the characteristics of modern medical structures, such as increased state intervention, institutionalisation, and professionalisation, only emerged during the mid to later eighteenth century. Although there was no legal barrier to Presbyterians pursuing a medical career, and many did so in Ulster in the early eighteenth century, trained professionals tended to be found in Dublin or larger towns. This left the provinces with a meagre supply of trained practitioners and the mass of population with little access to professional medical care. By the mid-nineteenth century, Islandmagee still lacked a 'medical practitioner' and the absence of a medical dispensary (state-funded institutions that provided medical care for sick poor) left 'the humbler or less affluent class [without] the means of obtaining medicine or medical advice'.[13] In common with the rest of the British Isles, Irish elites such as Dunbar would not have considered it socially acceptable to enter a provincial or metropolitan hospital or infirmary. In any case, they were not founded in any great number in provincial Ireland until the late eighteenth century, and even then they catered for a very small number of the curable, 'deserving' poor. Licensed, university-trained physicians did not come cheap, and although Dunbar may have been afforded the status of 'gentlewoman', she may have had little by way of personal fortune. Although she was a guest in the Haltridge house, hospitality and charity then as now had a limit, and it may have been beyond the family's means to bring a physician from Belfast or Antrim.

Faking It?

Apart from illness or disease, another explanation for Dunbar's condition was that she deliberately faked or simulated some or all her symptoms. If indeed she was a fraud, she was among good company, because by the early eighteenth century numerous such cases had been detected and well publicised in England and Scotland, as well as on the Continent. The extent to which this occurred should, however, not be overplayed. Imposture-like illness does not explain all possession cases or indeed all symptoms exhibited by individual demoniacs. Brian Levack has argued that after experiencing initial symptoms some 'simply assumed a role that was available to them in their religious culture' and therefore did not 'necessarily know they were acting'. In this reading, all cases of demonic possession, even those involving outright fraud, are 'understood as cultural performances that had meaning for the demoniacs, the minsters, and the audience'.[14]

In London in 1574, two young girls, Agnes Briggs and Rachel Pinder, simulated demonic possession before accusing a local woman of their bewitchment. In 1599, 25-year-old Marthe Brossier, from Romorantin in France, was exposed by priests, doctors and theologians as a fraud after failing numerous tests. She convulsed after being touched by ordinary water she had been led to believe had been blessed: a true demoniac would have only reacted adversely to the presence of genuine holy water. In 1604, Brian Gunter took advantage of the sudden onset of convulsions in his 16-year-old daughter Anne to accuse neighbours he had fallen out with in his village in Berkshire, England, of witchcraft. Brian went to extreme lengths to expand Anne's repertoire of possession symptoms. He thrust pins into her body while she slept and forced her to breathe in fumes of burning brimstone and to swallow oil to induce vomiting. In 1605–6, the newly minted scepticism of James I was instrumental in exposing Anne and her father as frauds and having them prosecuted for making false accusations. This was a major change in direction for a monarch who had previously written a book about the dangers of witchcraft in the 1590s and encouraged two major witch-hunts in Scotland. In Bilston, Staffordshire, in 1620, the 12-year-old son of a tenant farmer, William Perry, accused the elderly Joan Cocke of causing his possession by cursing him after they had an argument on his return home from school. Cocke was duly tried for Perry's bewitchment but found not guilty. Perry was then placed under the supervision of Thomas Morton, Bishop of Coventry and Litchfield, who soon came to the conclusion that the boy had counterfeited his possession under the tutelage of a mysterious Catholic priest. Perry had initially fooled physicians that his black-coloured urine was an indicator of the presence of demons, but surveillance conducted by the bishop's servants revealed he added black ink to his chamber pot after he urinated into it. He also placed an ink-drenched piece of cotton under the foreskin of his penis to be used in emergencies.[15] A year later, in 1621, Elizabeth Saunders taught Katherine Malpas to simulate possession to gain money from onlookers who took pity on her. In 1698 in Hammersmith, London, Sarah Fowles was tried at the Old Bailey (London's main criminal court) for pretending to be possessed and making a false accusation of witchcraft.[16]

The seventeenth century saw more deliberate impostures. Richard Hathaway, a blacksmith's apprentice from Southwark, whose early life, like so many victims and accused in witchcraft trials, we know very little about, accused Sarah Morduck or Moredike, the wife of a river worker, of bewitching him. Hathaway's possession exhibited itself in all the usual ways and his accusation was supported by his master, Thomas Welling, his wife, Elizabeth, the mass of the local population (including leading local non-conformists), and magistrate Sir Thomas Lane. It was, however, opposed by sceptical Church of England minister Dr Martin. Repeated physical and verbal attacks by Hathaway and the Wellings on Morduck forced her to leave her home and employment and move from Southwark into central London. She was unfortunately followed by accusers, who led a mob attack on her new home. Morduck eventually stood trial for witchcraft at Guildford Assizes in summer 1701 and was acquitted. Hathaway was deemed an imposter by the jury and later prosecuted by the Crown and tried at the Surrey Assizes on 25 March 1702. He was given six months' hard labour, pilloried, and flogged for fraud, assault, and rioting. It emerged later that the Wellings had used and embellished Hathaway's naturally occurring fits to wage a hate campaign (for reasons unknown) against Morduck. Hathaway, on the other hand, hoped to gain money and goods from his theatrics along with the undivided attention of the community. He even wrote an account of his possession to gain a wider audience, but the local bookseller he presented it to, Richard Ball, was so convinced he was an imposter he refused to publish it.[17] Even Scotland was not immune from imposture. In 1705, in the fishing village of Pittenweem, Scotland, Janet Cornfoot (one of her co-accused died in prison) was badly beaten and then crushed to death by a mob after she was acquitted of bewitching the 16-year-old son of a blacksmith, Patrick Morton. Morton faked his possession after the local minister, Patrick Cowper, read him a published account of the Christian Shaw case.[18]

It has been suggested in earlier chapters that the occurrence of demonic possession cases in non-conformist networks in Scotland and North America may have heightened awareness of the phenomenon in Ulster in the late seventeenth and early eighteenth century. The question therefore arises as to whether public exposure to knowledge of possession cases occurring elsewhere, in an age of judicial scepticism, influenced the way possession cases were perceived and handled in Ulster. Certainly Dunbar's claims to have been attacked in spirit form by women she had never met were repeatedly and rigorously tested and verified by touching tests and identity parades conducted without the victim's prior knowledge. The tests were even repeated when family members of the accused objected to the way in which they had been conducted.

Possession: a Dramatic Art

As Phillip Almond has suggested, 'possession was learned behaviour'.[19] Its symptoms were stereotyped and could be easily copied. As some of the above cases demonstrate, fraudulent demoniacs often learnt the cultural script of possession by being coached by family members or figures of authority. Others may have learned it from neighbours or by hearing sermons about possession or reading relevant passages of the Bible. Many demoniacs learnt about possession by reading accounts of other cases. In Nottingham in 1597, William Sommers began to show the signs of possession after he had taken bread and butter from an old woman. Before this incident and a formal accusation of witchcraft was made against the woman, Sommers had read an account of the possession of the Throckmorton children who, five years earlier, accused Agnes Samuel and her family of their bewitchment. In 1616, a young man named Henrie Smith had nine women executed at Leicester for sending their familiars to attack him. Smith had faked his symptoms after reading about the Throckmorton children and was eventually exposed as a fraud by King James I and the Archbishop of Canterbury, George Abbott. The published account of the possession of Christian Shaw not only inspired Patrick Morton's antics, but possibly had a hand in shaping the accusations in 1699 of two young girls who lived near her.[20] It is therefore possible that Dunbar learned the part of a demoniac by reading (or hearing about) published accounts of Scottish or American trials, or indeed the 1661 or 1698 Irish cases. The cultural script of possession that demoniacs followed was extended and expanded upon by responding and reacting to audience expectation. This explains why the range of their possession symptoms increased over weeks, sometimes months. The theatricality of possession was not lost on playwright William Shakespeare, who believed that exorcists and demoniacs were frauds and possession a dramatic performance in which the audience played a part.[21]

Even if Dunbar had faked her possession, using knowledge of past cases and the cultural cues of her 'audience', there is nothing to say that *all* of her behaviour was simulated. As her possession progressed, it could have been that the line between real and faked fit, trance or vision became blurred, and that simulated behaviour became un-simulated, and feigned pain became actual, physical suffering. There is also the possibility that she may have become increasingly convinced that she was genuinely possessed and began to exhibit the expected physical symptoms such as shaking, trances and hallucinations.

Believable Witches?

As we have seen, possession by direct demonic intervention (where the devil or demons chose their victims themselves without the agency of a witch) was associated with sin or moral transgression, as demons were thought to specifically target the ungodly. Given these associations, it is no wonder that Dunbar opted for a witch-centred explanation over direct, Satanic intervention. The question remains, however, as to who or what directed her towards her chosen suspects? As five of the eight women were called Janet, it could have been that Dunbar had a particular prejudice against this forename. It is far more likely that this was a coincidence, as Janet was a popular name in early modern Scotland, and presumably among the Scottish diaspora living in Ulster. This popularity is evidenced by the fact that Janet was the forename of nearly 500 accused witches (out of a total of 3,212 we have names for) in Scottish witchcraft cases between 1563 and 1736.[22] Furthermore, in common with her contemporaries, there is no real reason for us to disbelieve Dunbar's repeated claims that she had never met or spoken to the accused women in person prior to their spectral visits. This was unusual in possession cases, as the onset of symptoms was preceded by the receipt or refusal of charity, an argument or disagreement, or some sort of interpersonal or interfamilial conflict. The 9-year-old victim in the 1698 Antrim case, who apparently 'for beauty, education, or birth [was] inferior to none where she lived', became bewitched 'having innocently put into her mouth a Sorrel leaf, which was given to her by a witch that begged at the door, to whom she had first given a piece of bread, and then some beer'.[23] Mary Longdon had known Florence Newton three or four years before she refused her charity at Christmas time 1660. Longdon's refusal led to an angry exchange of words and a curse being uttered by Newton. The confrontation ended with Newton kissing Longdon's cheek. These words and actions were later interpreted as acts of magical aggression and ultimately taken as the cause of Longdon's bewitchment.[24]

Given her lack of prior relationships with the accused women, it could be that Dunbar was drawn to them because, culturally speaking, they were plausible, believable witches. In other words, they were just the type of people thought likely to use demonic, harmful magic. In common with many accused witches (see chapter 4) they had reputations for practising witchcraft. Samuel Molyneux noted in May 1711, the 'severall previous disturbances that severall others alleged to have suffered' at the hands of the accused women. The fact they had previously made 'frequent vaunts and threats of their own revenge and power' strengthened the case against them.[25] Furthermore, according to the pamphlet account, Janet Liston 'had been for a great many years under the repute of a witch, and her daughter [Elizabeth Sellor] for some time'. A reputation for witchcraft also played a part in convincing local elites of Florence Newton's guilt in 1661. The Mayor of Youghal, Richard Mayre, had been informed by 'three Aldermen' of the town that Newton had in the recent past kissed their children who 'died presently after'. Mayor Mayre also had a personal reason to side with Newton's accusers, as he and his family believed their infant child had died five weeks after Florence had kissed it.[26] Richard Godbeer noted that, in 1692, 'much of the evidence presented at Salem referred to events that had taken place several years before, in some cases a decade or more.'[27]

Some of the accused could also have been seen as believable witches in that they conformed to popular stereotypes concerning how witches looked. In England, by the end of the seventeenth century, this was so set in the popular mind as to have on occasion influenced the opinion of jurors and accusers. These witches were imagined as argumentative, envious, dishevelled, poor, old, wrinkled, often with failing eyesight, or carrying the outward signs of disease or mental illness. Even though this stereotype was removed from the reality of many of those accused of, and prosecuted for, witchcraft, it was this image that found its way into cheap print and pamphlets. Trial attendee Revd Tisdall suggested that people may have suspected Dunbar targeted the women because they looked 'diabolical' or witch-like:

> the supposed witches were eight in number, six of them with such strange variety of ill looks, that had the afflicted known them before, it might have given grounds to suspect she had singled them out for her tormentors, even from their diabolical appearances.[28]

Although Irish literary culture lacked a body of indigenous witchcraft prints and pamphlet accounts of famous trials this witch stereotype found its way to Ireland either in Scottish, English or North American witchcraft literature, or by word of mouth, carried to Ulster by settlers.

It could be that the women simply conformed to popular witch stereotypes and that was why they were accused by Dunbar, but by drilling deeper into what Tisdall meant by 'ill looks' and 'diabolical appearances', something more sinister seems to have been at work. At least five of the accused women were functionally or physically impaired or visually different in some way. Janet Liston was known as 'the lame woman' and described as having 'a large rolling eye' and 'very thick lips', while her daughter, Elizabeth Sellor, was small and 'lame of leg'. Janet Main had a birthmark on her chest and distorted joints in her hand due to severe arthritis. She is also described as having small brown eyes and a large mouth, which were set in a long, sallow face pitted with smallpox scars. The final two suspects we will meet in chapter 7 were also set apart by their appearance. Even by the standards of the early eighteenth century, when illness, disease and infirmity were far more parts of everyday life than today, disability nevertheless marked people as different, which in its turn often governed how they were treated; not least because disability was often read by contemporaries as reflecting inner corruption and sin. It was unsurprising then that the most corrupt of human beings, witches, who had renounced God to help the Devil to destroy their own communities, bore the outward, physical signs of their sin and apostasy. In 1624, playwright and poet Thomas Heywood noted with disgust, in a large folio volume dedicated to the virtues of strong women such as Queen Elizabeth I, that witches were in stark contrast 'stigmaticall and ouglie [ugly], insomuch, that it is growne into a common adage, *Deformis ut saga*, i.e. as deformed as a witch.'[29] This is not to say that disability was enough to cause a person to be accused of witchcraft, as there were simply 'too many people crippled by birth defects or accidents for such to become the case'.[30]

Their embodied difference also diminished their femininity in the eyes of contemporaries as they failed to meet accepted, idealised male standards of female beauty and appearance. Furthermore, to a greater or lesser degree the suspects also failed to meet contemporary codes of feminine behaviour and language. Women who did this, who challenged accepted, male standards of womanhood, were more likely to be accused of witchcraft in early modern Europe (see chapter 4). Most of the suspects in the Islandmagee case were neither passive, silent, chaste, subservient nor law-abiding. If Mary Dunbar, when not possessed, ticked all the boxes for how a 'good woman' should behave, the Islandmagee witches broke all the rules. This was illustrated in Dunbar's claim that, while in spirit form, they verbally abused and assaulted her and admitted to drinking strong alcohol. Janet Latimer had a bad reputation locally and Catherine McCalmont was regarded by her neighbours as uneducated, irreligious and of an 'ill fame'. Janet Main was commonly regarded as an 'ignorant' woman with a 'malicious temper', while one of the final suspects to be arrested (who will be discussed in the next chapter) was reported to smoke tobacco, curse and be prone to temper tantrums. Janet Liston and Elizabeth Sellor were brought to Knowehead House to confront Dunbar under duress. Indeed, most of the women at some point resisted the male-led interrogation, prosecution and conviction process using the limited educational, economic and social capital at their disposal. In some cases, the 'imperfect' bodies, acts of resistance and deviant behaviour that marked them out as believable witches was complemented by old, stained clothing. Janet Liston/Sellor was described as having a dirty face and wearing a dirty biggy or head covering, while another suspect (who we will meet in chapter 10) wore old clothes and a worn bonnet over unruly hair. In the context of criminal trials in Ireland, clothing and bodily appearance were understood as being able to be read to provide information 'about a person's social background, character, sense of guilt, and honesty'.[31] In the present case, old, ruined clothing not only reflected the low social status and poverty of the suspects but the type of corrupted inner lives expected of witches, just as the ragged clothing of the mysterious boy we met earlier pointed towards his true demonic nature.

Many Reasons Why

Dunbar may have chosen easy targets, but the question remains: why did she fake at least some of her symptoms in the first place? This is best answered by exploring the kind of life she would have led in Ulster at that time to reconstruct why she made the choices she did. As an unmarried, female adolescent, Mary Dunbar may have felt marginalised within her wider family group and community. Although early modern women were not as unassertive, subjugated, dependent, or confined to the domestic sphere as once thought, they were still less likely to be educated than their male counterparts, unable to go to university, sit in parliament or enter the professions. The experience of family life in the eighteenth century could be as varied as the personalities involved, but historians largely agree that overall relationships were certainly not cold, distant, or authoritarian and were often affectionate and warm. That is not to say children and young people were not ill-treated or abused or pushed to the margins of adult attention. In common with other economically privileged Presbyterian women, Dunbar would have been judged by the accepted, restricted standards of feminine behaviour, language and manners, even if it is admitted that early eighteenth-century society was slightly more permissive for 'gentlewomen' than it would be a century later. Given her level of Biblical knowledge, and what we know about Presbyterian gentry families at that time, it is almost certain she would have been raised in a religious household and subjected to strict standards of private and public worship.

In common with many British demoniacs, possession would have provided Dunbar with the attention, concern and sympathy of the local community and the Haltridge family. It also enabled her to move from the margins of adult attention to the centre, from invisibility to notoriety, and from a position of powerlessness to one of empowerment through the use and control of her body. Possession also allowed her to bend and even break female behavioural codes policed by men in a male-dominated society. Unlike the women she accused of witchcraft, Dunbar was able to challenge the patriarchal constraints placed on her without consequence. Demoniacs, after all, were not accountable for their own actions and were therefore liberated from normal rules of behaviour: they could scream, shout, blaspheme, curse, and act in a sexually inappropriate manner without reproach. They were therefore able to contest adult authority and smash the restrictions of a pious upbringing, including the demands of saying prayers and singing psalms when requested. Indeed, as Keith Thomas suggested decades ago, 'a conspicuous feature of the cases of possession about which details survive is that they frequently originated in a religious environment' and 'it could be plausibly urged that the victims were engaging in a hysterical reaction against the religious discipline and repression to which they had been subjected.'[32] Demoniacs were also able to overturn the strict age hierarchy that existed at that time, which expected children and adolescents to respect and obey their elders, by accusing older men and women of their bewitchment. Finally, one should not overlook the force of momentum, as once Dunbar's possession had been confirmed by leading men in the community, and the first suspects named, there was no turning back. Things had gone too far.

Margaret Spear

One problem with the imposture/cultural script argument is that it only accounts for Dunbar's possession and not the other supernatural phenomena witnessed in the Haltridge house. The most compelling of these was physical evidence, which included cloaks that had been stuffed with straw, broken windows, apron strings and cravats found mysteriously knotted, and sheets pulled off beds and rearranged in the shape of a corpse. Strange smells, noises heard in the night, and sightings of the demonic boy can be added to this list. Some of these phenomena were witnessed or heard before Dunbar arrived in Islandmagee, or when she was out of the room. The imposture argument also fails to explain how Dunbar was able to describe the suspects so accurately or pick them from a line-up when she supposedly had never seen or spoken to them before. The most straightforward explanation for this is that Mary Dunbar had an accomplice. The most likely candidate for this role was the Haltridge's young servant, Margaret Spear, who was the only witness to many of the demonic attacks on the elderly Ann. It may have been no coincidence that some of the more elaborate supernatural events, such as the smashing of the windows and the attempted Satanic sacrifice, occurred when James and his wife were absent from their home. This absence gave Spear free rein over the household. Spear had much to gain from orchestrating the obsession of Ann Haltridge. It provided a level of attention and freedom she would not have ordinarily gained as a young female servant in a Godly household. The mysterious death of her mistress made her the leading lady in a drama of her own creation. She may have even aimed to profit financially from it, as it provided a cover for an ultimately unsuccessful attempt to steal an expensive book and a turkey.

When Ann Haltridge died and the drama and the attention surrounding her subsided, Spear may have colluded with Dunbar to ensure its continuation. Dunbar's choice of 'believable' suspects could have been directed by Spear, who not only possessed local knowledge but may have harboured grudges against the women concerned. The distinctive nature of the physical characteristics and clothing of the suspects meant that Dunbar could have easily picked them out of the identity parade from the descriptions supplied to her by Spear. Furthermore, even when their approach was unannounced, or when her back was turned to the wall, Dunbar could have been warned by her accomplice. Spear could have supplied Dunbar with the names she knew of some of the suspects, which enabled the authorities to make arrests more swiftly than they would have done otherwise.

The timing of some of the supernatural disturbances that plagued the Haltridge household after Dunbar's arrival is also intriguing, as Spear was once more the only witness to many of them, such as the appearance of the demonic boy and the stone-throwing. Other phenomena occurred when Dunbar's symptoms were in temporary abeyance, leading one to suspect that this 'down-time' between fits and spectral attacks was Spear's cue to keep the tempo of the drama going and spectators in the house occupied while Dunbar prepared for the next performance. Knowing the house intimately, as Spear would have done, put her in a perfect position to plant the bewitched items throughout the house, smash windows, and unmake beds. Not all reported supernatural phenomena are explicable in these terms, since Spear was occasionally absent when they occurred, such as when a rag rose by itself in the kitchen and a demonic sound was heard just before McCalmont was interviewed by Revd Sinclair.

Conclusion

It is easy to imprint a modern medical diagnosis onto Dunbar's symptoms, whether it is of a mental or physical nature or a mixture of both, but there is no contemporary medical evidence to suggest she was suffering from a complaint of this kind. It seems more plausible that

Dunbar and her accomplice Margaret Spear followed a cultural script of demonic obsession and possession and faked at least some of the supernatural phenomena witnessed in the Haltridge house, which were then validated by the family and local community. The social and emotional needs which possession catered for provides a good reason as to why Dunbar orchestrated such an elaborate hoax in the first place. The theatre of possession allowed both Dunbar and Spear to move from the margins of adult attention to the centre. It allowed Dunbar to break free from the social and cultural restrictions of being a gentlewoman in a strict, religious family living in a male-dominated society. Spear and Dunbar accused the women they did because they were believable witches, having variously reputations for witchcraft, failing to meet accepted standards of appearance or beauty, publicly breaking social taboos regarding female morality, language or behaviour, and by resembling the accepted stereotype of what a witch was believed to look like. And rather than passively complying with the investigation and prosecution process, they resisted it at every opportunity.

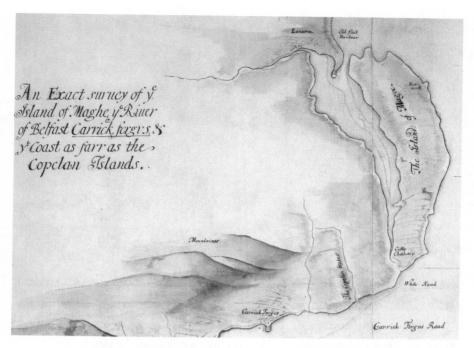

Fig. 1. This map from 1680 shows Islandmagee (Island of Magee), Larne (Lanarm), and Carrickfergus: 'A Colored Exact Map of Island Maghe, the River of Belfast, Carrickfergus …'. (Courtesy of the British Library, London)

Fig. 2. The old Presbyterian meetinghouse, Islandmagee, was demolished in 1900 to make way for the First Presbyterian Church, Islandmagee. (Reproduced from Dixon Donaldson, *Historical, Traditional and Descriptive Account of Islandmagee* (Islandmagee, 1927))

Fig. 3. This photograph was taken around 1920 and shows the front of Knowehead House, Islandmagee, where Mary Dunbar first became demonically possessed. (Reproduced from Donaldson, *History of Islandmagee*)

Fig. 4. The rear view of Knowehead House, c.1920. (Reproduced from Donaldson, *History of Islandmagee*)

Fig. 5, 'Witches dancing with demons at a Sabbat'. Francesco Maria Guazzo, *Compendium Maleficarum in Tres Libros Distinctum Ex Pluribus Authoribus* ... (1608). (Courtesy of the Library of Queen's University, Belfast)

Fig. 6. Men and women being baptised by the Devil in order to become witches, and consequently renouncing their original covenant with God. Guazzo, *Compendium Maleficarum*. (Courtesy of the Library of Queen's University, Belfast)

Above Fig. 7. This early eighteenth-century depiction of the 1593 'Witches of Warboys' case shows Alice Samuel conjuring up demons to do her evil work, while standing in a protective magical ring drawn in the dirt and lit by candles. Richard Boulton, *A Compleat History of Magick, Sorcery and Witchcraft* … (London, 2 vols, 1715–22), volume one, frontispiece. (Courtesy of the University of Glasgow Library)

Left Fig. 8. Joan Prentice's familiar, a ferret called 'Satan', sucking her blood from a 'devil's mark' located on her face. She was hanged on 5 July 1589 for witchcraft. Anon., *The Apprehension and Confession of Three Notorious Witches* … (London, 1589)

Fig. 9. This modern-day imagining of a pillory stands in Carrickfergus, County Antrim. (The author)

Opposite, top Fig. 10. This image of a child levitating appears on the title page of Joseph Glanvill's *Saducismus Triumphatus: or, Full and Plain Evidence Concerning Witches and Apparitions …* (London, 1682). Glanvill's book also contains a detailed account of the trial of Florence Newton in Youghal, County Cork in 1661. (Courtesy of the Library of Queen's University, Belfast)

Opposite, below Fig. 11. A witch receiving the 'Devil's mark', which in the early modern period was regarded as an indelible indicator of the recipient's allegiance to Satan. Glanvill, *Saducismus Triumphatus*. (Courtesy of the Library of Queen's University, Belfast)

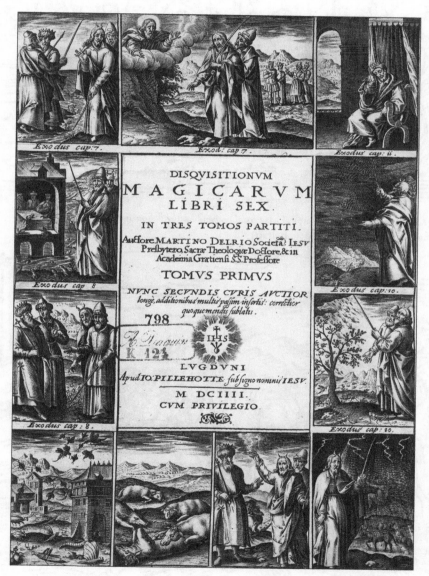

Fig. 12. The title page of an influential, early modern demonological work by Jesuit theologian Martin Del Rio, *Disquisitionum Magicarum* (1604). (Courtesy of the Library of Queen's University, Belfast)

Fig. 13. Witches boiling a baby. Guazzo, *Compendium Maleficarum*. (Courtesy of the Library of Queen's University, Belfast)

Fig. 14. A depiction of some witches digging up corpses for body parts to use in their 'spells'. Guazzo, *Compendium Maleficarum*. (Courtesy of the Library of Queen's University, Belfast)

Horror at Knowehead House

Demons in Church

Having been in Knowehead House just under a fortnight, Mary Dunbar awoke on Sunday, 11 March, with a strong 'desire to go to sermon' at the Presbyterian meetinghouse in Islandmagee. During this time, she had been reliant on people coming to Knowehead to see her, and public interest in her must have been waning in the aftermath of the arrest of six suspected witches. Church on a Sunday morning promised a new audience and perhaps the renewed attention of Revd Sinclair, whose role as chief investigator was gradually being taken over by others. During the service Dunbar sang psalms and listened to the minister's prayer, but she 'fell into a fit' as soon as the sermon began. She was quickly removed from the service so as not to disturb the congregation and eventually taken home.

This was not the first time the Devil had visited a County Antrim church. In his autobiography, written in the early 1660s but not published until the mid-eighteenth century, Robert Blair described how in Larne in 1630 some recent converts, who joined his church in the context of religious revival in east Ulster, had fitted during his Sunday service. The affected people later claimed their convulsions were 'the work of the Lord' and that they had been divinely possessed by the spirit of God. Blair noted that as 'daily the number' of converts 'increased ... both pastor and people' began to think their possession was inspired by Satan 'the destroyer', who 'playing the ape' had possessed the people 'to slander and disgrace the work of the Lord'. The following Sunday another demoniac screamed and convulsed, causing Blair to rebuke the 'lying spirit' for daring to disturb 'the worship of God', ordering it 'in the name and authority of Jesus Christ not to disturb that congregation' again. Blair noted with satisfaction that from that point on, 'we met with no more of that work' of the Devil.[1]

Describing Devilry

As her possession was caused by witchcraft and not direct Satanic intervention, there was to be no such quick fix for Mary Dunbar. When she arrived back at Knowehead, her condition worsened and she reported more spectral visitations, this time from 'an ill-coloured woman' who was 'blind of an eye, which was sunk in her head'. Although she had 'never heard [her] named' Dunbar nevertheless described her as being a 'little woman, her hair of a dark brown', her 'face drawn together by the small pox ... and a string of black beads about her neck, in a very ordinary habit'. Her 'fingers were drawn together and crooked in at the ends, having been all occasioned by falling in the fire, where she was burned'. Accompanying her was a woman the other 'witches' called 'Mrs Ann' who was 'red haired', 'of a middle stature' and 'marked with the small pox'. She also had a 'reddish face', 'unevenly set' teeth, and 'rough arms and course hands'. 'Mrs Ann' was described as wearing a 'good head-dress' with 'sometimes a plain muslin apron, sometimes one furbelowed,[2] sometimes a stamped one, and a mant of black and white mixture, at other times one of a brownish colour'.

Clothes in this period distinguished the social status and gender of the wearer. In small communities they may have also helped distinguish between individuals, given the fact that clothing was expensive to make or buy, with only the wealthy owning anything resembling an extensive wardrobe. The majority of clothing in that period went un-dyed as colourful garments (especially those of deepest black) were very expensive to produce. This may explain why Dunbar pointed out the colour as well as the type of the garments worn by the mysterious Mrs Ann: it was a further way she could help the authorities find her attacker.

On the strength of this description, a number of partially sighted women who lived in Islandmagee were brought before Dunbar, but on every occasion she showed no reaction and in doing so established their innocence.[3] At nine o'clock that evening, turf was thrown at houseguest Sheela McGee, with such 'great force' that it 'bruised her much', while a short time later the Haltridges' servant, Margaret Spear, complained her mouth and nose had been bloodied in the same way. At midnight, John Campbell and John Smith of Larne were sleeping in one of the upstairs bedrooms when they heard cats mewing and their door fly open. When Smith got up to close the door, he saw two people standing at the window who immediately vanished, leaving him extremely frightened. Around the same time, 'Mrs Jameson' and 'Mrs Stannus', wife of James Stannus, who were probably relatives of Dunbar,[4] were sleeping in the kitchen when they heard something strike the back of a chair. However, when James Blythe, who was among those keeping vigil that night, searched the room by candlelight, he found nothing. A little later, McGee was hit in her bed by the bottom of an old lantern that had been thrown at her, after which the house fell silent.

The Testimony of Mary Dunbar, 12 March 1711

More seizures followed the next morning when Dunbar was visited by the spectral form of the one-eyed woman. A few hours later, Mayor Clements arrived from Carrickfergus to take Dunbar's sworn testimony or deposition,[5] a document which provides, in her own words, an unparalleled insight into the young woman's view of events affecting her. When this deposition is compared to the pamphlet account, it becomes apparent that it is in fact the written-up answers to questions put to Dunbar by Clements.

Clements first asked Dunbar if 'the six women in custody'[6] were 'her tormentors'. She confirmed they were and stated that since their imprisonment 'none of them has troubled her'.[7] 'During these severall weeks,' Dunbar continued, she had been 'in a most grievous and violent manner tormented and afflicted with witches,' who made her 'fall very often into fainting and tormenting fitts,' took the 'power of tongue from her,' and afflicted her to the 'degree that she often thinks she is pierced to the heart and that her breasts are cut off.'[8] Dunbar then described how Latimer and Main 'did very much torment her, especially when Mr Sinclair, the dissenting minister, was praying with and for her, and told her they would hinder her of hearing his prayers.' Mayor Clements then asked Dunbar 'if there were any others that tormented her?' Dunbar told them that 'now only two appear to her', 'Mrs Ann' and 'another woman, blind of an eye'. She went on to state that the women had told her during one of their visitations that when Revd Robb said prayers for her, 'they would hinder her from hearing them'.[9] Interference with private prayer would have been taken particularly seriously in Presbyterian religious culture at that time, where praying 'provided a direct access to God', while for others it 'had a more practical role as curer of physical or supernatural ills'.[10]

In a manner perhaps befitting an early eighteenth-century English JP of a sceptical bent, Clements enquired as to why Dunbar in an earlier statement called Janet Latimer by the name of Elizabeth. The girl's explanation was that her knowledge about the suspects came from what they did and said when they 'did frequently appear to her (tho' invisible to her keepers and attenders)',[11] and that she specifically heard Latimer answer to the name of 'Elspy'. She went on to describe how the witches promised that they would 'destroy her if she would discover them; and they … would never leave off, till they put the whole family out of the house.' Clements then asked Revd Robb, who was assisting him, to pray for the girl, but as he did so she remained 'in a fit during the whole time'. Dunbar claimed afterwards to have heard none of it because of the spell cast by the two witches still at large. After her interview was over, Dunbar convulsed periodically until midnight, her tongue often doubled backwards down her throat.

Going to Larne, 13 March

Possibly to give the family a relief from the unrelenting ritual of seizures and supernatural disturbances, it was decided the next morning that Dunbar should be taken from Knowehead to the house of James Stannus in Larne.[12] The first part of Dunbar's journey to Larne was made on foot along the mile-long road on the shores of Larne Lough.[13] When her fits became so severe she was unable to walk, she was put on horseback with a rider placed in front of her and two men on either side. This was an ultimately unsuccessful attempt to prevent her from falling from the horse to the ground. The party then made the 2-mile boat trip across the Lough, during which Dunbar fitted almost continually. Arriving at Stannus's house two hours later, just after noon, Dunbar informed her new hosts that her fits had been caused by Janet Main, accompanied by the blind-eyed woman, who both appeared to her on the boat. Dunbar remained 'positive' that the woman was Main, even after she was warned, probably by Revd William Ogilvie, 'to take care of what she said, for Janet Main was in gaol, and so could give her no trouble'. Revd Ogilvie was the bookish, Scottish-born Presbyterian minister of Larne from 1699 until his death in September 1712.[14]

That afternoon and evening Dunbar fitted frequently, 'sometimes standing upon her head and feet at the same time, with her belly up like a bow'. The 'tormenting of bodies' into unusual shapes was a sign of possession that had Biblical precedent, and one occasionally displayed in Elizabethan demoniacs.[15] Even Dunbar's particular acrobatics had been seen before, as the Throckmorton children were reported to have had 'their bellies heaving up, their head and their heels still touching the ground'.[16] Dunbar was further heard speaking in a low voice, with her 'eyes open, steadfastly looking sometimes to one place and sometimes to another' in an unsuccessful bid to locate the witches responsible for her possession.

A renewed search of the countryside was begun to locate 'Mrs Ann' and her accomplice. It was not long before a number of women were found to loosely match Dunbar's description of her attackers, but all were released when they failed to produce a reaction when brought before the girl. Acting on information received from some neighbours, James Blythe travelled from Islandmagee to the Scotch Quarter of Carrickfergus to interview a woman who was blind in one eye. In tears, the woman informed Blythe that she had been sick for a long time and had just only recovered, but promised 'by the strength of God, she would be with her [Dunbar] in the morning'. The woman then broke down and wept bitterly. Just as Blythe was leaving her house, he noticed a woman he had never seen before making her way 'along the street smoking a pipe of tobacco'. The woman was called Janet Millar and matched Dunbar's description exactly. When 'challenged' by Blythe, Millar fell 'into a great rage' and 'cursed and swore horribly'. Blythe then threatened to arrest her, using a warrant signed by Mayor Clements, and she agreed to be tested for witchcraft by confronting Dunbar. Due to the lateness of the hour, Blythe allowed her to remain in Carrickfergus for the night and to make her own way to Larne in the morning.

The Arrest of Janet Millar, 14 March

At nine o'clock the next morning, the 'weeping' woman from Carrickfergus, along with another woman reportedly 'blind of an eye' from Larne, were brought before Dunbar, who categorically stated they were not her spectral attackers. Feeling sorry for the Carrickfergus woman, and no doubt adding to her growing aura of piety, Dunbar asked her cousin to get the woman 'something to eat and drink', as she had come a long way and was 'under a great concern for being suspected of witchcraft'. Dunbar, however, soon reverted to a trembling, sweating demonic when Janet Millar, who had been brought to Larne by her neighbours, came within a quarter of a mile of the Stannus house. When she entered her bedroom, Dunbar fell immediately into a convulsive fit and had to be held down once more by 'three men'. When asked whether Millar was one of her bewitchers, Dunbar replied, 'she knew her too well, and had seen her too often, to doubt she was the woman who had disturbed her.'[17]

Millar was tested in this manner several times before being taken into a barn by Revd Ogilvie, who then 'asked her several questions, as to her Christian faith, without receiving any satisfactory answer'. To most sceptical, modern minds, this inability to answer his questions may have stemmed from ignorance in Biblical matters, or simply from the shock of being accused of witchcraft, marched to another town, and interrogated in a barn by a clergyman she had never met before. Ogilvie then asked Millar why Dunbar convulsed in her presence and how the girl was able to describe her without previously knowing her, to which Millar answered, in 'a surly manner', that '"I believe the devil's in the lass".' Millar's response resonated with the gathered crowd in the Stannus house as a third test was called for, this time with the accused being brought into the room while the victim faced the other way. When Millar entered, Dunbar immediately fitted and screamed for 'them to take the Devil out of the roome'.[18] This was enough to convince the constable of Larne, Bryce Blan, to formally arrest Millar and organise her transportation to Carrickfergus gaol. Following the example of the earlier interrogation of Catherine McCalmond, or even the advice given in Bolton's handbook for JPs (see chapter 3), Blan searched Millar's house for magical objects, which revealed a 'ball of hair, made up ... with roots of herbs, and some combustible matter, with a needle five inches long through it'. He immediately threw the ball into the fire as it was widely believed this was the only way to remove its magical efficacy. Indeed, it was noted that after this had been done, Dunbar's tongue ceased curling down the back of her throat. The following year, in Hertfordshire, England, Anne Thorn would be cured of her demonic fits when a cake of feathers tied by a long thread was found in her pillow and burnt, much to the later annoyance of the trial judge, Justice Powell. To the community this act offered protection from potentially harmful magic; to Powell it represented a destruction of evidence.[19]

Janet Main Appears to Dunbar

An hour before the arrival of the suspects in Larne, Dunbar began to fit once more. When recovered, she related that she had just been visited in spectral form by the apparently incarcerated Janet Main. This convinced James Stannus to enquire if Main had indeed escaped from prison to renew her spectral attack on the girl. He immediately wrote a letter to Mayor Clements a few miles away in Carrickfergus, to which he received a reply the same day. This explained that the previous day, 13 March, Main and Liston had been taken out of prison by the gaoler (possibly Thomas Faulkner), where the former 'had her bolts struck off to spin' flax fibre into yarn, while the latter 'carded for her with her bolts on'. The processes of spinning and carding were followed by weaving the yarn into brown linen, which would then be bleached and pounded to produce finished cloth. Spinning was usually done in the home by women on hand-driven spinning wheels, while weaving was carried out by small independent producers using yarn made in their own homes or bought at market. Weavers were concentrated in east Ulster and often combined this trade with other employment, usually farming. It would seem, then, that the gaoler, who was being paid by County Antrim grand jury, was using free labour supplied by his prisoners to become part of the increasingly economically significant domestic Ulster linen industry.

After a hard day's labour, Main and Liston were taken back to gaol at eight o'clock that evening and bolted until seven o'clock the next morning, 14 March, when they returned to the gaoler's house for more spinning and carding. In short, the periods of time when Main did not have her wrists and (probably) legs chained and bolted coincided with the spectral attacks on Dunbar, the implication being that the shackles prevented her spirit leaving her body. Similarly, during the trial of Florence Newton for bewitching Mary Longdon in Cork in September 1661, it was revealed the victim 'had been very well when the said Florence was in bolts, and ill again when out of them'. Consequently, for the remainder of the trial, Newton had her hands 'manacled' and her legs chained and bolted to ensure she did not hurt Longdon.[20]

The Attack of the Spider Witch, 15 March

The next day Dunbar's fits continued as before, with 'Mrs Ann' frequently appearing to tell her that 'she should never know her name' and 'would never leave her till she would be her death'. This provided Dunbar with an explanation as to why 'Mrs Ann' was proving far more difficult to locate from her descriptions than previous suspects. Later Dunbar told of how during one of her fits, 'Mrs Ann' appeared to her in spectral form before leaving in the shape of a spider. John Getty, a merchant from Larne,[21] who was visiting the Stannus house, claimed that although he could not see 'Mrs Ann' he witnessed the spider leave the room. Another seizure followed, along with a further appearance of the 'witch' in her spectral and spider forms. This time Getty caught the spider, but when he opened his hand to examine it he found it had mysteriously disappeared. That evening 'Mrs Ann' visited the girl once more, laid 'upon her breast' and informed her that she would 'not so easily get her discovered as she had done the rest'. She then vanished in the form of a housefly, at which time Getty claimed to have felt something strike 'him on the right thigh'.

Shape-shifting witches, who variously changed into horses, apes, cats, dogs, wolves, bees, fish, and sea mammals, can be found in that period in most places in the British Isles and across continental Europe. They even surface in popular seventeenth-century English witchcraft pamphlets such as Thomas Potts's *Wonderfull Discoverie of Witches*, which details the trials of the Lancashire witches in 1612. If the notion of a shape-shifting witch, founded on folk traditions of classical and medieval times, was a part of early modern popular witchcraft belief, it was one that did not sit well with learned, elite writers of witchcraft. This was due to the fact that it implied the theologically unorthodox position that the Devil could overturn the natural order and perform miracles, when he could only perform illusions or lesser wonders. As has been discussed in chapter 4, shape-shifting witches took a more central position in Gaelic supernatural culture in the peripheral regions of the British Isles, especially in Ireland where 'butter-witches' turned into hares to steal milk. It may have been that by describing the shape-shifting of 'Mrs Ann', Dunbar was deliberately feeding into this body of popular beliefs in order to keep the narrative of her possession interesting to her audience. Furthermore, by choosing the form of a spider for the witch to transform into, she could guarantee its appearance in the room at some point, as well as providing, for the first time, verifiable, empirical evidence of the supernatural visits of her spectral attackers.

Counter-Magic and Cunning-Folk

The exertions of the last few days must have taken their toll on Mary Dunbar, because on Friday, 16 March, she was able to rest 'easy, having but some light fits that day'. The following day was marked by severe fitting and visitations by 'Mrs Ann', who threatened to 'destroy her' and promised she would never be discovered. Shortly afterwards, Dunbar claimed that the circulation of the blood in her arm had been cut off, causing intense pain. Upon inspection, it was found that a 'black woollen string, with eight knots upon it' had magically appeared; a 'fact' attested to by one of the men who had held her during her fits and who claimed to have seen 'nothing visible on her arms, when he took hold of them'.[22] The string was removed, but a few hours later, at twelve noon, Dunbar fell into another fit and afterwards her cloth head-dress was found tightly wound around her thigh with 'seven knots upon it'. Her mother, who had by that time joined her daughter in Larne, pointed out that this 'was the same [head-dress] that she had given her that morning, and had seen it tied about her head'.[23] Two hours later, Stannus and Revd Ogilvie cut a length of blue string with five knots in it from Dunbar's arm. This was followed by another fit and the discovery, by Armagh-born Church of Ireland curate of Larne, Revd William Skeffington,[24] of more knotted string, first around the girl's neck and then her waist, causing intense pain in her stomach and back. It was later discovered that this episode was an adverse reaction to the use of 'a counter-charm' procured by Dunbar's mother from 'a popish priest' and employed against her daughter's will during one of her fits. According to Tisdall, the charm contained 'the first chapter of St John in a paper' and was tied around the girl's neck.[25]

Written charms (often laid out on specially produced parchment) had a variety of magical purposes in the early modern period but were principally designed to protect or to cure those humans and livestock from the effects of witchcraft. Those designed for humans were not to be read or flaunted openly by the user and were often required to be kept close to the body. Most written charms had a strong religious element to them, containing Catholic exorcisms or passages from the Bible, and were usually supplied by 'beneficial' magical practitioners or cunning-folk.[26] Known all over Europe by different names, cunning-folk were a ubiquitous part of early modern culture, providing an array of magical services for an affordable fee: from love magic and fortune telling (often involving a prediction of whom a client would marry), to the detection of thieves or lost or stolen property. Cunning-folk also possessed a wide range of anti-witch measures. First of all, they diagnosed witchcraft in suspected victims, a part of their business that increased after 1660 when many trained medical professionals began backing away from supernatural diagnosis (see chapter 6). They also cured the symptoms of bewitchment, either by physically attacking or scratching the skin of the witch, or by helping ensure a suspect was dealt with by the law, or by breaking the spell of a witch using charms and herbs. Finally, cunning-folk helped detect specific witches (or at the very least confirm a client's suspicion), of which a common method was the heating of urine and hair, or sometimes thatch from a roof, placed in a kettle, pan or earthenware bottle over a fire. A form of sympathetic magic, this counter-spell would cause the urine in the bladder of the witch to become unbearably warm and the witch would reveal themselves when they sought relief by overturning the kettle. In recent research I have suggested that magical practitioners approximating European cunning-folk operated in Catholic, native Irish and Protestant settler communities in early modern Ireland. At a local, parish level in early modern, Gaelic, Catholic Ireland, there is evidence that some priests may have acted as de facto cunning-folk, or at the very least facilitated lay use of popular magic. This number includes the 'popish-priest' who provided Mary Dunbar's mother with a protective charm.[27] However, Irish cunning-folk usually came from the same walk of life as their clients, the lower, poorer end of society. They were occasionally paid with money, but usually with goods in kind for performing three main types of magical service: finding lost or stolen goods or occasionally hidden treasure; the diagnosis, detection and curing of witchcraft; and thirdly, in Gaelic-Irish and Catholic areas, protection against, and curing of, fairy attacks on livestock and humans. Written protective charms were also used in Catholic communities and these were largely produced by cunning-folk.

Although some of the methods and services they supplied were prohibited under the 1586 Irish Witchcraft Act, there is no surviving evidence that there was any concerted effort made by civil authorities to stamp out their activities. The three main religious denominations (Presbyterian, Church of Ireland, and Roman Catholic) nevertheless regarded the use and practice of popular magic as socially and religiously damaging. We have better records for Presbyterian church courts, so we know they reprimanded individual practitioners who came to their attention, up until the later eighteenth century. Church-based denunciation of cunning-folk, whatever the denomination, was articulated in much the same way in England and in Europe: that there was very little to differentiate popular magic from demonic, harmful magic, because if the former had any efficacy (and most agreed that fraud was the likely explanation in most instances) its power originated with the Devil.

In early modern and modern Ireland, cunning-folk were referred to in a variety of ways. In English, they were called elf doctors, fairy men, fairy women, and wise men and wise women. In Irish, they were known as bean chumhachtach (woman with supernatural powers), bean feasa (wise woman), doctúirí na síofraí (fairy doctors), and mná feasa (wise women).[28] In the modern period in particular, 'some of these terms were also used to describe charmers'.[29] Charmers or magical healers were different from cunning-folk. They specialised in curing naturally occurring illness or disease in humans or animals. In the modern period, they provided charms to deflect or cure the effects of the evil-eye, fairy, or witch attack. Charmers were both men and women, and their 'gifts' were usually inherited but occasionally derived from contact with fairies. The efficacy of a given cure or charm was dependent on a lack of commerciality. If the practitioner charged money or expected goods for using their gift, it would no longer work. Cailleach, which translated from the Irish means supernatural old woman or hag, in Irish folk tradition, depending on context, can refer either to witches who stole milk and butter or to a cunning person or a magical healer.

'Tho' Men Should Spew Pins and … Women Spit Straws'[30]

The next morning, Sunday, 18 March 1711, Dunbar informed James Stannus that 'Mrs Ann' had stuffed 'hair, feathers, and pins' down her throat to 'choak her'. 'Mrs Ann' also warned her that 'pen knives' would be used next, which 'would destroy her'. Afterwards the girl was bent double with agonising pain in her stomach until two in the afternoon, when she 'threw up some hair, a part of which appeared to be horsehair, by the coarseness of it'. That night Dunbar vomited several times, drawing forth 'five large pins, with wool and feathers'. As has been mentioned, vomiting foreign objects was a main feature of early modern possessions and particularly noticeable in the Youghal (1661) case.[31]

Dunbar's fits began in earnest on 20 March, when she added to the description already given of 'Mrs Ann' that she was middle-aged. James Blythe and John Smith reported that the previous evening, 19 March, they had interviewed a woman called Margaret Mitchell, from the parish of Kilroot, who was around this age and matched Dunbar's physical description. Threatened with arrest by a 'constable and a guard', Mitchell agreed, albeit 'with great reluctancy', to go to Larne of her own volition the next day. In 1683, Richard Dobbs wrote of the parish of Kilroot, which lies just north of Carrickfergus, that it was 'but small', being only a mile long, and 'the inhabitants (except my family and some half a dozen that live under me) all Presbyterians and Scotch, not one natural Irish in the parish, nor papist, and may afford 100 men.'[32] When Jonathan Swift, author of *Gulliver's Travels* and later Dean of St Patrick's Cathedral in Dublin, was installed as vicar of Kilroot in March 1695, he came to a neglected, poor parish overrun with Presbyterians. It also lacked a manse and an inhabitable church in which to preach to his handful of parishioners. Kilroot was one of three parishes, along with the rectory of Ballynure and the vicarage of Templecorran (Broadisland), that comprised the prebend of Kilroot. Swift had been appointed to this living a few months earlier by the Irish government. For numerous reasons, including its poverty and non-conformist nature, Swift left Kilroot in 1696. One can only imagine what Swift's literary comment on the Islandmagee case would have been had he still been living in County Antrim in 1711.

As promised, Mitchell made her way to Stannus's house on 20 March. Although 'a fear came upon' Dunbar on Mitchell's approach, it was nevertheless reported that there was 'not so great a trembling as before, when any of the rest' of the suspected witches had visited her. This lack of reaction was later explained by a counter-charm Dunbar had used to protect herself against Mitchell's magical attacks, this time procured from a 'Scotch gentleman who had been troubled himself by witches'. The Scotch gentlemen is not named in surviving records but his 'preservative' proved so effective that she was able to talk to Mitchell without fitting. 'And though in great terror,' Dunbar during this conversation 'accused her of being one of her greatest tormentors'. Just as he had done on Dunbar's arrival, Revd Ogilvie displayed the caution, common sense and moderate scepticism that for the most part typified the Irish Presbyterian Church's treatment of witchcraft accusations, by warning Dunbar 'to be cautious of what she did, in accusing any person of so great a crime'. Dunbar replied that 'she should answer to God' at Judgement Day if she were lying and that Mitchell was 'the person who went under the name of Mrs Ann amongst her tormentors'.

Perhaps feeling her testimony was being doubted, Dunbar seized the initiative and asked Blythe and Smith to let Mitchell go free, to see whether or not she would use her newfound freedom to attack her. The men complied and within the hour Dunbar fell into a fit, during which, almost in homage to the final days of Ann Haltridge's life, Dunbar pointed at the foot of her bed to where Mitchell apparently stood in spectral form. Upon recovery, she informed the men that Mitchell had promised not to torment her again if she agreed to 'not prosecute her'. A further seizure was followed by the revelation that Mitchell had threatened to cast images in wax of Blythe and Smith and 'roast them like larks before a fire, and ere it were long some of them should be as ill, and worse than she was'.[33] More concrete evidence of Mitchell's witchcraft came when Dunbar vomited 'a great many feathers', four large pins, and some buttons. It was later discovered the buttons had come from Blythe's 'vest' and had been in their rightful place just before the girl had convulsed.

Testing Times

The next day, 21 March, Mitchell was taken before Dunbar for the second time, with 'the preservative which she had from the Scotch gentlemen being laid' aside. Dunbar convulsed as soon as Mitchell appeared and recovered as soon as she left the room. She then stated for the record that this 'was the person who went under the name of Mrs Ann'.

On the strength of this, Blythe and Smith and John Logan, constable of the parish of Broadisland, formally arrested Mitchell. The incarceration of Mitchell should have improved Dunbar's condition, but in the early evening she experienced another severe fit and a debilitating pain spread throughout her body. She also vomited some 'linen thread, with seven knots upon it'. Her condition only improved at eleven o'clock that night when Constable Logan put leg chains and bolts on Mitchell during a stopover at the village of Ballycarry in Broadisland, on the way to Carrickfergus gaol. Just as they had done for Janet Main, the chains and bolts prevented Mitchell from conducting any further spectral attacks on Dunbar.

Only Witches Can Fly?

With Margaret Mitchell gaoled and bolted along with the other suspects, Dunbar enjoyed 'perfect health' for the next two days. However, just after twelve noon on 24 March, she was pulled by Janet Main in spectral form 'through the bed backwards ... to the floor' where she lay in pain for a 'considerable time'. Main had also threatened to drag Dunbar out of the casement window and drown her in a nearby well. This was followed by another fit, during which Main taunted her that she would 'destroy her' and 'put pins and feathers down her throat', while her companion, Janet Liston, also tried to lure her out of the window into the garden, to 'see the finest play, and hear the sweetest music that she ever saw or heard in her life'. After a series of severe fits and convulsions, Dunbar levitated above Stannus's expensive four-poster bed until she touched the canopy, despite the fact that 'James Blythe did all he could to hold her down'. Dunbar's levitation was a recognised, if rare, phenomenon in early modern times (see fig. 10). For example, when Richard Jones was bewitched by Jane Brooks in February 1658 in Shepton Mallet, Somerset, he was seen rising 30ft from the ground before floating over the garden wall.[34] This was not the only time Dunbar had defied natural laws and appeared to levitate. Witnesses had seen her float off her bed and appear to be gently lowered to the ground by invisible hands. She later explained that what onlookers had seen was a divinely thwarted attempt by the witches in their invisible, spectral forms to drag her to an open window and throw her out of it.[35] That these attacks occurred when Main and Liston were apparently out of harm's way in Carrickfergus gaol was later explained by the fact the women had had 'their bolts struck off, on purpose' just after midday to test whether 'they would at that time trouble the girl'.

'Struck Dumb', 25 March, Larne

After a restful night, the girl awoke the next day, 25 March, unable to speak but 'made signs for a Bible' to be brought to her on the premise that 'if she read the 2nd chapter of Job, she would have the power of her tongue'. Her speech was returned after reading up to 'the 9th verse' of the chapter. The use of the Bible in the battle against the Devil is one common to many demonic possession narratives, as it was believed to have 'the power to protect the demoniac as well as to banish demons'.[36] This passage was possibly selected because it informed her audience once more how her struggle against the forces of darkness, and her maintenance of devotion to God in the face of it, was similar to that experienced by Job in Biblical times. The next morning, 26 March, Dunbar vomited a pin she claimed had been put in her mouth a few days before by Main, having lain in her stomach for two days, but 'could give no account how' this had been achieved. With Main and Liston bolted once more, Dunbar rested easily 'in very good health' for the next two days, until 29 March, when she prepared to travel to Carrickfergus to attend the trial of the women she accused of bewitching her.

Back at Knowehead House: the Haunted School, 14 March

When Dunbar and her entourage left Islandmagee on 14 March, young Mrs Haltridge was left alone with her servant, Margaret Spear, as her husband James was still in Dublin. The 'disturbances in the house' over the last few weeks had left her emotionally fragile and so she asked a local 'schoolmaster who dwelt near them to bring his scholars and keep school in the parlour'. Within two hours of their arrival at Knowehead, however, 'seventeen stones [were] thrown against the door' of the room in which they were studying, 'with such force they all made great impressions in it', and Mrs Haltridge's partly burnt riding hood was found on the fire.

Legislation passed in the mid-seventeenth century dictated that schoolmasters had to be licensed (and thus approved) by a Church of Ireland bishop in order to teach legally. For a dissenting denomination that placed emphasis on literacy and education, this posed a potentially large problem for Ulster Presbyterians. Presbyterian schools nevertheless operated in Ulster, and were attached to churches and overseen by ministers and Elders. They provided prospective clergy and children of the congregation with a basic education. Although there is little evidence of a concerted effort by the Established Church to close down the Presbyterian school system, schoolmasters and individual institutions were periodically harassed by hotter Anglican clergy, particularly in the early eighteenth century. Nineteenth-century sources suggest that Presbyterian children in Islandmagee, from all walks of life, were receiving formal education from at least the mid-seventeenth century onwards. In 1800, a school teaching basic literacy, numeracy and religious education to just over twenty children was established in the session house of the Islandmagee meetinghouse, funded by the Synod of Ulster through their schools society.[37]

Neighbourhood Watch, 15 March–1 April

For the next five days, until 20 March, stones were hurled by unseen hands and strange noises were heard throughout the house as the family gathered their beds together 'for their greater security, being afraid to lie at a distance from one another'. Sensing the need of Mrs Haltridge and her children, many of her neighbours 'came every night to stay', with some of them sitting 'up all night, having a candle burning by them'. Despite this vigilance, clothes disappeared before reappearing days later and were 'sometimes found in the hag yard covered with straw, and at other times brought back and laid upon the floor'.[38] Scratching sounds were heard on the floorboards and bedposts, as if it 'were one's nails'. Invisible hands battered backs of chairs and keys were 'thrown in upon one of the beds or upon the floor'. The Haltridge 'children's gown-laces, cravats and shirts' were found to be 'strangely knotted'. One of them even had his 'shirt knotted at the corners whilst upon his back as he lay in bed'.

Sometime between Tuesday, 20 March, and Saturday, 24 March, James Haltridge returned from Dublin,[39] to a household in chaos. Bedclothes were torn from the beds, sometimes when children were sitting on them, or in well-lit rooms in front of adult visitors. There were also reports of assaults by invisible entities on various guests and family members with sticks and iron keys that had up until that point been missing. The day after the arrival home of her husband, young Mrs Haltridge, when preparing to go to the meetinghouse on Sunday, 25 March,[40] discovered her gloves and black hood were missing. That night a 'great knocking' was heard in the bedrooms upstairs and 'all things that could be knotted, had a great number of knots put upon them'. Furthermore, 'a pair of blankets being nicely folded up in the shape of a child' were found in Margaret Spear's 'bed in the kitchen', with Mrs Haltridge's 'black hood put as it were upon the head of it'. As on so many occasions before, Spear was first to discover this macabre sight and immediately 'called out [that] there was somebody in the bed'.

After 25 March, disturbances in the house intensified, the base line of which were stones hurled with force at unsuspecting householders and everyday objects being found with knots in them, from the 'horses and cows binding' to 'garters in a minute's time after having been removed' from legs. Margaret Spear's sheets were stripped from her bed and a riding-hood of a neighbour called Mary Lock was thrown in the fire. On the night of 28 March, Spear, being frightened, was allowed to leave her bed in the kitchen and sleep with the children. While in bed she felt a presence crawling slowly over her body, while pillows were taken from under the sleeping children and 'thrown at her with great force'. Several clods of earth were also thrown at her, bloodying her mouth and nose. On 29 March, bedclothes began taking the shape of corpses and loud scratching, knocking and laughing noises were heard all over the house. These manifestations lasted for a few days until 1 April 1711.

Demonic Possession and Obsession: a Symbiotic Relationship?

Although Dunbar's possession symptoms improved after 21 March, when the accused women were imprisoned and bolted, the attacks on the Haltridge family by a demonic spirit not only continued but intensified, lasting even beyond the day of the trial. This leaves us with the question as to how far the demonic haunting and Dunbar's possession were bound together? For example, if they were inextricably linked, why did the demonic entity in the house not follow the possessed girl and leave Knowehead in peace? A modern, sceptical answer to this question, albeit one founded on supposition, would be that the servant Margaret Spear, possibly aided and abetted by the Haltridge children, did not want to give up the attention and thrill of torturing the household just because Dunbar had left it. To contemporaries in Islandmagee, however, a more plausible explanation may have been that the witches had conjured up two distinct entities: one to possess Dunbar and one to haunt Knowehead House, along with the Haltridge family, their servants, visiting clergy, neighbours and friends.

The Trial, 31 March 1711

Travelling to the Assizes

On 29 March 1711, Mary Dunbar left James Stannus's house in Larne on horseback to travel 'to Carrickfergus ... to prosecute at the Assizes the eight women in custody'. Around two o'clock, however, she fitted and fell from James Blythe's horse. Loss of speech and regular fits convinced the party to stay the night at the house of a man called John Burns. That evening, around nine o'clock, Dunbar made signs for a Bible to be brought to her, and as she began reading John 14:6[1] her speech returned. She then told of how, earlier in the day, upon the road, a man appeared to her who had a long face, 'of an ordinary size' and 'light brown hair, a little curling at the ends, mixed with some grey hairs'. Dunbar also remarked upon his shabby appearance, noting that he wore 'an old bonnet upon his head, brown coloured clothes much worn'. Beside him stood 'an old woman, marked with the small pox, of a dark complexion, in ordinary clothes, of a middle size'. Accompanying her was 'a young woman, of about twenty years of age ... of a middle stature, her clothes pretty good, and of a light colour'. The spectres also told Dunbar that they would torment her even more 'than she had been yet'. Whatever protective effect Dunbar's earlier reading of the Scriptures had, it dissipated after 'about an hour' and her fitting returned.

At dawn the next morning, 30 March, 'it was borne in upon her' that if she read from Genesis 16:5[2], 'she should speak, which happened accordingly'. It is not clear from the pamphlet account how this idea was conveyed to her, but the assumption at the time was that it was the result of divine intervention. Dunbar and her party then took to the road, but 2 miles from Carrickfergus she was again 'struck dumb'. Her speech, however, returned a few hours later, around one o'clock in the afternoon, just in time for her to converse with a number of gentlemen and clergymen who had gathered to meet her at Carrickfergus courthouse. To these men, Dunbar apparently gave 'great satisfaction in relation to her trouble', or put more simply, she was able to convince them her possession was genuine. This group may have included Presbyterian ministers Revd James Cobham of Broadisland (Ballycarry) and Revd Patrick Adair (of Carrickfergus), as this was the first time they had encountered Dunbar and yet both men were able to give evidence at the trial a day later. Adair and Cobham both knew Robert Sinclair, minister of Islandmagee, as all three had been representatives of the Presbytery of Belfast at the Synod of Ulster held in Belfast the previous June.[3] We will hear more about Revd Adair (died 1717) in a following chapter, but it is interesting to note that he came from a family with a deep interest in the supernatural. His father, also a Presbyterian minister called Patrick Adair (died 1694), detailed the murder by witchcraft of James Shaw and his wife in 1672 in his as-yet unpublished history of the Presbyterian Church in Ireland. More importantly, he supplied preeminent natural philosopher Robert Boyle (died 1691) 'with instances of preternatural phenomenon in 1687–8'. Towards the end of his life Boyle became particularly interested in gathering verified cases of spirits, demons and witches as evidence of the existence of the spirit world, and by extension of God. As such, he formed part of a loosely affiliated group of anti-atheist, anti-Sadducee writers, many of whom were clergymen interested in the 'new science'.[4] It may have been that a new audience of important men was too great an allure for Dunbar to pass up by remaining silent. If her symptoms were a deliberate and conscious subterfuge, periods of silence were a good way to ensure she did not incriminate herself on the eve of a trial on which the whole county had its eyes. In this pattern of speech loss and return, occasioned by reading certain parts of the Bible, there was an unspoken, implicit agreement between Dunbar and her audience, that it was not the girl who was choosing what Biblical passages to read, at certain times, to regain her speech, but the providential hand of God guiding her to them. In any case, at about 3 a.m., she experienced 'several fainting fits, and was dumb till four in the morning of the 31st' March, the day of the trial.

At that time, Dunbar once again made 'signs for a Bible' and reading from Exodus, 'the third and thirteen chapters', her speech returned.[5] Dunbar then revealed that the women and man she had just met on the road had visited her and told her that she 'should not be able to discover them as she had done the rest, and should not be able to speak one word from five in the morning till four at night'. This promised bout of silence held particular significance because criminal trials in that period would not have been expected to last this long, ensuring Dunbar would avoid having to speak in court. Furthermore, the sudden appearance of three new witches provided a way to explain any post-trial symptoms, thereby facilitating a relapse and prolonging her possession drama. Dunbar's muteness has some precedent in the annals of English witchcraft trials. In March 1662, when Amy Denny and Rose Cullender were tried for the possession of 11-year-old Elizabeth Pacy and her 9-year-old sister Deborah, the victims had been groomed to be star witnesses but were unable to give evidence on the day: Deborah 'was held in such extreme manner, that her parents wholly despaired of her life, and therefore could not bring her to the Assizes', and Elizabeth, who did attend the trial, 'could not speak one word all the time'.[6]

Trial Preliminaries

As has been suggested, Irish courts, along with many other aspects of the legal system, were extremely similar to those in England. The twice-yearly Assizes for County Antrim were held in Carrickfergus in the county courthouse in a building maintained by the grand jury. It was built at the same time (nearly 100 years previously) as the county gaol it stood next to at the head of Main Street.[7] As Neal Garnham has pointed out, 'the majority of courtrooms would have been of some antiquity, and as a consequence were probably constructed along the lines of English originals' containing 'an elevated bench for the judiciary, two boxes for the grand and trial juries, and perhaps some seating for the court officials and spectators ... prisoners were required to stand in the open court, or be confined to a large communal dock.'[8] In 1716, the County Antrim grand jury had iron plates (embedded with spikes) fitted to the dock in Carrickfergus Assize room, 'for the better securing of prisoners' and to stop people sitting on it, 'which often proved offensive to the court'.[9]

Assize towns came to life when the court convened, as people poured in to experience legal dramas as well as to shop, conduct business, participate in civic duties, and attend charity balls, taverns, feasts, markets, fairs, and auctions. The spectacle of the Assizes began with the arrival of the trial judges, who were government employees plucked from one of Dublin's three common law courts. Twice a year, Assize justices worked one of the five court circuits that divided Ireland, hearing all the cases JPs and grand juries had prepared for them. In theory, two justices were to be assigned to each circuit, but in practice it was often only one.[10] In spring 1711, however, two justices, James MacCartney and Anthony Upton, were appointed to the North-East Assize circuit. The North-East circuit of Ulster started in the town of Drogheda before moving on to Dundalk, County Louth, Downpatrick, County Down, Carrickfergus, County Antrim, and Armagh, County Armagh. It finished in Monaghan, County Monaghan.[11] Given that the county was split by party tensions, it may have been thought prudent that Whigs and Tories each had a representative on the bench, of which more will be said in the next chapter.

Unfortunately, there is no surviving documentary evidence detailing what happened immediately before the trial of the Islandmagee witches. It is more than probable, however, that a number of preliminary procedures were gone through just as they were in Assize courts in other parts of the country.[12] Before a trial took place, parish and county officers submitted statements and depositions and other evidences (in the Islandmagee case supplied by Mayor Clements), which were then passed to the clerks of the court who used them to draft bills of indictment for the consideration of the grand jury. Pretrial depositions therefore played a very important role in the indictment process, and we are lucky enough to have been left with a full set for the first Islandmagee trial. Grand juries had, at a county level, a number of administrative, economic, and political as well as legal roles, and were composed of between twelve and twenty-three men plucked from the wealthy higher reaches of county society. Grand juries often represented particular factions or family groups within the county and members were likely to sit on panels over extended periods.[13] In theory, those involved in the earlier investigation and gaoling of the Islandmagee witches could have exercised influence over the grand jury, or may have even sat on it. Although a list of the grand jury presiding at Carrickfergus Assizes does not survive for spring 1711, it does for the following year, spring 1712, and none of the seventeen gentry listed there had any prior involvement with the Islandmagee case. Of course, there is no way of telling if the grand juries of spring 1711 and spring 1712 consisted of the same men, but the grand jury list for the next Assize session, that of late summer 1712, shows that ten out of the seventeen appearing on it were also sitting at the previous session, indicating at least some consistency of tenure.[14]

County Antrim High Sheriffs were, in theory, appointed annually by the government, but in practice this was done by leading, large, resident landowners. After the passing of the Test Act in 1704, sheriffs were expected to take communion, while in office, in a Church of Ireland church. Mayor Edward Clements of Straid, County Antrim, was first appointed to the office in 1707, and again in 1716. In 1711, the position was held by his brother, Andrew Clements, who was also resident in Straid.[15] Sheriffs were unpaid officials who, among a host of other duties carried out in the county, ensured all witnesses and local officers, from coroners to JPs and constables, were in the court on the day of the Assizes. From among attendant constables, they also chose a number of bailiffs to assist the court. Irish grand juries, unlike their English counterparts, did not interview witnesses in person and instead reviewed, in private, written bills prepared for them by clerks of the court. They then decided if the evidence warranted a trial, and if this was the case a *Billa Vera*, or True Bill, was issued and the accused were then arraigned. The new Bill of Indictment was read out by the clerk of the court and the defendants were then required to plead guilty or not guilty: only a small number of those indicted in Ireland at that time pleaded guilty to serious charges. Defendants who pleaded guilty were removed from the court to await sentencing, while those who chose the not-guilty route, including the eight women in our case, went on to the next stage of the trial process. A final check was made to see if the prosecutors of the case were in court (in this case Dunbar or her representatives) before a trial jury (petty jury) of twelve men was chosen and sworn in under oath by the sheriff. The defendants were then brought into the court and, for the benefit of the petty jury, the indictment was read once more.

The Trial Begins

The trial of the eight Islandmagee witches began an hour or two earlier than most criminal trials in Ireland, at six o'clock in the morning. Dunbar and some of the witnesses and trial attendees had been awake until at least four in the morning, so they must have been very tired, having had little or no sleep. Just as proceedings began, the petty jury informed presiding judges, Justice of the Common Pleas Anthony Upton, and Justice of the Queen's Bench James MacCartney, that 'some facts, antecedent' to the bewitchment of Dunbar should 'be enquired into'.[16] Petty juries had an important role in the criminal justice system as they not only delivered verdicts but 'could also force the hand of the justices of Assize in deciding to what sentence convicted offenders received' and even helped to secure pardons.[17] Their request, however, was 'overruled by the bench'. It is unclear if this decision was reached by one or both of the presiding judges, but it is telling that no mention is made in surviving sources of any disagreement arising on this issue between the two men. Revd Tisdall, who is our main guide to the trial itself, having taken notes 'from the mouths of the sworn witnesses', regarded this exclusion of evidence relating to the death of Mrs Ann Haltridge as 'very unaccountable, considering the great dependence' the cases had on one another, 'which doubtless were, a series of the same preternatural causes and effects; and would have reflected much light to each other'.[18] The 'neighbourhood', after all, generally believed that the old woman had been 'bewitched to death' by the same witches who went on to attack Dunbar.[19]

Tisdall was the son of William Tisdall senior, a former Sheriff of Carrickfergus between 1690 and 1694. Educated at Trinity College,

Dublin, William junior became Church of Ireland vicar of Layde, Skerry and Racavan, County Antrim, in 1706, rector of Drumcree, County Armagh, in 1711, and vicar of Belfast in 1712. Tisdall was a friend of Jonathan Swift and the men 'bonded over their mutual distain for the Dissenters', both having 'served as clerics in the Scottish heartlands ... of the northeast during a period of Presbyterian expansion'. Their relationship soured after 1704 when Tisdall told him he wished to ask Swift's companion, Esther Johnson (Stella), to marry him. Tisdall owned property in Carrickfergus, which along with his High Church, Tory politics explains his attendance at the trial.[20]

The reasons for the reticence of the judges to use their discretionary power to hear evidence relating to Ann's bewitchment and death can only be guessed at. They may have simply wished to avoid adding another layer of complexity to a trial which was already comparatively complex. Although eighteenth-century Irish Assize judges 'acted to clarify points of uncertainty, and provided legal interpretations for the court', their identification 'of legal caveats tended to be more often in the favour of the accused than the prosecutor'.[21] If evidence concerning the death of Ann Haltridge was heard, it could have led to the eight women being indicted for the far more serious offence of using witchcraft to kill, which under the 1586 Irish Witchcraft Act was a capital crime that carried the death penalty. Most eighteenth-century judges did not take the death penalty lightly, nor did they particularly enjoy passing it. Justice Upton, who later instructed the jury to acquit the accused, may have also been aware of the situation in England, where the death sentence had not been passed for witchcraft since the execution of Alice Molland at Devon Assizes in 1685.

After the petty jury's interjection, the prosecution of the defendants began. The eight women did not have legal representation or counsel as this was rare in Irish criminal trials, and the case for the prosecution was led by the injured party and not by lawyers. Overall, the involvement of lawyers in most criminal proceedings at that time was relatively small. As 'neither counsel nor attorney' was 'employed against the prisoners', Mary Dunbar would have been expected to lead the prosecution herself. She was unable to perform this role having experienced a serious of seizures almost immediately after the trial began. This left her unable to speak, nor hear 'very well, except in her fits, when she neither heard nor saw anybody that was with her'. Tisdall later noted that he had seen Dunbar in court, 'cast her eyes about, in a wild distracted manner, and it was then thought she was recovering from her fit, and it was hoped she would give in her own evidence'. 'As they were raising her up,' he continued, 'she sunk into the arms of a person who held her, closed her eyes, and seemed perfectly senseless and motionless.' After the trial, Tisdall spoke to Dunbar, who had by this time recovered her speech, and she informed him that 'she knew not where she was when in court; that she had been afflicted all that time by three persons, of whom she gave a particular description, both of their proportions, habits, hair, features, and complexion.'[22]

Dunbar's inability to take part ensured these unusually complex proceedings lost direction. Tisdall believed the situation was made worse by the fact:

> there was no lawyer to manage the trial, so that the evidence not being produced in any order, the circumstances of time and place were so perplexed and confused, that were it for so many glaring matters of fact which pierced through all the clouds that could be raised, men might have gone away without having either discovered truth, or satisfied their curiosities.[23]

Tisdall noted that the situation 'was taken notice of by the council at the bar, and one of them declared, had any of them been assigned to manage the trial and evidence, they would have willingly done it without any fee.'[24]

Nineteen witnesses for the prosecution were eventually called and gave evidence under oath: one was a woman and four were Presbyterian clergymen.[25] William Tisdall recounts that of these witnesses, six gave detailed and lengthy testimonies, but he unfortunately failed to state who they were. He merely noted that they were 'of good repute for understanding and integrity, and seemingly of good fashion and substance, and the most considerable persons in the neighbourhood where the facts happened.'[26] Given this description, it is likely the group included some of the clerical witnesses and pre-trial deponents, in particular those who were also important figures in their communities, such as James Blythe, Hugh Wilson, Charles Lennan, William Fenton, and Hugh Donaldson. The evidence the witnesses gave is detailed in Tisdall's letter, but because what was recounted has been discussed in earlier chapters there is no need to repeat it here.[27] Along with witness testimony, physical evidence was produced in court in the form of 'a great quantity of things ... sworn to be what she [Mary Dunbar] had vomited out of her throat'. Tisdall related that he had held these objects in his hand and 'found there was a great quantity of feathers, cotton, yarn, pins, and two large waistcoat buttons'.[28] Tisdall also related that during the trial, when witnesses described how Dunbar had identified the women from their names or physical appearance, the defendants were 'called to the bar to compare them with the descriptions given by the afflicted at several times'. Tisdall went on to state that 'it is really inconceivable to imagine how exactly they all agreed to the descriptions given; though it was confessed they never seen the afflicted, nor the afflicted them.'[29]

After prosecution witnesses had been heard, witnesses for the defence could, theoretically, give evidence. However, no defence witnesses were called to speak on behalf of the accused women. This was common practice in most criminal trials at that time, particularly in non-capital cases. Consequently, Justices Upton and MacCartney 'ordered the prisoners at the bar to offer what they could to the court, in their own defence'.[30] Tisdall described how the accused 'positively denied the facts charged against them, and one of them with the worst look, and the most suspected, called the great God of heaven and earth to witness that she was injured.'[31] It was at this point, 'the characters of each person was inquired into' and it was found that 'some of them were of an ill fame'.[32] It has been suggested in earlier chapters that Janet Latimer, Janet Main, and Janet Millar behaved in ways that would have contravened respectable female behaviour and speech in relation to the standards of their tight-knit, Presbyterian communities: they smoked pipes; drank wine; cursed; wore old, stained clothes; and resisted arrest and the interrogation process. Some of them even had long reputations for practising witchcraft and had threatened to bewitch their neighbours in the past. These negative attributes were heightened by the contrast they represented to Mary Dunbar (and, indeed, the witnesses for the prosecution) who towered above them in reputation, social status, perceived physical beauty, education and Christian piety. This contrast was so striking that even outsiders such as Samuel Molyneux, who did not question 'the reality of the witchcraft', was 'really inclinable to determine in her [Dunbar's] favour'.[33]

William Tisdall, on the other hand, argued that the reputations of the accused women were not informed by 'any facts, or rumour of facts' but 'rather due to their ill looks'. He went on to suggest that 'most of them had received the communion ... that several of them had been laborious, industrious people', and had been known to pray publicly and privately within their family groups. Tisdall also pointed out that the eight women had learnt the Lord's Prayer in the short time they were in prison.[34] He had to admit, however, that this and other outward acts of piety did not fully exonerate those accused of witchcraft because, in common with their master Satan, witches were not above 'the basest and vilest acts of hypocrisy'.[35] Tisdall may have had a point that the 'witch-like' appearances of some of the suspects, compounded by various physical impairments and other visual differences, made them believable witches and the accusations laid against them more plausible. However, the idea that they were mostly respectable, church-going women is hard to maintain in the face of overwhelming evidence to the contrary. As we shall see in the next chapter, Tisdall's attempt to rehabilitate some of the defendants' reputations was based on a desire to exonerate all of them for religious and political reasons. Tisdall obviously had no idea the influence this inaccurate portrayal of the Islandmagee witches would have on future generations of writers, historians and journalists (see chapter 11).

Summing-Up

When all the testimony and evidence had been heard, it was usually left to the judiciary to sum up the case, a service the petty jury particularly needed in complex cases such as this. Summing-up was one of the main ways Assize judges could influence the jury and thus the outcome of a trial. Tisdall reported that, 'Judge Upton summoned up the whole evidence, with great exactness and perspicuity, notwithstanding the confused manner in which it was ordered.'[36] Educated at

Oxford University, Upton was in politics a Tory and had been a barrister in England before being made Justice of the Common Pleas after the accession of Queen Anne to the throne. He committed suicide in 1718 by cutting his throat while suffering from acute mental illness.[37] His view of witchcraft, and more importantly the prosecution of suspected witches, had been formed in the English legal system. During his speech to the petty jury, Upton demonstrated a straightforward elite view of witches, as those who harmed using magical powers provided by Satan after they had made a pact with him. He also admitted that, although 'he could not doubt but the whole matter was preternatural, and diabolical', he nevertheless 'conceived, that had the persons accused been really witches, and in compact with the Devil, it could be hardly presumed they should be such constant attendants upon divine service, both in public and private.' He then advised the jury that they 'could not bring them in guilty upon the sole testimony of the afflicted person's visionary images'.[38] Although becoming popular by the mid-seventeenth century, spectral evidence was treated with scepticism by some English legal authorities, particularly in possession cases.

In short, Justice Upton's continued belief in witchcraft but scepticism towards the evidence of instances of it was an example of the pervasive judicial scepticism (discussed in chapter 4) which helped bring European witch-hunting to an end in the late seventeenth and eighteenth centuries. This judicial scepticism was particularly prominent in an early eighteenth-century trial, which Upton, coming from an English legal background, may have been aware of. Chief Justice Sir John Holt, in his questioning of witnesses and handling of evidence, repeatedly aided the prosecution case against Richard Hathaway in March 1702 for deliberately faking his possession to make a false accusation of witchcraft against Sarah Morduck. Holt even prompted a witness to reveal that Hathaway had pretended 'to be dumb', and made sure it was made clear to the jury that a demoniac's fits could be easily feigned. In his summing-up, which no doubt helped them to arrive at a guilty verdict without having to leave the courtroom, Holt pointed out that Hathaway had been tricked by local sceptics, including local Anglican minister Dr Martin, into revealing that he had faked his method of easing his symptoms of possession: the scratching of Morduck until she bled.

Holt also reminded the jury that the pins Hathaway had claimed to have vomited had actually been kept in his trouser pockets before being transferred to his mouth.[39]

Justice James MacCartney also made a final speech to the jury, but unlike Upton, who had advised them to acquit the defendants, he suggested that they 'might, from the evidence, bring them in guilty'.[40] Justice MacCartney was the eldest son of prominent Belfast merchant, and Surveyor-General of Ulster, George MacCartney (died 1691), and at the time of the trial was 60 years of age, twenty years older than Upton.[41]

The Verdict

After the prosecution had delivered its evidence, which the judges had summed up, it was time for the trial or petty jury to deliver a verdict. This had to be unanimous. Twelve-man juries ideally were to be plucked from the 'middling sort', but in practice they often came from lower down the social ladder. Catholics were prohibited from serving as jurors in cases involving foreign enlistment or the enforcement of the Penal Laws (and related civil bills) after 1709. Unfortunately, there are no surviving jury lists to tell us who made up the panel at the trial of the Islandmagee witches. As petty juries were drawn from all over the county, it is unlikely that jurors in the Islandmagee case would have been directly involved with the accusation or prosecution of the accused witches, but it is conceivable. It is almost certain that they would have had at least some prior knowledge of the case, which could have impacted upon their decision-making processes. Furthermore, it was not above certain sheriffs to select panels who were likely to return a desired verdict. It may be significant that the sheriff at that time, Andrew Clements, who selected the Carrickfergus jury, was the brother of Mayor Clements, who was not only convinced of the guilt of the Islandmagee witches but instrumental in bringing them to court. Any of these suppositions could offer an explanation as to why, according to William Tisdall, the petty jury was so 'predetermined against the witches'.[42]

When the jury 'brought in their verdict' it declared they believed the defendants 'were guilty of exercising of witchcraft on the body of Mary Dunbar'. In normal circumstances, this verdict would have been announced to the court by the foreman and the prisoners would have been removed to await judgement or sentencing. They would have then been brought back into the courtroom and paraded before the judges who, after enquiring whether any mitigating circumstances existed, such as a plea of pregnancy, passed sentence. As was discussed in chapter 4, the sentence for those convicted for a first offence of practising witchcraft short of causing death was set by the 1586 Irish witchcraft statute: twelve months' imprisonment and four stints, for six hours at a time, in the pillory in a market town on market day, while they named their offences and apologised for them. Market days were important days in the urban and rural calendar and pillorying convicted criminals at that time ensured maximum audiences, thereby increasing the punitive effect of the sentence. It was this punishment, 'to be imprisoned twelve months, and to be pilloried four times', that Upton and MacCartney handed down to the eight women. The pillory was situated outside Worraigh Tower in Carrickfergus, and close to the spot where the original stood a replica set has been erected (see fig. 9). The trial lasted from 'six in the morning, until two in the afternoon', which was extremely long by the standards of Assize trials in general, even capital cases.

It is a sad fact of historical research, and genealogy in particular, that the poor leave very little to posterity in documentary form. This observation becomes truer the further one goes back in time. We do not know how the women served their sentences or what they did afterwards. There are no surviving death certificates, gravestones, or prison records. It has been suggested that spending time in Carrickfergus gaol would have been an unpleasant and unhealthy experience, and as nineteenth-century folklore had it (see chapter 11), the women 'were severely pelted in the pillory, with boiled cabbage stalks, and the like, by which one of them had an eye beaten out'.[43] Although there is no documentary evidence supporting this claim, it nevertheless made a deep impression on writers for the remainder of the century. Whatever was thrown at them, and whatever its impact, being bent over, on public display, for hours on end, must have been a deeply humiliating and painful experience.

A Political Witch-Hunt?

William Tisdall and Anti-Presbyterianism

In common with Justice Upton, Revd William Tisdall was convinced that the 'extraordinary facts' of the Islandmagee case 'proved upon oath, in the course of the evidence, were all preternatural' and could not be explained 'by any human reason'. They might have been preternatural, or beyond what was natural, but that does not mean they represented a miracle or an act of witchcraft. Tisdall claimed that the time of miracles had passed with the Apostolic Age, which had ceased with the death of Jesus Christ's last Apostle. This was a common stance for Anglican clergymen to take when they wished to stay within the bounds of theological orthodoxy. They often argued that after the Apostolic Age, seemingly miraculous phenomena were most likely to be the Devil's work, especially when 'wrought for bad ends' such as in cases of witchcraft and possession. Tisdall did not harbour doubts about the existence of diabolical witchcraft, only that the present case was not a verifiable example of it.

Tisdall consequently agreed with Justice Upton that the eight women on trial should not have been 'found guilty' of causing Dunbar's 'fits, or possessions'. Tisdall's ultimately unrequited desire for the acquittal of the Islandmagee witches lay (in part) in an explicit distrust of the girl's spectral evidence. This was not because he thought Dunbar was lying, but because he believed the Devil had conveyed 'to her imagination' the images of the 'prisoners at the bar'. Satan, in other words, had created an illusion to cause Dunbar to see the spectres of the accused women. This was just the type of trick the devil would play to 'have innocent persons arraigned, accused, lose their reputations, and perhaps their lives'. Tisdall went on to give Biblical precedents where God had allowed the Devil to 'represent the images of innocent persons' by taking the form of a saint in heaven, viz. that of Samuel to Saul, by the mediation of the witch of Endor'.[1] These precedents were given to counter an argument often made in support of spectral evidence, that God would not let innocent people suffer as a result of the Devil's deceptions.

As has been mentioned, the worthiness of spectral evidence as proof of witchcraft had come under increased scrutiny in later seventeenth-century England. It was also treated with caution by magistrates gathering evidence during the preliminary stages of the Salem trials in 1692. As Wendal Craker pointed out, during the trial itself 'spectral evidence was not allowed to stand by itself as evidence before the court'. Whenever possible, they looked to strengthen it with other forms of evidence, including confession. Father and son, Increase and Cotton Mather, were even more critical of spectral evidence. Increase was an author and a Puritan clergymen, and more involved in the Salem trials that his son. In late 1692 he condemned spectral testimony for much the same reasons as Tisdall, believing that it ultimately relied on evidence supplied by the Devil. To the argument that a benevolent God would not allow this sort of injustice to occur, Increase stated that such a defence wrongly placed limits on His power and sovereignty by subjecting Him to human laws and justice.[2]

Along with the influence of judicial scepticism, religious conflict and party politics may explain Tisdall's position, as well as the mixed messages coming from the bench at the end of the trial. A High-Church of Ireland Tory, it is unsurprising that Tisdall would have been wary of giving legal sanction to a charge of witchcraft made and defended by the very section of society he feared and distrusted, Ulster Presbyterians. Furthermore, by explaining away Dunbar's symptoms in terms of direct demonic intervention and hallucination, Tisdall was able to publicly contradict and oppose the Presbyterian-Whig faction he believed controlled Carrickfergus corporation, including Mayor Edward Clements.[3]

David Hayton has argued that although Clements and his group were without a doubt Whigs sympathetic to Presbyterianism, they were nominally Anglican.[4] As we shall see, Tisdall also had little time for one of the prosecution witnesses, Presbyterian minister of Carrickfergus Patrick Adair.

Tisdall's distrust of Clements and his associates was founded on a deeper antagonism towards Presbyterians in Ireland and their Whig supporters. Tisdall was utterly convinced their growing population and increasing economic and political power, along with an increasingly organised and visible Church, made Presbyterianism the greatest single threat to the Established Church and state in Ireland. By virtue of several hard-hitting pamphlets published in the first two decades of the eighteenth century, he became a leading polemicist in the denouncement of the toleration of Presbyterian worship, schools and seminaries, and regarded as utterly abhorrent any extension of full civil liberties to them.[5] Tisdall was, unfortunately for Presbyterians, not alone in holding such opinions. After James II had been defeated at the Boyne, the Presbyterians who had fought alongside Anglicans on the side of William of Orange were left in a precarious legal position, and it was during these years that animosity between the two denominations reached crisis point. The Acts of Uniformity of 1560 and 1665 had made attendance at an Anglican parish church compulsory, effectively banned dissenting schools and colleges (see chapter 7), and imposed a £100 fine on ministers administering communion who had not been ordained by an Anglican bishop. By the late seventeenth century, these laws went largely unenforced, but any notion that they would be repealed was quashed in the Irish parliamentary sessions of 1692 and 1695. Official religious toleration would not be extended to Protestant dissenters in Ireland until 1719, during the reign of George I. In England it had been extended to all moderate Protestant non-conformists in 1689, while in Scotland a Presbyterian national Church had been established. High-Church elements in the Church of Ireland now demanded the seventeenth-century laws discussed be more rigorously implemented. This call reached a high point in late 1710, when their natural political supporters, the Tory party, were swept into power. Although factions within the Anglican, Established Church in Ireland had been, from the end of the seventeenth century, using the apparatus of church courts to sporadically attack Presbyterian marriage, funerals and education, this type of antagonism became more marked in this period. Moves were also made to prevent new Presbyterian congregations being set up in Drogheda, County Louth (1708) and Belturbet, County Cavan (1712). The annual grant, the *regium donum*, given by the crown to the Presbyterian General Synod of Ulster to support poorer non-conformist clergy, was withdrawn. Although religious toleration was theoretically denied to them, there was no barrier to Presbyterians entering public office, and after the conclusion of the Williamite wars in Ireland in 1691 they took increasing control of borough corporations in Belfast, Derry, and Carrickfergus.

In Carrickfergus and Belfast, Presbyterians were made mayor, with Belfast electing a non-conformist MP to the Irish parliament. Many of the burgesses of borough corporations in Derry, Belfast and, to a lesser extent, Coleraine, if not Carrickfergus, were Presbyterian. Increasing political prominence was accompanied by an increase in militia officers, and Presbyterian JPs were suspected by 'hotter' Anglicans of protecting and favouring their co-religionists. Such fears were to some extent allayed by the introduction of a sacramental test, or Test Act, to Ireland. This was achieved by 'tacking' a clause onto the end of a far-reaching Penal Law aimed at curtailing various civil liberties of Irish Catholics, namely the 1704 Act 'To Prevent the Further Growth of Popery'. This clause was added by the English Privy Council (an executive arm of the government) in London, which retained the right to amend draft legislation, or heads of bills, sent to it for approval by the Irish parliament. The amended bill returned to Dublin excluded from the majority of municipal or crown offices anyone who had not taken the sacrament of Holy Communion according to the rites of the Church of Ireland.[6]

As a result, the office of High Sheriff became a monopoly for Anglican conformists, and Presbyterian members of the corporations of Derry and Coleraine resigned *en masse* in late 1704, while those in Belfast lost their positions a few years later. It has been calculated by Robert Whan that around twenty-five Presbyterian JPs resigned their commissions in 1704, which ensured a decline in Presbyterian influence in important arms of local government. Although Presbyterian constables were not excluded from office by the Test Act, their election was now subject to the control of members of the Church of Ireland. Protestant dissenters were also excluded from holding commissions in the militia and army.[7] Unsurprisingly, the Test Act, which was not repealed until 1780, was fiercely opposed by northern Presbyterians, not least because it placed a stigma on a community that had fought in the past for the maintenance of the Protestant interest in Ireland. More importantly, it convinced some of the already small number of substantial Presbyterian landowners to drift towards the Church of Ireland. Already distinct from Anglicans because of their religion, culture, and Scottish heritage, Presbyterians became increasingly socially distanced from parish institutions and associations after this time.

Party Politics and Witchcraft

This problem of Protestant Dissent and how the Established Church should deal with it played a central role in the conflict between the Whig and Tory parties during the reign of Queen Anne (1702–14). This dominated parliamentary, governmental and, to a lesser extent, popular politics in that period. Due to the differing political, economic, religious and social realities in England and Ireland, Irish Whigs and Tories in Ireland were ideologically divergent in some important respects to their English counterparts. Given they were a minority controlling what was in effect a Catholic country, few Irish Tories could allow themselves the luxury of ambivalence on the issue of whether the Glorious Revolution of 1688, which removed pro-Catholic James II from the throne, was justified.[8] Similarly, there was reluctance to discuss the issue of who should succeed Queen Anne, whether a Catholic who had a hereditary claim to the throne or a Protestant from the German, Hanoverian line who had none. What Irish Tories did do that was broadly in line with their English brethren was style themselves the true defenders of the personage of Queen Anne and the defenders of the Anglican faith. The Irish Tory party was the Church party, the true home of High-Churchmen like

Tisdall, who defended the rights and privileges of the Church of Ireland. This stance was in practice inseparable from an intense dislike of Presbyterians.

Whigs, on the other hand, were eager to preserve the rights of the Irish parliament from perceived encroachment by Crown, government and parliament in Westminster. Although many Whigs were committed Anglicans, they were often more favourably disposed towards Protestant dissenters. Few, however, publicly supported the Repeal of the Test Act of 1704. Whigs also considered Roman Catholics as sleeper agents for the spectre of international 'popery' who were intent on killing Protestants, taking back their land, dismantling the Protestant Church and state, and putting a Catholic Jacobite on the throne: the exiled James Francis Edward Stuart, the 'Old Pretender'. It was this hostility that made Whigs in parliament natural supporters of enacting new Penal Laws to further restrict Catholic religious and civil liberties and to toughen and enforce old ones. They were also critical of High-Churchmen for being 'soft' on the issue of Catholicism and for interfering in secular politics. This Whig attitude to Catholicism was displayed in a typical state sermon preached in 1722 by Robert Howard, the Irish-born and educated Whig rector of St Bride's in Dublin, and later Bishop of Killala and Achonry:

> Thus encouraged from abroad [France], and hoping for like success, they [Irish Catholics] have fixed their eyes on Rome [the Pope] and a Popish successor [the 'Old Pretender'], to whom only, they acknowledge their civil and religious allegiance is due, and please themselves to hear of his proficiency ... in biogttry and heights of popish superstition.[9]

Party tensions were also running high in Carrickfergus near the end of Queen Anne's reign, a drama in which Tisdall played a supporting role. In early 1708, some Whigs sitting on the grand jury at the court of Quarter Sessions at Ballymena drew up a loyal address in support of the Repeal of the 1704 Test Act. This was eventually printed in a Dublin newspaper in August of that year. A month later, Tories in the town claimed in a London newspaper that the address had been published without the consent of Carrickfergus corporation and had been doctored to make it pro-repeal when the original was not. Later Tisdall would claim that Revd Patrick Adair had penned the fraudulent address himself before getting his associates to sign it. The accusation was later found to be baseless.[10] Edward Mathews, Church of Ireland curate of Carrickfergus, and a High-Church Tory, accused Patrick Adair of avoiding military (militia) duty in the same year during a Jacobite invasion scare, and tradition has it that the accusation caused a brawl between the two men in a Carrickfergus street.[11]

Three years later, in 1711, Tory Alderman of Carrickfergus Samuel Davys petitioned the Irish Privy Council in Dublin to prevent Edward Clements's re-election as mayor. With the backing of Tories in government, Davys became mayor for the following two years. In such circumstances it is unsurprising that High-Churchman Revd Matthew French, curate of Belfast and chaplain in ordinary to Tory Duke of Ormond, was picked to deliver the Tory party line in a sermon delivered at the County Antrim spring Assizes.[12] In the 1713 election, the Davys family returned two Tory MPs to parliament and Mathews preached a High-Church sermon in which he called for the state to protect the Church by all legal means necessary. He also linked Whigs and Presbyterians to republicanism and political radicalism.[13] In March/April 1714, riding high on the Tory and High-Church backlash elsewhere, Tory members of County Antrim grand jury, along with some JPs and gentry, presented a loyal address (drawn up during the Carrickfergus Assizes) to Queen Anne that lionised leading Irish Tories in the Dublin parliament while attacking their Whig opponents.[14] In the summer of the same year, Carrickfergus Tories confiscated Presbyterian catechisms being sold in the marketplace and threatened to nail up their meetinghouse.[15] William Tisdall, Edward Matthews, Matthew French and others also sent another loyal address to Queen Anne, this time praising the 1704 Test Act for keeping Presbyterian-Whig influence in local politics to a minimum.[16]

Although party politics in Carrickfergus was not usually a matter of ballot and election, they were very important to those involved with the Islandmagee case, including Tisdall and the trial judges. Consequently, a confirmed English Tory such as Justice Upton, who in common with many of his party would be removed from office when the Whigs came to power after the accession of George I in 1715, may have found it objectionable to side with a prosecution composed of Presbyterians and Whigs. This was especially true in a town where party tensions were running so high. Justice MacCartney, on the other hand, was an Anglican Whig who would be removed from his position as Second Justice of the Queen's bench to make way for a Tory after the Islandmagee witchcraft trial ended. His star rose during the reign of George I along with the fortunes of other Irish Whigs.[17] It is thus perfectly understandable why MacCartney would choose to back the prosecution of the Islandmagee witches: to spite his Tory opposite number and support the Whig cause.

Politics, Parties and Witchcraft in England After 1710

Although the Islandmagee witchcraft trial provided a public space for some prominent Whigs and Tories to articulate their political opposition to one another, the party politicisation of witchcraft in Ireland should not be overstated. The fact that Mayor Edward Clements was a Whig and friendly to Presbyterians no doubt made it easier for him to take Dunbar's accusations seriously enough to warrant a full investigation. This decision would prove pivotal in turning her accusations into prosecutions, and ultimately criminal convictions. However, witchcraft only became a party issue in Ireland on the day of the trial and never became a part of the ideological armoury of most Irish Whigs and Tories.

In England, witchcraft also became a political battleground for the Whig and Tory parties in the early eighteenth century, but the situation there was very different. Firstly, it proved far more divisive over a longer period, and was intimately related not only to judicial scepticism and a decline in trials but to a challenge to belief in witchcraft itself. In contrast to Ireland, English Tories supported traditional witchcraft belief, whilst Whigs began to distance themselves from it. This development reached its climax during the trial of Jane Wenham in 1712. The accusation against Wenham originated in a parish where party tensions ran at fever pitch, and it was local High-Church Tories who took up her prosecution. Wenham, after all, was suspected of being variously a dissenter and an atheist. However, confirmed Whigs such as Bishop Francis Hutchinson, who had attended Wenham's trial, opposed her prosecution and conviction.[18] The pamphlet debate that followed her conviction comprised ten tracts and laid out the party fault-lines of witchcraft belief. The Tory side was headed by Francis Bragge, who, motivated by party considerations and the prospect of turning a publishing profit, upheld traditional witchcraft belief. Bragge regarded it as compatible with contemporary medical opinion and the 'new science', but more importantly saw it as a tool to increase belief in the supernatural, the spirit world and, by implication, God. The latter he regarded as a small step on the way to protecting the Established Church, which was considered by Tories as the best defence against atheism and irreligion. A smaller number of tracts were published in answer to Bragge in which supporters of witchcraft were tainted with Catholicism and superstition. These tracts also employed well-worn sceptical arguments, such as the fact that the Scriptures did not contain any real justification for witch-hunting and that there were natural and medical explanations for the possession of Wenham's victim, Ann Thorn. Associating witchcraft with irrationality and weakness in understanding, they accused supporters of witch-hunting of manipulating the fears and emotions of the mass of population in order to control them.

This sceptical, Whiggish view of witchcraft can be linked to a series of intellectual, social, political and religious shifts that made up the early English enlightenment. Although orthodox Protestantism in England and Ireland agreed that the age of modern miracles had passed, and that those who claimed the spirit of God worked directly through them were not to be trusted, some English elites in the early eighteenth century, especially those of a Whiggish bent, were challenging other aspects of a magical, moral universe that their Irish counterparts seemed afraid to touch. The Devil was increasingly seen as a metaphor for evil rather than the greater deluder, tempter and cheat who traversed the earthly plain. Among the more forward-thinking, liberal Whigs, Hell was no longer seen as a localised place of torment reserved for the sinful as an afterlife punishment, and spiritual essences were less likely to interfere in the lives of men and women. Witchcraft was also increasingly linked to the popular culture of the lower orders and therefore best avoided by those who considered themselves educated, urbane, polite, and mannered. The natural outcome of witchcraft belief, trials, also clashed with the Whiggish vision of an ideal society, which was at once polite, ordered, stable, and mercantile. If moderate, rational religion helped people accept their divinely allotted place in this world, witchcraft belief was its anti-type. After all, witchcraft accusations and prosecutions divided communities, threatened social order, and disturbed the peace. The Wenham trial had proven this. Thousands of people turned up to visit the accused in prison and an unprecedented number gathered for her trial.

After the second decade of the eighteenth century, this sceptical position became more mainstream among the middle and upper classes in England, who increasingly saw belief in witchcraft as inherently politicised and best left alone. The middle decades of the century saw this scepticism harden into outright disbelief within the culture of a minority of disproportionately vocal, wealthy, and politically and socially influential male elites. Under their watchful eye, witch trials officially ended in England, Scotland and Wales in 1736 with the repeal of existing witch statutes. Those elites excluded from the Whig-Hanoverian regime and mainstream politics (Roman Catholics, radicals, high-flying Tories, and Wesleyan and early Primitive Methodists), however, fervently clung to traditional witch beliefs, as did a minority of Church of England and Protestant non-conformist clergy. In early to mid-eighteenth-century Scotland, some Godly elites in the Church of Scotland proved reluctant to relinquish traditional demonology. Most of the gentry and members of the professional classes, however, eventually pulled away from belief in witchcraft in a wider process of social and cultural distancing from the mass of the population. In Ireland, by the mid-eighteenth century, some Irish Protestant elites, especially Anglicans, began to publicly distance themselves from traditional belief in witchcraft. The eighteenth-century, minority Anglican position that belief in witchcraft was 'superstitious' and the product of an age of unreason that was corrected only by the rationalism of the Enlightenment became the standard public position in the nineteenth century, for Catholics and Protestants alike. This is not to say that (in private at least) some of the rural middle classes did not continue to entertain the possibility, or fear at some level the effects of witchcraft. The 1586 Irish Witchcraft Act was eventually repealed in early 1821. This decline in belief should not be overstated, because the mass of the population in Great Britain and Ireland continued to believe in, fear, punish, and protect themselves against witchcraft.

Second Trial,
11 September 1711

William Sellor

After the trial ended, William Tisdall was able to interview Mary Dunbar because her speech had returned as a result of her signing for, and reading, a passage from the Bible, 'the 40th Psalm and 13th verse': 'Be pleased, O' Lord, to deliver me O' Lord, make haste to help me.'[1] The interpretation intended to be drawn by onlookers from this episode was clear. Mary was saved from her demonically inspired tormentors by divine intervention because she was pious and therefore worthy of God's help. As has been mentioned, Mary then informed Tisdall that the two women and a man who appeared to her in spectral form during the trial were responsible for her speech loss and had threatened to 'put pen knives down her throat'. They were the same people she had met the previous day.

Eventually, at five o'clock that evening, Dunbar set out on horseback to her mother's house in Castlereagh, County Down. She soon relapsed and only 'got home that night' after 'three or four fits upon the road'. It was reported that the next day, 'the first of April, she was very ill, and had several violent fainting fits, and put out of her mouth several pins, and feathers'. In the 'intervals' between seizures, Dunbar 'declared they were put into her mouth by her tormentors'. During the next week, she suffered many more 'fainting fits' and vomited 'twenty pins and a considerable number of feathers'. On 8 April 1711, however, she was able to provide some fresh information. She claimed the man she had met on the road to court, who was of medium height, had a long face, grey-brown, curly hair and wore old brown clothes, had visited once more in spectral form. This time he 'threatened to kill her' if she told authorities about him and his accomplices. Dunbar's precise description of his clothes and physical appearance ensured the man was soon identified as William Sellor, husband of Janet Liston and father to Elizabeth Sellor.

A warrant was issued on 10 April for Sellor's arrest but not for the two mysterious women, of which nothing more is heard. As his warrant was being served, he managed to flee his Islandmagee home, but was captured shortly afterwards, 4 miles away. His decision to abscond was reasonable given that his wife and daughter had just been convicted and imprisoned on the strength of Dunbar's allegations. After his capture, Sellor was forced to confront the girl, who it was reported in the pamphlet account, 'did not accuse him for fear of his threatening; so he was let go', presumably by a local constable. Two days later, Dunbar told of how Sellor (once more in spectral form) had threatened to kill her again but this time with a butcher's knife, 'the blade of which was broken and welded together'. Dunbar then claimed William had followed through on his threat and stabbed her just below the right shoulder blade. It was noted by eyewitnesses 'that the place being looked [at] there was a visible mark' or wound on Dunbar's body.

The next day, 13 April 1711, Dunbar's friends in Islandmagee were informed (possibly by the girl's mother) of her torments and injuries and an unnamed constable finally arrested Sellor, but not before he assaulted his guard, John Brown, with a 'drinking horn'. It is assumed that Sellor was held in County Antrim gaol to await trial just like his wife and daughter before him. His stay would not have been measured like theirs in days or weeks, but in months. He was eventually tried 'and found guilty' on 11 September 1711 at the summer session of County Antrim Assizes held at Carrickfergus.[2] The two presiding justices in his case, who in the summer of 1711 were working 'the north-east Circuit' of the Ulster Assizes, had markedly different political outlooks. Born in Staffordshire in England in 1656, Sir Richard

Levinge in 1711 was middle-aged, a politician (he had previously served as an MP in both English and Irish parliaments), a gifted lawyer and a moderate Tory in politics. In early 1711, he was appointed Attorney General of Ireland by Tory Lord Lieutenant of Ireland, James Butler, second Duke of Ormond. When the Whig party came to power after the Hanoverian accession in 1715, Ormond renounced the new regime to become a Jacobite supporter of the exiled 'Old Pretender'. The second Assize justice, Henry Echlin, was a Whig and second baron of the Irish Court of Exchequer. Born in County Down, he was an avid book collector and approaching 60 years of age in 1711.[3] Surviving records for Sellor's trial are maddeningly sparse and amount to little more than a few lines in the surviving pamphlet account. It is therefore impossible to know if political antagonism caused Levinge and Echlin to reach separate decisions with regards Sellor's guilt. In other words, did wider Whig and Tory party conflict colour the legal judgement of Levinge and Echlin just as it had done a few months earlier with MacCartney and Upton?

No matter the politics involved, Dunbar's fate would have had important consequences for William Sellor. A stark but devastating report published in a Dublin newspaper on 24 April 1711, just over three weeks after the first trial, stated: 'Dublin. We have an account that the young gentlewoman, that was tormented by the *witches*, lately tryed at Carrickfergus, is dead.'[4] Unfortunately, the cause of Mary's death is not mentioned, here or anywhere else. A plausible but ultimately unproveable explanation is that the observable knife wound in Dunbar's shoulder led to a slow, painful death through blood loss or infection. Mary Dunbar's end was an unusual outcome in demonic possession cases. As Philip Almond has put it, 'the drama' of demonic possession 'ended only when the demoniac, delivered from the Devil and returned to normality, was integrated back into the human community'.[5] Consequently, many demoniacs disappear from the historical record after their trials and no more can be discovered about their later lives. An exception is Christian Shaw, who in Scotland in the 1690s had seven people executed on the strength of her accusations. Shaw later married a minister, set up a thread-making business, and became the accepted founder of the industry in Paisley, Scotland.

Dunbar's death would have turned Sellor's initial, lesser offence of harming by witchcraft into a capital crime, for which the punishment was execution by hanging. William would have been the last witch convicted in Ireland under the 1586 Irish Witchcraft Act, and the only Islandmagee witch put to death. Sellor was also the only man formally tried for witchcraft in Ireland. Although men were certainly brought before Protestant church courts by clergymen and elders in the later seventeenth and eighteenth centuries for magical offences such as divination, none were accused of witchcraft. It is possible that the lack of male witches is the result of uneven record survival and the documents detailing them were simply lost. Certainly, as the next chapter will suggest, male witches were far from unknown in nineteenth- and early twentieth-century Ireland.

An extensive search of existing newspapers and other sources in archives and libraries in Britain and Ireland has failed to uncover further documents relating to Sellor beyond what is related here. The barest genealogical data is impossible to find. There is no surviving will, nor any baptismal, marriage or death record. William Sellor's case raises another question: what was different about him that made him a target for Mary Dunbar's accusation in the first place, and more importantly made it stick? To find any type of answer to this question it is best to consider briefly male witches in early modern Europe. Men made up around 20 per cent of all those tried for witchcraft in early modern Europe, but until recently they have been sidelined in debates concerning the role of gender in trials. Traditionally, male witches were regarded as collateral damage: men who found themselves caught up in large-scale trials (especially on the Continent) when the witch stereotype of an older female began to disintegrate, or were accused because of their association with suspected women. This association often brought with it an antisocial feminisation, where male witches took on supposedly female characteristics such as spite, envy, wantonness, and intellectual fragility or weak-mindedness.

In recent years, this interpretation has been developed, and occasionally challenged, through regional analysis and case studies of individual trials. Research has shown that accusers and witch-hunters in Tuscany and in some of the German states used witchcraft prosecution to target opponents and rivals for political, social and financial reasons. In Scotland, the number of men prosecuted for witchcraft declined during large witch-hunts, but those believed to have dabbled in elite magic or sorcery for political ends, or who were practising cunning-folk, were particularly susceptible to accusation. In the Catholic Duchy of Carinthia in Austria, young, male, wandering vagrants prone to begging were vulnerable to charges of witchcraft. Robert Walinski-Kiehl has argued that in early modern Germany men accused of witchcraft had often 'violated expectations of masculinity embodied in the ideal of the honest, reliable, married, household head' and 'they tended to display the following negative social and moral characteristics: bringing the family into debt, involvement in questionable business practices, theft, drunkenness, gambling, bigamy, and adultery.'[6] Malcolm Gaskill has pointed out that while many English male witches had no known association with female counterparts, they often failed to meet contemporary standards of masculinity, where 'self-restraint and recourse to law … were elevated as the highest ideas across the social order'.[7]

William Sellor was unkempt, had a bad temper, drank alcohol (from a 'horn'), tried to evade local agents of law enforcement, and had allowed his wife and daughter, who were his moral and legal responsibilities, to stray into the clutches of the Devil. He was not an honest, pious head of a household, and as such had strayed very far from the model of accepted masculinity. This made it easier for his neighbours to believe he was a man capable of the diabolical deeds attributed to him by Dunbar. This is not to say that familial association with convicted witches (as the head of a 'witch-family', no less) did not play a role. As suggested in chapter 4, in early modern Europe, reputations for practising witchcraft were not only transferred inter-generationally, from parents to children, but from husband to wife and vice versa. In this case, from Janet Liston to Elizabeth Sellor, and from Janet to William Sellor. Necessity may also have been the mother of invention here, as Dunbar needed, whether consciously or subconsciously, to prolong her possession, and William Sellor was the perfect candidate. She may have been able to describe him to prosecutors because of an earlier meeting during the interrogation or testing of his wife. There is no historical record, however, of any such meeting.

Back at Knowehead House

The supernatural disturbances continued unabated at Knowehead House for nearly two weeks after the first trial. From 29 March until 1 April 1711, 'bed clothes' were once more 'made up in the shape of a corpse' and 'great noises, such as scratching, knocking, laughing' were heard in empty rooms. On 2 April, while alone, Margaret Spear witnessed a bolster pillow, dressed in her master's bed-gown, walk slowly by itself 'out of the room into the kitchen'. She 'at first thought it was a boy, but being afraid ran into a room where there were tailors working, and told them, who came immediately out and saw it [the pillow] standing against the wall.' Accompanied by 'the throwing of stones', the noises in the house continued for the next five days and only ceased when a sword was waved in the direction they were thought to be coming from.

From 8 to 12 April, the noises 'changed from knocking to whistling louder than usually a man can do.' People in the house heard 'several tunes very distinctly' such as 'the Jolly Batchelors'.[8] When dogs were sent to search for the source of the whistling, it transformed into an ominous hissing sound. The demonic presence also 'often struck the children upon the heads when in bed'. During this time, Mary Twinam, who was staying in the house, felt a presence climb 'over her in the bed several times', and the same entity pulled local man 'John Spire very strongly by the hat, when it was on his head'. When Spire 'was sitting on the children's bed side, of a sudden the clothes were taken off the bed, and rolled about his head, and several things thrown at him'. Occasionally, the presence would 'make a noise like ducks, sometimes clap, sometimes draw the curtains of Mr Hattridge's bed backwards and forwards, and then make the bed shake terribly.'

The supernatural disturbances stopped suddenly on 13 April when William Sellor was imprisoned. At the precise time this happened, Islandmagee man Robert McKillock 'saw two men run down towards' his house 'and mount two black horses'. This was interpreted in a culturally specific way. Sellor had continued where the other witches had left off and had attacked Knowehead with the aid of two demons, until his imprisonment behind iron bars had stripped him of his power over them and they rode back to Hell. This abrupt cessation of supernatural activity would have silenced anyone still convinced that the demonic presence in the Haltridge house was commanded by something other than human will.

Conclusion

The trial of the eight women did not end the drama that had unfolded in north-east Ulster in late 1710 and early 1711. Supernatural disturbances in Knowehead House escalated after their trial and ceased only with the arrest of the ninth and final Islandmagee witch, William Sellor. Mary Dunbar claimed that he had continued on with the diabolical attacks orchestrated by his wife and daughter and the other witches. He cut a believable witch figure because he challenged contemporary modes of male behaviour and through his role of as head of a 'witch-family'. Sellor was eventually arrested and convicted of bewitching Mary, who had died shortly after the first trial, turning his crime into a capital offence for which the punishment was death by hanging. If his sentence was carried out, he would have been the only man executed for witchcraft in Ireland.

After Lives

Continuing Belief in Witchcraft

The trial of nine people in County Antrim in 1711 was the last successful prosecution for witchcraft in Ireland, a year ahead of England (1712) and sixteen years before Scotland (1727). Just as in England, America and continental Europe, the decline in trials and repeal of witchcraft laws did not end popular belief in witchcraft in Ireland. It remained strong in both Catholic and Protestant rural farming communities throughout the country up until at least the mid-twentieth century. By the late eighteenth century, Irish belief in witchcraft was no longer as divided across ethnic and religious lines as it had been in earlier centuries. It now represented a mixture of older Gaelic-Irish ideas concerning butter and milk stealing and the harmful witchcraft associated with Protestant settler culture. While not particularly demonic, this new witch figure was, in certain circumstances, a significant threat to humans, livestock, and agricultural produce.

A variety of rites, rituals, charms, cures, and magical objects were available to Irish people in the nineteenth and twentieth century to detect, deflect, or punish the harmful magic of suspected witches. These were wielded by professionals (charmers, fortune-tellers, cunning-folk) as well as well-informed amateurs. Although no longer a crime after 1821, those affected by witchcraft, all over Ireland, continued to seek the intervention of the law up until the mid-twentieth century. Seemingly everyday crimes such as theft, slander, and assault were occasionally underpinned by an accusation of witchcraft. These accusations were usually made by tenant farmers, male and female, and directed at neighbours and co-religionists (Protestants accused Protestants, and Catholics accused Catholics) in the context of recurrent political, social and economic crisis, especially after the Great Famine of the 1840s. Certain legal developments made it easier for ordinary people to lodge official complaints, such as the establishment of metropolitan and provincial police forces and the extension of Police Courts and Petty Sessions. These lower courts of summary jurisdiction allowed magistrates to pass verdicts on lesser crimes, set fines, and hand down short prison sentences without a jury. When deemed serious enough, magistrates passed cases to higher criminal courts such as the Quarter Sessions and the Assizes.

Witchcraft and the Law

Two main types of criminal cases involving witchcraft came before Irish courts in the nineteenth century. The first was when suspected witches used the courts to fight back against accusers, charging them with assault but occasionally with slander or breach of the peace. In November 1861, at Mitchelstown Petty Sessions, County Cork, 'complainant Thomas Quinn charged John Condon, his wife, and their son, John Condon, with assaulting him after they had accused him of bewitching their pigs and preventing them from eating for a week.'[1] James Jamieson appeared before Belfast Police Court in June 1870 for assaulting complainant Alice Hunter and stealing her shawl. The court heard that Jamieson had been informed by a local magical practitioner, or 'cow doctor', that Hunter had bewitched his cattle cows, halting their production of milk. Jamieson was then given instructions to perform a counter-spell (based on the principles of sympathetic magic) to restore the flow of milk. He was told to burn an item of Hunter's clothing under the noses of the afflicted livestock. Acting on this advice Jamieson confronted Hunter, took her shawl by force, and burned it in the prescribed manner. Presiding Regional Magistrate E. Orme condemned the credulity of both parties, but as Jamieson was, in the eyes of the law, guilty of assault and theft he fined him 20s and ordered him to replace Hunter's shawl.[2] In July 1908, at Belturbet Petty Sessions in County Cavan, James McCaffrey complained that 70-year-old Catholic Mary McCaffrey 'had committed a breach of the peace by using "abusive and threatening language" towards him'. McCaffery had accused him of practising witchcraft and his wife Alice of transforming into the shape of a hare to steal his butter. Possibly acting under legal advice, McCaffrey withdrew the complaint and the case was dropped.[3]

Bewitched parties and/or their relatives also accused suspected witches of theft of milk and butter. Theft, of course, was a crime, but the method they claimed had been used to purloin the milk was not, namely magic. At Cavan Quarter Sessions in December 1850, John Mulligan, a respectable farmer, was acquitted of stealing milk from the cows of his neighbour and complainant, Rose Fitzpatrick. It emerged during the trial that Fitzpatrick had been accusing people in the local area of bewitching her cows and preventing their milk from being churned into butter for over thirty years. Mulligan came under her suspicion when her cows became ill after the pair quarrelled over the ownership of a house and land. This case could have easily occurred centuries earlier as it centred on inexplicable misfortune arising in the context of interpersonal tensions and social conflict. Before turning to the law, Fitzpatrick had (unsuccessfully) employed the services of a cunning-person to return her milk and butter.[4]

The second main type of crime involving witchcraft was when suspected witches found themselves in legal hot water, having been accused of slander or assault when they answered an accusation of witchcraft with harsh words, fists, and occasionally knives and firearms. At Cahir Petty Sessions, County Tipperary, in October 1895, William Burke was charged with assaulting Thomas Meehan by hitting him with a reaping hook after he accused his wife of stealing butter from his cows. Burke was found guilty, bound to keep the peace for a year, and fined the princely sum of £20.[5]

Islandmagee

After years of searching, I have been unable to find any criminal cases arising from witchcraft accusations made in Islandmagee. This does not mean that belief in witchcraft disappeared from the area, or that it no longer influenced the way people lived their lives. In April 1840, James Boyle, who was working as a collector for the Ordnance Survey Memoirs of Ireland, and charged with researching and reporting on the landscape, society, culture, and economy of Islandmagee, noted that, 'in no part of Ireland are the people more generally and inveterately superstitious than here,' where 'most of the better educated class implicitly believe in witchcraft, fairies, brownies and enchantments'.[6] In the eighteenth and nineteenth centuries, locals reported seeing the Devil in the shape of a black dog or a pig, and were known to consult charmers and cunning-folk to find lost or stolen goods, or to cure a range of ailments and afflictions, including those thought to have had supernatural causes.[7] Protective or apotropaic magic remained a key feature of popular culture there up until the twentieth century. Silver coins were placed in milking pails and flowers strewn on thresholds of byres and barns to prevent witches and fairies harming livestock and interrupting milk or butter production. Witch-, elf-, or hag-stones (naturally occurring holed stones or pebbles) were hung in cowsheds to protect livestock against fairy and butter-witch attack.[8] Two witch-stones were used by farmers in Islandmagee up until the 1970s and are currently housed in the Ulster Folk and Transport Museum (UFTM), which opened in 1964 in Cultra, County Down, about 7 miles east of Belfast.[9] Responses to questionnaires concerning a range of folk beliefs sent out in the early 1960s by the UFTM confirm that 'witch-stones' were used in Islandmagee to prevent 'anyone who practiced the black art … witch[ing] the [butter] churn',[10] thereby safeguarding 'cows from being bewitched'.[11]

In other words, by the nineteenth century, Protestants living in Islandmagee had absorbed practices and beliefs traditionally associated with Gaelic-Irish butter witchcraft. However, belief in witchcraft in Islandmagee was unique in that it was informed by the shared memory of the 1711 trials. This social and folk memory provided proof that witchcraft was real, and that the Islandmagee witches had practised it and been justly punished as a result. It was transmitted from generation to generation (especially among descendants of those involved in the case who were still living on the peninsula) by a rich oral tradition and places associated with the trials, where the supernatural power of the convicted witches was thought to linger. Knowehead House was studiously avoided at night by local people, including those considered well educated or middle class, and tales of ghosts and spirit sightings near to the house circulated in the early twentieth century. In the mid-1870s, the *Belfast News Letter* reported on sightings by locals of the spirits of the Islandmagee witches dancing on the 'Rocking Stone' at night. The 'Rocking Stone' was a huge boulder that sat (as it does to this day) on the hillside overlooking Brown's Bay on the northern tip of the peninsula. It may have inspired fear at night, but museums and archives in Northern Ireland hold photographs that show children and well-dressed tourists sitting on and around it during the day in the late nineteenth and early twentieth century.[12]

In 1927, in his local history of Islandmagee, the headmaster of Kilcoan National School in Islandmagee, Dixon Donaldson (whom we have already met briefly), described what he called a 'Witch Stone'. It was 'about two hundredweight, with indents corresponding to the thumb and fingers' and lay in the townland of Balloo, midway up the peninsula on the eastern side and directly across from Kilcoan More where Knowehead House stood.[13] Donaldson explained that in 'recent times' (the early twentieth century) the stone and its immediate environs were 'given a wide berth by the superstitious after night-fall'. This avoidance was rooted in its association with convicted Islandmagee 'witch' Catherine McCalmond in a 'story' that had 'been handed down' to successive generations. It told that McCalmond had been:

gathering sticks for the fire as the constable approached, and on seeing him she dropped the sticks and flung herself upon the stone, from which the limb of the law had difficulty in removing her; the marks of her fingers (or claw) were afterwards noticed on the stone.[14]

Writing in 2024, I have been researching the Islandmagee trials on and off for nearly sixteen years, and during that time I have talked to a variety of people (including my own students at Ulster University) who grew up in or near Islandmagee or were currently living there. In 2019, I met descendants of Janet Latimer on a BBC television programme.[15] I had the pleasure of talking to local people during the planning stages of an exhibition based on the trial that I and colleagues at Ulster University worked on with Carrickfergus Museum in September 2023. From this admittedly anecdotal evidence, it seems that the memory and folklore of the trial remained strong in the area. A full-length oral history and folklore project is sorely needed to collect and analyse these narratives which can tell us so much about difficult heritage and history and how communities remember traumatic events. It is apparent from modern folklore that, as in previous centuries, stories of the Islandmagee witches have been passed down through a variety of family and community networks. As any folklorist will tell you, folklore is never static and is constantly evolving. Unsurprisingly, people today are less likely to apportion guilt or blame to the convicted witches or link them to a lingering supernatural threat. Places associated with the witches in local folklore and folk history have also changed over the years. The 'Rocking Stone' is not mentioned much, having been replaced with the Gobbins Cliffs and the Ballylumford Dolmen (also known as the 'Druid's Altar') as places associated with the 'witches'. Ballylumford Dolmen is a portal tomb probably dating from Neolithic times and located in the townland of the same name at the north-west tip of Islandmagee.

Commemoration

These objects and places may have invigorated the memory and folk history of the trial, but they also worked as informal commemoration of the convicted 'witches'. Since the first edition of this book was published in 2013, two memorials have been erected, and both put a more positive spin on the case than previous, informal commemoration. The first is a simple memorial stone plaque placed outside of the Gobbins Visitor Centre in Islandmagee in March 2023 by Mid and East Antrim Council.

It contains the following inscription:

> In memory of the eight women and one man convicted in a witchcraft trial in Carrickfergus in 1711. All were from Islandmagee and the surrounding area: Janet Carson, Janet Latimer, Janet Main, Janet Millar, Janet Liston, Margaret Mitchell, Catherine McCalmond, Elizabeth Sellor and William Sellor.

Due to a variety of factors, including some opposition from councillors within local government (specifically the legacy Larne council), it took nearly eight years for the plaque to be laid. By that time the Islandmagee Community Development Association had commissioned and erected its own commemorative piece of public art, the 'Willow "White" Witch'. This life-size depiction of a woman with long hair is constructed of twigs and sticks. The sculpture was completed in 2021 and placed at the entrance to the peninsula. It commemorates the Islandmagee witches while moving beyond their painful memory to reimagine the witch figure as a modern pagan 'white' witch, who is at one with nature and gathers plants and herbs in her basket to heal rather than harm.

Cultural Afterlife

If the Islandmagee case remained an important part of local culture in the modern period, a different view of it and historic Irish witch trials in general was committed to paper by journalists, historians, writers, and artists. From the late nineteenth century to the late twentieth century the history of Irish witchcraft was 'written by those working outside of academic history', who together created a remarkably resilient narrative of Irish witchcraft. Gaelic, Catholic Ireland was shown to be free of belief in witchcraft in the medieval and early modern period, and witchcraft in Protestant Ireland was restricted to a handful of infamous cases, including the trials of Florence Newton in 1661 and the Islandmagee witches. Modern Ireland was generally regarded as disenchanted, where belief in witchcraft no longer held sway because it was far more enlightened and rational than it had been during the time of the witch trials. Early modern witch trials were now regarded as the product of lower-class ignorance and superstition, and upper-class religious bigotry. Historical writing in that period also gendered historic witchcraft as female, even when a sizeable minority of suspected witches coming before Irish courts in the nineteenth century were male. By showing Irish witches as innocent, pious and nurturing victims, and thus worthy of pity, historians were able to reinforce contemporary male views of what constituted a 'good' woman. Viewed through this distorting lens, the Islandmagee witches were robbed of their agency and resistance, which as we have seen was part of the reason they made such believable witches in the first place. William Sellor was unsurprisingly left out of nearly all historical narratives from that period.[16]

In the early to mid-1800s, journalists 'weaponised' and 'brought to a mass market' this increasingly accepted version of the history of Ireland's relationship with witchcraft. Stories of historic witch trials were occasionally written up to fill empty pages of provincial newspapers, to cater to a growing readership in an era of expansion of journalism and the Irish newspaper industry. These cases were exceptionalised as the type of case that no longer troubled modern, rational Ireland, even when, in another part of often the same newspaper, criminal cases involving witchcraft were reported with attention-grabbing headlines. The Islandmagee witches featured heavily in these journalistic trips into Ireland's witch-hunting past.[17] The trials were explained away as rare Irish lapses into the irrationality, ignorance and religious extremism that drove witch-hunts elsewhere in early modern Europe. Modern coverage also tended to emphasise the innocence, piety and frailty of the female Islandmagee witches in the face of an uncaring legal system. William Sellor is overlooked, and a myth, popularised in the early nineteenth century by local historian of Carrickfergus, Samuel McSkimin, that one of the witches lost an eye while being pelted with cabbage stalks in the pillory, proved irresistible to many commentators.

Newspaper coverage of the trial became increasingly political in the late nineteenth century as Irish national identity was reframed and refashioned and the press became divided across unionist and nationalist lines. Nationalists were at that time increasing their demand for self-governance, while unionists wished to maintain the union with

Britain. Journalists writing in newspapers based in Southern Ireland with nationalist-leaning editors and an overwhelmingly Catholic readership used the case to suggest that belief in harmful magic was foreign to Ireland, brought there by Scottish immigration and British imperialism. Unionist newspapers, operating in the north of the country, in a region with the highest concentration of Protestants, continued to employ the enlightenment rhetoric described above to distance themselves from historic witch-hunting. They were now, however, careful to sidestep the fact that most early Irish witch trials occurred in Scottish and English diaspora communities. This allowed them to avoid the criticism that the discussion of such matters obscured the positive social and cultural benefits that union with Britain brought. By the mid-twentieth century, journalists writing in a local newspaper, the *Larne Times*, started to medicalise Mary Dunbar's accusation by regarding it as the product of mental illness and the prosecution process as the actions of a persecuting Church and state. In one instance, in the *Ballymena Observer* on 27 January 1939, the trial was seen as having been spearheaded by professionally minded male doctors determined to root out troublesome women who threatened their medical practice. These were, of course, explanations that would come to dominate the popular discourse of early modern witch-hunting in the later twentieth century.

The early twentieth century also saw the trials influence creative writing as authors began to use the peninsula as a suitable setting, given its history, for stories involving witchcraft and magic. Islandmagee was reimagined as a place shrouded in superstition and teetering on the edge of civilisation. In July 1910, in the 'Poet's Corner' section of the *Larne Times*, John A. Harrison's poem 'Lines on Islandmagee, Co. Antrim' saw the memory of the trial as being kept alive by the folk tales that enlivened the nightscape: 'And full oft we have shuddered at tales heard at e'en/Of the glamours and spells of its witches of old/These still practise their arts, as in days that are past.'[18] Harrison was writing before the rise of self-identifying pagan witchcraft in the late twentieth century, so the last line was acknowledging continuing belief in harmful witchcraft in the peninsula. Poet and novelist Margaret Teresa Pender, who was born in County Antrim in 1850, set a short story in Islandmagee that was later serialised in a newspaper in 1913. Like most of her work, it was a historical narrative imbued with strong nationalistic overtones. Seventeenth-century Islandmagee itself was characterised as a strange, bewitched, desolate landscape where 'Caura na Calligh' (Caura the hag), a Gaelic-Irish fortune-teller, lived in a cave on the Gobbins Cliffs. In the story, Caura, an Irish-speaking Catholic, is prosecuted for witchcraft by marauding Protestant soldiers who had arrived in Ulster as part of a Scottish invading force.[19]

In the mid-twentieth century, Irish writers begun to base their creative outputs directly on the events of 1711. Chief among this work was Belfast-born playwright and novelist Olga Fielden's one-act play, *Witches in Eden*, first published in 1948.[20] The published play was well received,[21] but it was not performed until March 1951 by Larne-based amateur dramatic society the 'Tangent Players', for the Larne Drama Festival,[22] where it won the prize for best non-dialect play.[23] The play was produced once more for the festival in March 1975 by the Larne Drama Circle.[24] It was not performed again until November 2023, when I, Dr Victoria McCollum, Dr Lisa Fitzpatrick, director Kat Woods and staff and students at Ulster University staged a new production for Riverside Theatre, Coleraine.

Fielden's play was the first based on an Irish witch trial and was set over the course of an evening. It centres on JP Andrew Fergusson's investigation into Mary Dunbar's witchcraft allegations. As the play progresses, Fergusson is placed in an untenable position when Dunbar accuses his wife and daughter, Janet Mean Fergusson and Ann Fergusson, along with an old poor, blind woman, Sarah, of witchcraft. Mary's accusation of the Fergusson women is rooted in romantic jealousy of Ann, who once courted her fiancé, James Blythe. The play ends with the women's guilt being put beyond doubt when they are brought secretly into Dunbar's bedroom and identified not by sight but by their demonic presence. The curtain comes down to the Revd Tobias Sinclare (based on Revd Robert Sinclair) praying on his knees for the return of Dunbar's health. Fielden altered aspects of the 1711 case for dramatic effect. Unlike the real-life 'witches', the suspected women in the play are well behaved and respectable and do not challenge societal norms or resist the prosecution process. Resistance or agency in the play is shown by male characters.

Fielden invented characters (Sarah) and provided others (James, Janet, and Ann) with new backstories and romantic entanglements to account for their behaviour. Fielden also worked to establish the 'otherness' of Islandmagee and its people:

[Rev. Tobias] Sinclare: They're a queer people in Islandmagee, Haltridge, You're not a man of these parts, but I am, and I'll say they're as queer a people as you'd find in the length and breadth of the land. [James] Haltridge: Don't I know it! Didn't they put spells on that white heifer of mine only last spring because I bought her over the head of John Wilson.[25]

Conclusion

The trial of the Islandmagee witches did not die with Mary Dunbar or William Sellor, and lived on in the memory of people living in or near Islandmagee and in places associated with it. In the nineteenth and twentieth century, it shaped how lingering belief in witchcraft was understood in the peninsula. The case was also remembered between the early nineteenth and mid-twentieth centuries by historians, journalists, dramatists, poets, and novelists. This work created an accepted narrative of Irish witchcraft and magic as exceptional and gendered it as female. It also painted Ireland as a disenchanted land by obscuring continuing belief in witchcraft and the criminal cases for assault, theft, and slander (among other things) that arose from it. Witchcraft belief was not held in a vacuum and Ireland remained awash with belief in, and practice of, popular magic. These gendered and politicised stereotypes of Irish witchcraft were not challenged until the late twentieth and twenty-first century by academic historians like myself and poets, artists, novelists, and playwrights, including Adrian Rice, Martina Devlin, and Sarah Shiel, who re-investigated and reimagined the trials of the Islandmagee witches.[26]

12

Some Conclusions

The idea that there were no witch trials in Ireland, and that Irish people did not believe at some level in witches or accuse each other of witchcraft, is, after a decade or so of research, no longer tenable. In early modern Protestant Ireland, people were accused, prosecuted, tried, and convicted for witchcraft, if nowhere near on the scale of the British Isles and some places in continental Europe. This book has suggested that the lack of witch-hunting in early modern Ireland was primarily rooted in the fact that most of the population, the Gaelic-speaking, Catholic Irish, did not accuse each other of the crime of witchcraft. In Gaelic-Irish culture, and other Gaelic-speaking parts of the British Isles, witches did not pose the same level of threat to life and property that they did in most of Western Europe. There was therefore little need to avail of the court system to punish those responsible, find closure, cease ongoing magical attacks, and/ or prevent future ones.

Gaelic-Irish witches were not demonically inspired and did not attack humans or usually kill livestock, but rather interrupted dairy production at certain times during the ritual year. They were also more easily challenged and countered by magical means. Death and lingering illness in humans and livestock in this culture was often blamed on other supernatural causes such as cursing, the evil-eye, and the fairies. The fact that fairies could also interrupt milk and butter production further lessened the perceived threat level of Gaelic-Irish witches. In late seventeenth- and early eighteenth-century Ulster, where ideas concerning demonic witchcraft did influence popular culture, most accusations did not become prosecutions because of the arbitration skill of the Presbyterian clergy working through Church courts, the actions of local law enforcement agents, and the growing influence of judicial scepticism on the educated.

The Islandmagee case was an aberration in that these checks and balances failed to operate. Mary Dunbar was able to convince the wider community that her possession was genuine and that it was caused by the malice of witches who deserved to be punished using the full force of the law. Compared with some parts of Europe, where witch-hunting was severe, it was relatively difficult to have someone prosecuted for witchcraft in Ireland, where the legal system was largely based on that of England. The whole community had to be behind the accusation, including local elites who controlled the legal machinery of prosecution, and be willing to stand up in court and give evidence. Before the trial even began, the local gentry serving on the grand jury had to be convinced by local magistrates that the evidence presented was enough to warrant a trial in the county's main criminal court. During the trial itself, the petty jury, comprised of the middling and lower sort, had to be able to bring in a majority guilty verdict. This was made easier if an Assize judge was amenable to the case for the prosecution. A toxic combination of converging circumstances ensured that nearly all these elements were present in the Islandmagee case. More importantly, and unusually for that time, local clergymen Sinclair and Robb sidelined denominational difference and conflict to back Dunbar's accusation and ensure the trial was handled by legal authorities and not their respective Churches.

The Presbyterian clergy, gentry, and even 'the commoner sort' in Islandmagee and Larne genuinely believed that the accused women were guilty of Dunbar's bewitchment. After all, they lived in a magical moral universe where the earthly activities of God, Satan, good and evil spirits, witches, and ghosts constantly interfered in daily life. In the years after the Glorious Revolution, Presbyterian communities in Ulster, who must have struggled to cope with the large numbers arriving from Scotland, felt the political stability, religious deliverance and social legitimacy they had hoped for in their new homeland begin to disintegrate. In a Calvinist religious culture that was already theologically very sensitive to belief in the Devil and his works, it was all too easy in periods of crisis such as these to believe that as the chosen people, the true upholders of the Christian faith, they had been singled out for special punishment. Dunbar herself embodied this struggle of piety over evil, something she was at pains to point out with repeated allusions to the Biblical story of Job. Furthermore, in England and in Calvinist networks around the world, there had been a spate of similar cases, occuring during the death throes of the British witch-hunts, which made Dunbar's claims much easier to believe.

The local community's support of Dunbar's claims may be explained by the fact that she possessed a good reputation, was of a high social standing, and met expected standards of female appearance, behaviour and morality. Ironically, it was the behavioural constraints imposed by these standards, along with the strict age hierarchy, that motivated Dunbar to fake at least some of her symptoms. It is also probable Dunbar learnt the script of the demoniac by reading about other, well-publicised possession cases in Scotland and colonial America. Dunbar is easy to paint as a villain, but although her actions had terrible consequences, they can be seen as acts of resistance against societal norms imposed on her in a highly religious, male-dominated society. There is no evidence that her symptoms were caused by physical or mental illness, but it must be remembered that she died a few weeks after the first trial. She would not live to see her 'attackers' pilloried, or William Sellor convicted of her bewitchment.

Dunbar's claims were lent credibility because at least four of the convicted 'witches' had reputations for practising witchcraft, including members of the Sellor 'witch family'. Most of the accused clung to the margins of an increasingly isolated Presbyterian community in County Antrim by virtue of their poverty, lack of education, and the challenge their looks, behaviour and reputations posed to accepted models of femininity and masculinity. Some were unchurched and accused of having low morals, while others engaged in what was considered at the time to be antisocial behaviour. They also did not passively or obediently accept their fate, and instead resisted the prosecution process in any way they could. These were just the type of people expected to fall into the clutches of the Devil and to practise witchcraft. They were believable witches. Their visual difference and physical impairment further marked them out, and in combination with old and stained clothing hinted at inner corruption and sin. The recent, mysterious death (generally believed to have been caused by witchcraft) of Ann Haltridge lent Dunbar's accusation further weight, as did the fact that her possession was matched by almost continual supernatural disturbance in Knowehead House. This was believed to have been orchestrated by the same demonic presence that had targeted Ann and then Mary. Although some of these phenomena defied natural explanation, others point strongly in the direction of the Haltridges' young servant, Margaret Spear, whose motivations for such a cruel charade may have been similar to Dunbar's. The party-political conflict then raging in east Antrim also seeped into the trial and persuaded Justice MacCartney to back local Presbyterian Whigs, including Mayor Clements, and direct the petty jury to bring in a guilty verdict.

Judicial scepticism in relation to witchcraft cases was increasingly evident in legal circles in seventeenth-century Europe, including the British Isles, and made for a heightened awareness of the problems of proving witchcraft using traditional proofs such as spectral evidence. This was important in cases of demonic possession because of the well-publicised cases of fraud which had been uncovered during the early modern period. This sceptical frame of mind can even be detected in the Islandmagee case: not only did local clergy and agents of law enforcement in Islandmagee rigorously test Dunbar's spectral evidence through identity parades and probing questions, but during the trial itself overtly sceptical arguments were made by Justice Upton and seconded afterwards by Revd Tisdall. In Ireland, however, there was no immediate weakening of belief in witchcraft, or in a world-view in which God and the Devil and other supernatural forces interfered directly in people's lives. Indeed, belief in and fear of witches survived in Ireland, changing and adapting to the forces of modernity well into the twentieth century.

The human cost of the Islandmagee case should not be underestimated because the convicted women were not burnt or hanged for their 'crimes', as in other parts of early modern Europe. The punishments handed down to the Islandmagee witches were not light given the conditions in gaols at this time, and they were publicly humiliated in the pillory on market days, most probably in front of large crowds. Members of the Sellor 'witch family' were particularly affected, as mother, father and daughter were all convicted of witchcraft and William may have paid the ultimate price on the gallows. The social stigma and suspicion of being accused of witchcraft and dealing with the Devil would have undoubtedly clung to the reputations of the witches themselves and to the generations that followed. The trial also haunted the beliefs, tales and culture of Islandmagee for centuries, and provided generations of writers with the material needed to articulate their own views of Irish witchcraft.

Notes

Preface (First Edition)

1   *The Dublin Intelligence Containing A Fully And Impartial Account Of The Foreign And Domestick News*, Saturday, 14 April 1711. In 1711 this newspaper was printed by Francis Dickson at the Union Coffee-house 'on Cork-Hill', Dublin, and contained a mixture of local and international news. For a description of the county Assizes, a system of provincial criminal courts in England and Ireland, see chapters 4 and 8.

2   For a discussion of how the Islandmagee trials were culturally represented in nineteenth- and twentieth-century journalism, non-fiction, visual imagery, and creative writing, see chapter 11 and Andrew Sneddon, *Representing Magic in Modern Ireland: Belief, History, and Culture* (Cambridge, 2022); idem., 'Witchcraft Belief, Representation and Memory in Modern Ireland', in *Cultural and Social History*, 16/3 (2019): 251–70.

3   Dixon Donaldson, *History of Islandmagee* (Islandmagee, 1927, repr. 2002): 44–8.

4   St John D. Seymour, *Irish Witchcraft and Demonology* (Baltimore, 1913): 118–27.

5   For example see: Patrick F. Byrne, *Witchcraft in Ireland* (1969, repr. Dublin, 1973); 38–47; Bob Curran, *Ireland's Witches: a Bewitched Land* (Dublin, 2005): 60–79.

6   See Charles McConnell, *The Witches of Islandmagee* (Carrickfergus, 2000).

7   See Gilbert Geis and Ivan Bunn, *A Trial of Witches: a Seventeenth-Century Witchcraft Prosecution* (London, 1997), for the trial of Amy Denny and Rose Cullender in Bury St Edmunds, Suffolk, in 1662. For the mass trial of the 'Pendle witches' in Lancaster in 1612, see Robert Poole (ed.), *The Lancashire Witches: Histories and Stories* (Manchester, 2002); idem., *The Wonderful Discovery of Witches* (Lancaster, 2011); Phillip C. Almond, *The Lancashire Witches: a Chronicle of Sorcery and Death on Pendle Hill* (London, 2012).

8   For more on these sources, see Author's Notes section, Notes on Sources and Referencing.

9   William Tisdall, 'Account of the Trial of Eight Reputed Witches, 4 April 1711', in *Hibernian Magazine* (1775): 47–51; Samuel Molyneux to Thomas Molyneux, 14 May 1711 (TCD, Ms 889, f.31r-31v.).

Preface (Second Edition)

1 Andrew Sneddon, '"Creative" Micro Histories, Difficult Heritage, and "Dark" Public History: the Islandmagee Witches (1711) Project', in *Preternature*, 11/1 (2022): 113.

Author's Notes

1 This section on original documents is taken from my introduction to: Andrew Sneddon, Shannon Devlin (eds), 'Documents from the Trial of the "Islandmagee Witches" at Carrickfergus Assizes, County Antrim, Ireland, 1711', https://w1711. org/originaldocs/ [last accessed 26 September 2024].

2 *A NARRATIVE Of the Sufferings of a Young Girl called MARY DUNBAR, who was Strangely Molested by SPIRITS and WITCHES, at Mr. James Hattridge's House, Parish of Island Magee, near Carrickfergus, in the County of Antrim, and Province of Ulster, in Ireland, and in some Other Places to which she was Removed during the Time of her Disorder, as also of the Aforesaid Mr. Hattridge's house being Haunted with Spirits in the Latter End of 1710 and the Beginning of 1711* (Belfast, 1st ed., 1822).

3 J.R.R. Adams, 'The Belfast Almanacs and Directories of Joseph Smyth', in *The Linen Hall Review*, 8/1 (Spring, 1991): 14

4 Unfortunately, four pages of this pamphlet have been lost (43, 44, 45, 46). This represents about half of the appended Tisdall letter. Thanks to Dr Shannon Devlin for helping to track down this edition.

5 Sneddon, *Representing Magic*: 39.

6 For this correspondence, see: Public Record Office of Northern Ireland [PRONI], Benn Papers: D3113/6/92; D3113/7, 100, 151, 152, 155, 199. Benn must have given Porter the McSkimin pamphlet before 1868, because in March of that year Porter lent his copy to William Pinkerton: William Pinkerton to George Benn, 16 March 1868 (PRONI, Benn Papers, D3113/7/149).

7 Classon Porter, *Witches, Warlocks and Ghosts* (Belfast, 1885): 2.

8 Tisdall, 'Account of the Trial': 47–51.

9 *THE ISLANDMAGEE WITCHES, A NARRATIVE of the Sufferings of a Young Girl called MARY DUNBAR, Who was Strangely Molested by Spirits and Witches, at Mr. James Hattridge's House, ISLANDMAGEE, NEAR CARRICKFERGUS, In the County of Antrim and Province of Ulster in Ireland, and in Some Other Places to which she was Removed during the Time of her Disorder, as also of the Aforesaid Mr. Hattridge's House being Haunted with Spirits in the Latter End of 1710 and the Beginning of 1711* (Belfast, 2nd ed., c.1920) This publication date is inferred from the type of paper and font used, and its private publication from the fact that no publisher name or place of publication is given. Thanks to staff at Belfast Central Library for their help in establishing a probable/possible publication date.

10 R.M. Young (ed.), *Historical Notices of Old Belfast and its Vicinity* ... (Belfast, 1896): 161–4.

11 Pinkerton to Benn, 16 March 1868 (PRONI, D3113/7/149).

12 'Examinations and Depositions taken in the County Antrim Respecting Witches',
March 1711 (TCD, Dublin Philosophical Society Papers, Ms 883/2): 273–85.

13 A manuscript of sworn evidence given by witnesses on the day of Florence Newton's
trial in 1661 does survive and is held in the archives of the Royal Society in London.
For a transcription of this document: Andrew Sneddon, "Florence Newton's Trial for
Witchcraft, Cork, 1661', in *Irish Historical Studies*, 43/164 (2019): 298–319.

14 Donaldson, *History of Islandmagee*: 48.

15 McSkimin (ed.), *The Islandmagee Witches*: 19.

Chapter 1

1 Donaldson, *History of Islandmagee*: 42–3; Donald Harmon Akenson, *Between Two
Revolutions: Islandmagee, County Antrim, 1798–1920* (Ontario, 1979): 31–4; Dean
William Henry's Topographical Survey of the Coast of County Antrim, c.1740
(PRONI, Transcripts, T/2521/3/5): 140–1.

2 'Description of the County of Antrim, by Richard Dobbs, Esq.' 1683, in George Hill
(ed.), *An Historical Account of the MacDonnells of Antrim: Including Notices of Some Other
Septs, Irish and Scottish* (Belfast, 1873): 376, 378, 379. Hill's publication was based on a
transcription of the report (dated 3 May 1683) on County Antrim that Richard Dobbs
submitted to William Molyneux. It is now held in Trinity College, Dublin (hereafter
TCD): Account of Carrickfergus and Antrim, 1683 (TCD, Papers of William and
Samuel Molyneux, 1662–1745, Ms 883/1): 181–210. Some manuscript notes written by
Dobbs for this report also survive: Richard Dobbs, 'Oberv[ation]s aboute Carrickfergus',
1683 (PRONI, Dobbs Papers, 1568–1917, D162/6). Just as violence against settlers
unleashed during and after the 1641 rebellion was afterwards depicted in Protestant
mythology as an extermination perpetrated by savage Irish Catholics, the murder of
Islandmagee Catholics in 1642 became, in oppositional polemic and politicised folklore,
a massacre of 3,000 local men, women and children by a Protestant garrison stationed
in Carrickfergus: T.W. Moody, 'Irish History and Irish Mythology', in *Hermathena*,
124 (1978): 10; John Gibney, 'What about Islandmagee? Another Version of the 1641
Rebellion', in *History Ireland*, 21/1 (2013): 22–5; Akenson, *Two Revolutions*: 32–3, 139–40.

3 Donaldson, *History of Islandmagee*: 107.

4 'Hearth Money Roll for the County of Antrim for the Year 1669, Upper Part
of Islandmagee', in Donaldson, *History of Islandmagee*: 41; Angélique Day, Patrick
McWilliams (eds.), *Ordnance Survey Memoirs of Ireland* [OSMI]: *Parishes of County Antrim X,
1830–1, 1833–5, 1839–40, East Antrim, Glynn, Inver, Kilroot, and Templecorran* (Belfast, 1994):
82. The OSMI were parish accounts for the north of Ireland designed to accompany
the new 6in ordnance survey maps. They were compiled in the 1830s and early 1840s
by several collectors and covered a range of topics including topography, local history,
and folklore. The OSMI were published in Belfast in the 1990s: Angélique Day, Patrick
McWilliams (eds.), *Ordnance Survey Memoirs of Ireland* (Belfast, 40 vols, 1990–98).

5 Donaldson, *History of Islandmagee*: 48, 108. The effective 'killing-range' of a musket
at that time was 100 yards, in other words, the point at which a musket-ball in flight
began to fall to the ground.

6   Revd John Haltridge, Islandmagee, will [no longer extant], Islandmagee 1697 (PRONI, pre-1858 wills index, Connor Diocesan wills).

7   William MacKenzie, *History of Galloway, from the Earliest Time to the Present Time* (2 vols, 1841), ii, 28, appendix; Minutes of the Antrim Presbytery, 14 Nov. 1690 (PRONI, Minutes of Antrim Presbytery Meeting, 1673–91, D/1759/1/A/2); Ian McBride, *Eighteenth-Century Ireland* (Dublin, 2009): 180.

8   Donaldson, *History of Islandmagee*: 108; Jean Agnew, *Belfast Merchant Families in the Seventeenth-Century* (Dublin, 1996): 255–6; W.D. Killen, *History of the Congregation of the Presbyterian Church in Ireland* (Belfast, 1886):162; Robert Whan, 'Presbyterians in Ulster, 1680–1730: a Social and Political Study' (Unpublished PhD thesis, Queen's University Belfast, May 2009), chapters 1–3; ibid., *The Presbyterians of Ulster, 1680–1730* (Woodbridge, 2013): 15–38, 99–123; Will of William Haltridge of Dromore, County Down, 4 Nov. 1691 (PRONI, Transcripts, Bound volume of Copy Extracts from Prerogative and Down Diocese Wills, 1657–1850, T403/1: 40).

9   The book Ann Haltridge was reading was likely to have been Alexander Wedderburn, *David's Testament Opened Up in Fourty Sermons ...* (Edinburgh, 1705).

10   *A Contemporary Narrative of the Proceedings against Dame Alice Kyteler, Prosecuted for Sorcery in 1324* by Richard de Ledrede, Bishop of Ossory, 1324, Thomas Wright (ed.) (London, 1843): 1–3; Philip C. Almond, *The Devil: a New Biography* (Ithaca, 2014): 156; Ronald Hutton, *The Witch: The History of Fear, From Ancient Times to the Present* (London, 2017): 270–1. Kyteler was tried and convicted in absentia after evading arrest by fleeing to England. Her alleged co-conspirators were not so lucky and were variously banished, flogged, and excommunicated. Petronella de Midia was tortured and burned alive. It has been suggested this case was not a politically motivated heresy and demonic conspiracy trial but was in fact the first witchcraft trial in European history: Maeve Brigid Callan, *The Templars, the Witch, and the Wild Irish: Vengeance and Heresy in Medieval Ireland* (Ithaca, 2015): 77–148.

11   Reginald Scot, 'The Discoverie of Witchcraft, 1584', Montague Summers (ed.) (New York, 1930, repr. 1972): 217–26; Brian P. Levack, *The Witch-hunt in Early Modern Europe* (Harlow, 3rd edn., 2006): 33–4, 38–9, 62–3; Julian Goodare, *The European Witch-hunt* (Abingdon, 2016): 63–4, 278; Hutton, *The Witch*, 99–101. For medieval antecedents of early modern demonic magic: Richard Kieckhefer, Revised and Expanded, *Magic in the Middle Ages* (Cambridge, 3rd edn, 2022), chapter 8.

12   Antrim Presbytery minutes, 3 Sep. 1672 (PRONI, D1759/1/A/2): 54.

13   Patrick Adair, 'A True Narrative of the Rise and Progress of the Presbyterian Church in Ireland ... 1623–70', W.D. Killen (ed.) (Belfast, 1866): 299–300.

14   A piece of cloth in which people were buried which left the head and feet exposed.

15   *OSMI, x: 43*.

16   Randal Leathes was Ruling Elder in Islandmagee in 1710, while John Man was Ruling Elder in 1714. See Donaldson, *History of Islandmagee*: 109.

17   Cited in Raymond Gillespie, '"Into Another Intensity", Prayer in Irish Non-conformity, 1650–1700', in Kevin Herlihy (ed.), *The Religion of Irish Dissent 1650–1800* (Dublin, 1996): 43. For more on this case: Andrew Sneddon, *Witchcraft and Magic in Ireland* (Basingstoke, 2015): 78.

18 S.J. Connolly, *Religion, Law and Power: The Making of Protestant Ireland, 1660–1760* (Oxford, 1992): 43, 145–7; Whan, *Presbyterians in Ulster*: 148, 48.

19 *OSMI*, x: 41.

20 Connolly, *Religion, Law and Power*: 167.

21 Leanne Calvert, '"He Came to her Bed Pretending Courtship": Sex, Courtship and the Making of Marriage in Ulster, 1750–1844', in *Irish Historical Studies*, 42/162 (2018): 248–50 (quotes at 249–50).

22 Katherine Hodgkin, 'Reasoning with Unreason: Visions, Witchcraft, and Madness in Early Modern England' in, Stuart Clark (ed.), *Languages of Witchcraft: Narrative, Ideology and Meaning in Early Modern Culture* (Hampshire, 2001): 218.

23 Richard Chamberlayne, *Lithobolia: or, the Stone-Throwing Devil ...* (London, 1698). For a detailed examination of this case: Emerson W. Baker, *The Devil of Great Island: Witchcraft and Conflict in Early New England* (Basingstoke, 2007).

24 Raymond Gillespie, *Devoted People: Belief and Religion in Early Modern Ireland* (Manchester, 1997): 110–3.

25 Hester Ann Rogers, 'Cadwallader Acteson's Ghost', Cork, 1788 (MAM/FL/33/1/4, Fletcher-Tooth collection, Methodist Archives and Research Centre, John Rylands Research Institute and Library, Manchester); Luke Holloway, Martha McGill, 'The Conversion of a Cork Candle-Maker: An Account by Hester Ann Rogers (1788)', in *Wesley and Methodist Studies*, 14/2 (2022): 191–205. The manuscript was written by Rogers (died 1794), a Methodist writer resident in Ireland with connections to John Wesley, and transcribed by Wesley's biographer Elizabeth Ritchie (died 1835). Thanks to Dr McGill for providing me with copies of these documents.

26 *Strabane Journal*, 13 Nov. 1786.

27 Richard Baxter, *The Certainty of the World of Spirits. And Consequently, of the Immortality of Souls ...* (London, 1691): 218–20.

28 Carnmoney Session minutes, 27 June, 8 July 1702 (PRONI, MIC 1P/37/4: 47).

Chapter 2

1 James and his three brothers, John, Robert and William, are mentioned in their uncle's will, but their sister is not: Will of William Haltridge, 4 Nov. 1691 (PRONI T403/1: 40).

2 Tisdall, 'Account of the Trial': 47. The pamphlet account states that Dunbar was 'a slender girl of fifteen or sixteen years of age', which is around two years younger than Tisdall's estimation.

3 Tisdall, 'Account of the Trial': 47.

4 Samuel Molyneux to Thomas Molyneux, 14 May 1711 (TCD, Ms 889, ff 31r-31v.).

5 See John Dunbar to George Rawdon, 31 Jul. 1661 (Huntington Library, California, Hastings (Irish) Papers, HA 14644); Thomas Stanhope to Arthur Rawdon, 16 Jan. 1684 (Huntington Library, California, Hastings (Irish) Papers, HA 15824); Copy of Registers and Baptisms from Lisburn Cathedral, 1640–1806 (PRONI, Stewart of Ards Papers, D/1823/5). I thank Brenda Collins for supplying me with these references.

6   Stana Nenadic, 'Necessities: Food and Clothing in the Long Eighteenth Century',
    in Elizabeth Foyster and Christopher A. Whatley (eds), *A History of Everyday Life in
    Scotland, 1600 to 1800* (Edinburgh, 2010): 141.
7   Sympathetic magic uses actions and objects that resemble, are associated with
    symbolically, or have made physical contact with the person the 'magician' seeks
    to harm or influence. For more on sympathetic magic: Ze Hong, 'A Cognitive
    Account of Manipulative Sympathetic Magic', in *Religion, Brain & Behavior*, 12/3
    (2022): 254–70.
8   Cited in James Sharpe, *Instruments of Darkness: Witchcraft in Early Modern England*
    (Philadelphia, 1996, repr., 1997): 152.
9   Sir William Aston's Transcript of Florence Newton's Trial for Witchcraft, Cork
    1661 (Royal Society, London [RS], RB 1/37/5, ff 96r–102v). This manuscript
    contains witness statements given at the Youghal trial. As already mentioned above,
    I transcribed, annotated and published this manuscript as: Andrew Sneddon, 'Select
    Document: Florence Newton's Trial for Witchcraft, Cork, 1661: Sir William
    Aston's transcript', in *Irish Historical Studies*, 43/164 (2019): 298–319. Youghal,
    County Cork, contained just over 2,300 inhabitants at that time.
10 Daniel Higgs, *The Wonderfull and True Relation of the Bewitching a Young Girle in
    Ireland* ... (1699): 6–7.
11 Tisdall, 'Account of the Trial': 48.
12 See: Matthew 12:22, 4:24, 9:32–3, and Mark 1:39.
13 Brian P. Levack, *The Devil Within: Possession & Exorcism in the Christian West*
    (London, 2013): 3.
14 Philip C. Almond, *The Devil: A New Biography* (Ithaca, 2014): 142.
15 See Philip C. Almond, *Demonic Possession and Exorcism in Early Modern England:
    Contemporary Texts and their Cultural Contexts* (Cambridge, 2004): 1, 22–3.
16 Anon, *The Most Strange and Admirable Discoverie of the Witches of Warboys* ...
    (London, 1593).
17 Almond, *Devil*: 161.
18 Dispossessions were carried out on demoniacs Richard Rothwell and John Fox
    (1612), the children of George Muschamp (1650), and Richard Dugdale (1690). For
    Dugdale, see Francis Hutchinson, *An Historical Essay Concerning Witchcraft* ... (1st ed.,
    London, 1718): 124–8. For the Church of England and exorcism in the sixteenth
    and seventeenth centuries: Francis Young, *A History of Anglican Exorcism: Deliverance
    and Demonology in Church Ritual* (London, 2018): 17–64.
19 Gillespie, *Devoted People*: 7.
20 Francis Young, *A History of Exorcism in Catholic Christianity* (London, 2016): 135–6.
21 Vera Moynes (ed.), *Irish Jesuit Annual Letters 1604–1674* (2 vols, Dublin, 2019), i,
    331–2; Alma O'Donnell, 'Jesuit Involvement in Exorcisms in Seventeenth-century
    Ireland', in Mary Ann Lyons, Brian Mac Cuarta SJ (eds), *The Jesuit Mission in early
    modern Ireland, 1560–1760* (Dublin, 2022). The Counter-Reformation was a religious
    and cultural reform movement and Catholicism's chief response to the Protestant
    Reformations of the sixteenth century. The Society of Jesus (the Jesuits) was a
    religious order of the Roman Catholic Church founded in 1540 by Ignatius Loyola.

22 Sneddon, 'Florence Newton': 303.

23 Higgs, *Wonderful True Relation:* 6.

24 Higgs, *Wonderful True Relation*: 7; Andrew Sneddon, 'Medicine, Belief, Witchcraft and Demonic Possession in late Seventeenth-Century Ulster', in *Medical Humanities*, 42/2 (2016): 1–6; Sneddon, *Witchcraft and Magic in Ireland*: 68–9.

25 Anon., *Sadducismus Debellatus, or a True Narrative of the Sorceries and Witchcrafts Exercis'd by the Devil and his Instruments Upon Mrs Christian Shaw* ... (London, 1698): 1–38; Brian P. Levack, *Witch-hunting in Scotland, Law, Politics and Religion* (Abingdon, 2008): 115–20, 125–9.

26 See also, Deposition of William Hatley, Islandmagee, 5 Mar. 1711 (TCD, Samuel Molyneux Papers, Ms 883/2): 281.

27 Alison Rowlands, 'Not "the Usual Suspects"? Male Witches, Witchcraft, and Masculinities in Early Modern Europe', in Alison Rowlands (ed.), *Witchcraft and Masculinities in Early Modern Europe* (Basingstoke, 2009): 13.

28 Tisdall, 'Account of the Trial': 48.

29 Ibid.

30 Deposition of James Hill, Islandmagee, 5 Mar. 1711 (TCD, Samuel Molyneux Papers, Ms 883/2).

31 William Fenton was Ruling Elder for Islandmagee in 1705, and was wealthy enough to leave a will: William Fenton, Islandmagee, will [no longer extant], Islandmagee 1724 (PRONI, pre-1858 wills index, Connor Diocesan wills); Donaldson, *History of Islandmagee*: 108.

32 For an early eighteenth-century Church of Ireland clergyman David Robb is an unusually shadowy figure. He is not mentioned in graduation lists of the universities where the majority (if not all) of Irish Anglican clergymen were educated (Cambridge, Oxford, and Trinity College, Dublin). He is also missing from the published succession list of the clergy of the diocese of Connor. This latter omission may be to do with the fact that the clerical rector of Islandmagee, Owen Lloyd, was also the Dean of Connor and employed curates to do his preaching and pastoral work for him. If Robb were indeed a 'stipendary' curate it is possible he would not have been listed anywhere but in vestry or visitation records, which the compiler of the succession list may not have had access to: Canon J.B. Leslie, *Clergy of Connor: From Patrician Times to the Present Day* (Belfast, 1993): 129, 156–7, 446. This argument is made stronger by the fact that the trial depositions mention 'Mr. Robb, the curate': Deposition of Mary Dunbar, 12 Mar. 1711 (TCD, Samuel Molyneux Papers, Ms 883/2: 275). Bishop of Down and Connor, Francis Hutchinson, in a list he compiled of the clergymen of his diocese in the 1720s, records Robb as being curate of the parish of Islandmagee: Bishop Francis Hutchinson's commonplace book, c.1721–30 (PRONI, Diocesan records, DIO/1/22/1: 152).

33 Donaldson, *History of Islandmagee*: 99; *OSMI*, x, 20.

34 Tisdall, 'Account of the Trial': 48.

35 For this case, see: James Sharpe, *The Bewitching of Anne Gunter: a Horrible and True Story of Football, Witchcraft, Murder and the King of England* (London, 1999): 160, and Clive Holmes, 'Women: Witnesses and Witches', in *Past and Present*, 140/1 (1993): 65.

36 Sneddon, 'Florence Newton': 303.
37 Hutchinson, *Historical Essay*: 131–2; See also Mark Knights, *The Devil in Disguise: Deception, Declusion and Fanaticism in the early English Enlightenment* (Oxford, 2011): 220–8.
38 See George Gifford, *A Dialogue Concerning Witches and Witchcraftes* (1593); Alan Macfarlane, 'A Tudor Anthropologist: George Gifford's Discourse and Dialogue', in Sidney Anglo (ed.), *The Damned Art: Essays in the Literature of Witchcraft* (Routledge, 1977): 152; James Hitchcock, 'George Gifford and Puritan Witch Beliefs', in *Archiv für Reformationsgeschichte*, 58 (1967): 97–8.
39 For example, see Revelations 14:10; 19:20; 20:10; 21:18.
40 Anon., *A Brief Narration of the Possession, Dispossession, and Repossession of William Sommers* ... (London, 1589) in, Almond, *Demonic Possession*: 285.
41 See Kathleen R. Sands, *Demon Possession in Elizabethan England* (London, 2004): 32.

Chapter 3

1 *OSMI*, x, 30.
2 Samuel McSkimin, *The History and Antiquities of the County of the Town of Carrickfergus, County Antrim* ... (Belfast, 1811) 43, 69–71, 164–6; Elizabeth J. McCrum (ed.), *The History and Antiquities of the County of the Town of Carrickfergus by Samuel McSkimin* (Belfast, 1909):418–9, 433, 475–6; Irvin Ehrenpreis, *Swift, the Man, His Works, and the Age, volume 1, Mr Swift and his Contemporaries* (Welwyn Garden City, Herts, 1962, repr. 1964): 163; Andrew Clements, Straid, will [no longer extant], 1718 (PRONI, pre-1858 wills index, Connor Diocesan wills).
3 Deposition of James Blythe, of Bank [-Head, Larne], County Antrim, 5 Mar. 1711 (TCD, Samuel Molyneux Papers, Ms 883/2: 281).
4 Donaldson, *History of Islandmagee*: 109.
5 William Brown, Islandmagee, will [no longer extant], 1738 (PRONI, pre-1858 wills index, Connor Diocesan wills); Donaldson, *History of Islandmagee*: 109.
6 Robert Holmes, Islandmagee, will [no longer extant], 1721 (PRONI, pre-1858 Wills Index, Connor Diocesan wills); Donaldson, *History of Islandmagee*: 108–9.
7 Dixon Donaldson suggests that Blythe was a constable in Islandmagee but provides no evidence to support this theory, see Donaldson, *History of Islandmagee*: 46.
8 Richard Bolton, *A Justice of the Peace for Ireland* ... (Dublin, 2nd edn, 1638): 97–8.
9 Hutton, *The Witch*: 270–6 (quotes at 271).
10 Thomas Benskin, *A True and Impartial Relation of the Informations against Three Witches, viz. Temperance Lloyd, Mary Trembles, and Susanna Edwards* ... (London, 1682): 11; Gaskill, *Witchfinders: a Seventeenth Century Tragedy* (London, 2005): 4, 29, 44; Goodare, *European Witch-hunt*: 62. For a discussion of how the narrative of this case was manipulated by Benskin for the benefit of his readers: Stephen Timmons, 'Witchcraft and Rebellion in late Seventeenth-century Devon', in *Journal of Early Modern History*, 10/4 (2006): 317–22.
11 Hutton, *The Witch*: 272.
12 Tisdall, 'Account of the Trial': 48.

13 Ibid.

14 Templepatrick Session minutes, 27 July 1647 (PRONI, Templepatrick Non-Subscribing Presbyterian Church Records, CR4/12/B/1: 23); Robert Armstrong, 'The Irish Alternative: Scottish and English Presbyterianism in Ireland', in Robert Armstrong and Tadhg Ó hAnnracháin (eds), *Insular Christianity: Alternative Models of the Church in Britain and Ireland, c.1570–c.1700* (Manchester, 2013): 210.

15 Antrim Presbytery minutes, 14 Feb. 1655/6 (PRONI, MS D/1759/1/A/1: 93–4).

16 Mark S. Sweetnam (ed.), *The Minutes of the Ministers' Meeting 1654–8* (Dublin, 2012): 14.

17 Sneddon, *Witchcraft and Magic in Ireland*: 66. See also, next chapter.

18 Connor Session minutes, 5 May 1701 (Presbyterian Historical Society, Belfast [hereafter PHSB], Connor Session Book, 1693–1703: 11).

19 Connor Session minutes, 8 May 1701 (PHSB: 11).

20 Carnmoney Session minutes, 5 Apr. 1721 (PRONI, MIC 1P/37/4).

21 Aghadowey Session minutes, 26 Nov. 1723 (PHS., Aghadowey Session minutes: 132).

22 Aghadowey Session minutes, 1 Apr. 1724 (PHS., Aghadowey Session minutes: 133).

Chapter 4

1 These figures are taken from Goodare, *European Witch-Hunt*: 27; idem., 'Introduction', in Julian Goodare (ed.), *The Scottish Witch-hunt in Context* (Manchester, 2002): 1; Levack, *Witch-hunting in Scotland*: 2.

2 These criteria were formulated by E.C. Lapoint, see: 'Irish Immunity to Witch-hunting, 1534–1711', in *Eire-Ireland*, 27 (1992): 80.

3 Timothy Godwin to William Wake, 28 Dec. 1720 (Christ Church, Oxford, Wake Letters, vol. 13, no. 216).

4 Archbishop King to Cotton Mather, 3 Oct. 1693 (TCD, Ms 1995–2008/300); Connolly, *Religion, Law, and Power*: 196. Cotton Mather was peripherally involved in the Salem witch trials in the 1690s and wrote a book about them: *The Wonders of the Invisible World: Being an Account of the Tryals of Several Witches Lately Executed in New England ...* (London, 1693).

5 Anon, *An Excellent New Ballad* (Dublin, 1726).

6 Bishop Hutchinson's commonplace book, Oct. 1726 (PRONI MS DIO/1/22/1, un-paginated section).

7 Bishop Hutchinson's commonplace book (PRONI MS DIO/1/22/1, undated 'witchcraft' page placed at the start of the volume).

8 John Cother, *Strange and Wonderful News from the County of Wicklow in Ireland ...* (London, 1678): 1–6.

9 Thomas Riggs, *The Tryal and Conviction of Thomas Riggs and John Woods Pretended Prophets, who were Try'd at Drogheda, April 13, 1712. With the Recorder's Speech to the Jury, and Several Speeches Made by the Judge* (Dublin, 1712); 'Council Book of the Corporation of Drogheda, volume 1, 1649–1734' ed. T. Gogarty (Drogheda, 1915): 307, 312–3; Jane Bonnell to John Strype, 25 Oct. 1709

(Cambridge University Library, Add. Ms 5, ff 160r–160v); John Moult, *Warnings of the Eternal Spirit, to the city of Dublin, Pronounc'd by the Mouths of John Moult, Guy Nutt and John Parker* (Dublin, 1710); Thomas Dutton to James Cunningham, 2 May 1711 (Mitchell Library Glasgow, Moir Collection Letters, 1709–40: 6); Sneddon, *Witchcraft and Magic in Ireland*: 105–6; Hillel Schwartz, *The French Prophets: the History of a Millenarian Group in Eighteenth-Century England* (California, 1980): 136, 154–5, 165, 172.

10   Herbert F. Hore, 'Irish Bardism in 1561 (Continued)', in *Ulster Journal of Archaeology*, 6 (1858): 209.

11   'Red Book of the Privy Council', 1544, in *Historical Manuscripts Commission* [hereafter HMC], 15th Report, appendix, part iii, the Manuscripts of Charles Halliday, esq., of Dublin, *Acts of the Privy Council in Ireland, 1556–71* (London, 1897): 277; Seymour, *Irish Witchcraft and Demonology*: 59.

12   Christopher Wandesford to [John Bramhall], 4 Sept. 1640 (Huntington Library, San Marino, California, Hastings Collection, Irish papers, HA 15969: 6); Colin Breen, *Dunluce Castle: History and Archaeology* (Dublin, 2012): 130–3, 139, 160–3.

13   Raymond Gillespie, 'Ireland', in Richard M. Golden (ed.), *Encyclopedia of Witchcraft: The Western Tradition* (4 vols, Denver and Oxford, 2007), ii, 568.

14   Madeline Shanahan, '"When Cheifest Rebell Feede": Food, Fosterage and Fear in Early Modern Ireland', in *Food, Culture & Society* 27/4 (2024): 14.

15   33 Henry VIII c.8 [England], 'An Act Against Conjurations, Witchcrafts, Sorcery, and Enchantments' (1541); 5 Elizabeth I, c.16 [England], 'An Act Against Conjuration, Enchantments and Witchcrafts' (1563); I James I c.12 [England], 'An Act Against Conjuration, Witchcraft and Dealing with Evil and Wicked Spirits' (1604); Julian Goodare, 'The Scottish Witchcraft Act', in *Church History*, 74/1 (2005): 39–67. The Scottish Witchcraft Act was passed in June 1563 by the Scottish Parliament and was more concerned with reprimanding cunning-folk and their clients than dealing with witchcraft.

16   5 Elizabeth I, c.16 (1563); 28 Elizabeth I, c.2 [Ireland], 'An Act Against Witchcraft and Sorcerie' (1586).

17   28 Elizabeth I, c.2 [Ire]. The full text of 1586 Irish Witchcraft Act can be found in: *The Statutes at Large, Passed in the Parliaments Held in Ireland* ... (Dublin, 13 vols, 1786), i, 403–5). For a more detailed discussion of this legislation, see: Sneddon, *Witchcraft and Magic in Ireland*, chapter 2.

18   Neal Garnham, 'How Violent was Eighteenth-Century Ireland?', in *Irish Historical Studies*, 30/119 (1997): 388.

19   Robin Briggs, *Witches & Neighbours: The Social and Cultural Context of European Witchcraft* (Oxford, 2nd ed., 2002): 215.

20   Figures taken from: Raisa Maria Toivo, 'Witchcraft and Gender', in Johannes Dillinger (ed.), *The Routledge History of Witchcraft* (Abingdon, 2020): 219–20.

21   James Butler, Duke of Ormond, to Archbishop of Dublin, Michael Boyle, 8 May 1669 (Bodleian, Oxford, Carte MS 50, f.28r). See also: James Butler, Duke of Ormond to Captain George Matthews, 25 May 1669 (Bodleian, Oxford, Carte MS 50, f.34). Thanks to Dr Peter Elmer for supplying these references.

22 Copy of Ms containing collections of Sir James Ware, 4 Oct. 1630 (Dublin City Archives [hereafter DCA], Gilbert Ms 169, ii, f. 204).

23 Thomas Jervis to Humphrey Owen, Dublin, 21 Mar. 1668, in W.J. Smith (ed.), *Herbert Correspondence: the Sixteenth and Seventeenth-Century Letters of the Herberts of Chirbury* (Dublin, 1963).

24 For this case: Crawford Gribben, *God's Irishmen: Theological Debates in Cromwellian Ireland* (Oxford, 2007): 140.

25 Diocese of Killaloe Court Book, 10 Aug. 1704 (British Library [hereafter BL], Add. Ms 31881, f. 150r); Yvonne Petry, '"Many Things Surpass our Knowledge": An Early Modern Surgeon on Magic, Witchcraft and Demonic Possession', in *Social History of Medicine*, 25/1 (2011): 55.

26 Christopher Crofts to Sir John Perceval, 15 Mar. 1685/6, in *HMC, Egmont Manuscripts* (2 vols, Dublin, 1909), ii: 181–2.

27 Memoirs of Roger Boyle, First Earl of Orrery (BL, Sloane Ms 4227, f. 81r.). Thanks to Peter Elmer for providing this reference. For Boyle, see Peter Elmer, *Miraculous Conformist: Valentine Greatrakes, the Body Politic, and the Politics of Healing in Restoration Britain* (Oxford, 2012): 132–3.

Chapter 5

1 The Quarter Sessions in Ireland were held four times a year and were presided over, in theory, by several justices of the peace, but in practice it was often fewer. Presentments or indictments for any crime could be laid before Quarter Sessions but they were strictly prohibited from trying criminal cases involving treason or felonies such as murder or witchcraft. These serious crimes had to be passed on to higher criminal courts such as the County Assizes. Quarter Sessions were thus restricted to dealing with lesser crimes such as riot, corruption, assault, and matters of religion or public morality: Neal Garnham, *The Courts, Crime and the Criminal Law in Ireland, 1692–1760* (Dublin, 1996): 76–8.

2 Calvert, 'Sex, Courtship and Marriage in Ulster': 244–64 (quote at 263).

3 McSkimin, *Carrickfergus*, 1811: 41, 58–9; Anon., 'A Description of the Town and County of Carrickfergus', in *Belfast Monthly Magazine*, 1/5 (1808): 323; William Pinkerton, 'The "Pallace" of Carrickfergus', in *Ulster Journal of Archaeology*, 7 (1859): 1; 'Charter of Carrickfergus', in *Belfast Monthly Magazine*, 24/23 (1810): 289; Angélique Day, Patrick McWilliams (eds), *OSMI: Parishes of County Antrim XIV, 1832, 1839–40, Carrickfergus* (Belfast, 1996): 20–1; John Howard, *An Account of Principal Lazarettos in Europe* ... (Warrington, 1789): 98. For John Howard see, Ole Peter Grell, 'A Journey of Body and Soul: the Significance of the Hospitals in Southern, Catholic Europe for John Howard's Views of Health Care and the Creation of the Utopian Hospital', in Ole Peter Grell, Andrew Cunningham, Bernd Roeck (eds), *Health Care and Poor Relief in 18th and 19th Century Southern Europe* (Aldershot, 2005): 289–316.

4 Howard, *An Account of Principal Lazarettos*: 98.

5   Anon., 'Description of the Town of Carrickfergus': 323; *OSMI*, xiv: 20–1.

6   County Antrim Grand Jury Presentments, Quarter Sessions/Assizes, 3 Oct. 1711, 15 Apr., 7 Oct. 1713, 6 Oct. 1714, 26 Mar., 27 Apr., 6 Oct. 1715 (PRONI, County Antrim Grand Jury Presentments 1714–21, ANT/4/1/1).

7   Ibid., 17 Jul. 1713, 27 Apr., 13 Jul. 1715, 12 Apr. 1716.

8   The following events of 5 March are related in the pamphlet account. Charles Lennan's deposition, however, placed them in a slightly different chronological order: Deposition of Charles Lennan, 10 Mar. 1711 (TCD, Ms 883/2: 279).

9   The early eighteenth century saw Ireland take on the 'role as a garrison for the largest part of Britain's standing army' amid 'ongoing concerns over internal security and a possible Jacobite invasion': Charles Ivar McGrath, 'Politics, 1692–1730', in Jane Ohlmeyer (ed.), *The Cambridge History of Ireland, Volume II, 1550–1730* (4 vols, Cambridge, 2018, repr. 2020): 137.

10 Rena Maguire, Jordana Maguire, 'Practical Magic: An Analysis of the Origins of Horse Skull Deposition in Irish Post-medieval Structures', in *Ulster Journal of Archaeology*, 77 (2022): 105–12 (quote at 108).

11 Anon., *Saddicismus Debellatus, or True Narrative ... Christian Shaw*: 37; Levack, *Witch-hunting in Scotland*: 120.

12 Smallpox is a contagious, potentially fatal disease caused by the variola virus and distinguished by fever, a rash, and pustules on the skin, which eventually scab over to leave pitted, deep scars. In the early eighteenth century, before inoculation and (afterwards) vaccination was accessible to a significant proportion of the population, smallpox was one of the most lethal epidemic diseases in Britain and Ireland, with the young being especially vulnerable. See: Deborah Brunton, 'Smallpox Inoculation and Demographic Trends in Eighteenth-century Scotland', in *Medical History*, 36/4 (1992): 403–10, 422–4; idem., 'The Problems of Implementation: the Failure and Success of Public Vaccination in Ireland, 1840–73', in Greta Jones, Elizabeth Jones (eds), *Medicine, Disease and the State in Ireland, 1650–1940* (Cork, 1999): 139–40; John Landers, 'Age Patterns of Mortality in London During the 'Long Eighteenth Century': a Test of the 'High Potential' Model of Metropolitan Mortality', in *Journal of Social History of Medicine*, 3/1 (1990): 52–5.

13 Cited in S.J. Connolly, 'A Woman's Life in mid-eighteenth-century Ireland: the Case of Letitia Bushe', in *Historical Journal*, 43/2 (2000): 433, 443.

14 Account of Carrickfergus and Antrim, 1683 (TCD, Ms 883/1: 199, 200, 206); 'A Description of the Town and County of Carrickfergus': 332; McSkimin, *History of Carrickfergus, 1811*: 40–1; Pinkerton, 'The "Pallace" of Carrickfergus': 1.

15 Deposition of Hugh Wilson, 10 Mar. 1711 (TCD, Ms 883/2: 278).

16 For eighteenth-century witchcraft book-owning (and presumably reading) Protestants, including Church of Ireland clergymen: Sneddon, *Witchcraft and Magic in Ireland*: 22–3, 106; Stuart Clark, 'Satanic Libraries: Marsh's Witchcraft Books' in, Muriel McCarthy and Ann Simmons (eds), *The Making of Marsh's Library: Learning, Politics and Religion in Ireland, 1650–1750* (Dublin, 2004): 99–116.

17 Wilson Deposition (TCD, Ms 883/2: 278).

18 Wilson and Lennan Depositions (TCD, Ms 883/2: 277–9).

19 Wilson Deposition (TCD, Ms 883/2: 278).
20 Almond, *Demonic Possession*: 33.
21 These women would later be accused of bewitching Mary Dunbar, see chapter 7.
22 This is the first mention of Mr Campbell, whom Dixon Donaldson refers to as John Campbell: Donaldson, *History of Islandmagee*: 46.

Chapter 6

1 Levack, *Devil Within*: 133–34.
2 C. L'Estange Ewen, *Witchcraft and Demonianism* … (London, 1933): 375.
3 See: Andrew Pickering, 'Great News from the West of England: Witchcraft and Strange Vomiting in a Somerset Village', in *Magic, Ritual, and Witchcraft*, 13/1 (2018): 71–97.
4 Sands, *Demon Possession in Elizabethan England*: 18.
5 Sharpe, *Instruments of Darkness*: 223.
6 'The Life of Mr Robert Blair, Minister of St Andrews, Containing his Autobiography, from 1593 to 1636', Thomas McCrie (ed.) (Dublin, 1848): 89; Thomas Witherow, *Historical and Literary Memorials of Presbyterianism in Ireland* (London and Belfast, 1879): 7–10.
7 Levack, *Devil Within*: 129–30.
8 Ibid., 117.
9 Sir Thomas Browne, 'Religio Medici', 1642, Robin Robbins (ed.) (Oxford, 1972): 32–3.
10 Transcript of Commonwealth Papers, 9 Feb., 15 Nov. 1656 (Allen Library, Dublin, Jennings Ms J2/Box 263, item 14).
11 Browne, 'Religio Medici': 32.
12 Anon., *Saddicismus Debellatus, or True Narrative … Christian Shaw*: 2–3, 41.
13 *OSMI*, x: 31.
14 Levack, *Devil Within*: 147–53 (quotes at 147–48).
15 Richard Baddeley, *The Boy of Bilson* … (London, 1622): 45–75; Hutchinson, *Historical Essay*: 217–24.
16 Hutchinson, *Historical Essay*: 46. No mention is made of this case in *The Proceedings of the Old Bailey, 1674–1913*, www.oldbaileyonline.org/ [last accessed June 2023].
17 Anon., *The Tryal of Richard Hathaway Upon an Information for Being a Cheat and Imposter* … (London, 1702): 1–30; C. L'Estrange Ewen, *Witch-hunting and Witch Trials: the Indictments for Witchcraft from the Records of 1313 Assizes held for the Home circuit, 1559–1736* (New York, 1929): 264–5; Knights, *Devil in Disguise*: 217–9: there seems to be no contemporary evidence to back up the assertion (219) that Morduck was tried twice for bewitching Richard Hathaway.
18 For this case: P.G. Maxwell Stuart, *Witch-hunters: Professional Prickers, Unbewitchers and Witch Finders of the Renaissance* (Stroud, 2003, repr., 2006): 104–5, 116–8; Levack, *Witch-hunting in Scotland*: 120, 145–58.
19 Almond, *Demonic Possession*: 40.

20 Margaret Murdoch and Margaret Laird accused more than twenty people of their bewitchment: Levack, *Witch-hunting in Scotland*: 116–21. For a discussion of the William Sommers case in its political, cultural and religious context: Marion Gibson, *Possession, Puritanism and Print: Darrell, Harsnett, Shakespeare and the Elizabethan Exorcism Controversy* (London, 2006): 72–101.
21 Phillip Almond lists Shakespeare's plays that deal with possession as: *King Lear* (Act 4, Scene 1; Act 4, Scene 6); *Twelfth Night* (Act 3, Scene 4; Act 4, Scene 2); *Comedy of Errors* (Act 4, Scene 4); Almond, *Demonic Possession*: 41n.316.
22 *The Survey of Scottish Witchcraft, 1563–1736,* witches.hca.ed.ac.uk [last accessed June 2023].
23 Higgs, *Wonderful True Relation*: 6.
24 Sir William Aston's transcript (RS, Boyle papers, RB 1/37/5, f 97r).
25 Samuel Molyneux to Thomas Molyneux, 14 May 1711 (TCD, Ms 889, f.31v.)
26 Sir William Aston's transcript 1661 (RS, RB 1/37/5, ff 101v–102r [quotes at f.101v]).
27 Richard Godbeer, *The Devil's Dominion, Magic and Religion in Early New England* (Cambridge, 1992): 181–2.
28 Tisdall, 'Account of the Trial': 48.
29 Thomas Heywood, *Gunaikeion: or, Nine Bookes of Various History Concerninge Women* ... (2nd ed., London, 1624): 399.
30 John M. Theilman, 'Disease or Disability: the Conceptual Relationship in Medieval and Early Modern England', in Wendy J. Turner and Tory Vandeventer Pearman (eds), *The Treatment of Disabled Persons in Medieval Europe* ... (Lewiston, New York, 2010): 225.
31 Katie Barclay, 'Performing Emotion and Reading the Male Body in the Irish Court, c. 1800–1845', in *Journal of Social History*, 51/2 (2017): 293.
32 Thomas, *Religion and Decline of Magic*: 480.

Chapter 7

1 'Life of Mr Robert Blair': 89; Witherow, *Historical and Literary Memorials of Presbyterianism*: 7–10.
2 Meaning that it contained a frill or decorative trim.
3 Deposition of John Smith, of Larne, 14 Mar. 1711 (TCD, Samuel Molyneux Papers, Ms 883/2: 276). This testimony was given to Mayor Edward Clements in Carrickfergus.
4 Porter, *Witches, Warlocks, and Ghosts*: 8.
5 Deposition of Mary Dunbar, 12 Mar. 1711 (TCD, Samuel Molyneux Papers, Ms 883/2: 274–6).
6 Janet Carson, Janet Liston, Elizabeth Sellor, Janet Main, Catherine McCalmond, and Janet Latimer.
7 Dunbar Deposition, 12 Mar. 1711 (TCD, Ms 883/2: 275).
8 Ibid., 274–5.

9   Dunbar Deposition, 12 Mar. 1711 (TCD, Ms 883/2: 275–6).
10 Gillespie, "Into Another Intensity", Prayer in Irish Non-conformity': 47.
11 Dunbar Deposition, 12 Mar. 1711 (TCD Ms 883/2: 275).
12 James Stannus took over this apparently substantial house in the late seventeenth or early eighteenth century, from Nicholas Netterville, see: Classon Porter, *Congregational Memoirs of the Old Presbyterian Congregation of Larne and Kilwaughter* (Larne, 1929): 46n.
13 Donaldson, *History of Islandmagee*: 46.
14 Porter, *Congregational Memoirs of Larne*: 21, 45, 48.
15 Anon., *A Brief Narration of the Possession, Dispossession and Re-possession of William Sommers*: 260.
16 Anon, *The Most Strange and Admirable Discovery of the Three Witches of Warboys*: 82–3.
17 The following episode is also described in John Smith's deposition, 14 Mar. 1711 (TCD, Ms 883/2: 276–7).
18 Deposition of Bryce Blan, constable, 14 Mar. 1711 (TCD, Samuel Molyneux Papers, Ms 883/2: 277).
19 Francis Bragge, *A Full and Impartial Account of the Discovery of Sorcery and Witchcraft Practis'd by Jane Wenham of Walkerne in Hertfordshire* … (London, 2nd edn, 1712): 22; Knights, *Devil in Disguise*: 226–7.
20 Sir William Aston's transcript 1661 (RS, RB 1/37/5, ff 98r–98v [quotes at f.98v]).
21 See: David Dobson, *Scottish-Irish Links, 1575–1725, part 3* (Baltimore, Maryland, 2001, repr. 2003): 70.
22 Tisdall, 'Account of the Trial': 48.
23 Tisdall, 'Account of the Trial': 49. This account of the incident differs slightly from the anonymous pamphlet account, in that it states the head-dress 'had also seven double knots and one single one', instead of seven knots.
24 Porter, *Congregational Memoir of Larne*: 45; Fred Rankin (ed.), *Clergy of Down and Dromore* (Belfast): part II, 95, 195.
25 Tisdall, 'Account of the Trial': 49. A similar type of charm was used in another possession case in early eighteenth-century England: Anon., *Tryal of Richard Hathaway*: 15–6.
26 See Owen Davies, *Popular Magic in English History* (London, 2003, repr. 2007), chapter 6.
27 This could have been Roman Catholic clergyman Edmond Moore, whose ecclesiastical charges, in the early eighteenth century, encompassed the Larne area: J. O'Laverty, *An Historical Account of Diocese of Down and Connor, Ancient and Modern* (5 vols, Dublin, 1878-95), iii, 109–10.
28 These terms are listed in: Richard, Jenkins, 'The Transformations of Biddy Early: from Local Reports of Magical Healing to Globalised New Age Fantasy', in *Folklore*, 118/2 (2007): 162–82.
29 Sneddon, *Representing Magic*: 8.
30 Anon., *An Excellent New Ballad* (Dublin, 1726).
31 Sir William Aston's transcript 1661 (RS, RB 1/37/5, ff 97v, 99v).
32 Cited in, Ehrenpreis, *Swift, the Man, his Works, volume 1*: 160; Louis A. Landa, *Swift and the Church of Ireland* (Oxford, 1954): 18.

33 Although this incident is related in the pamphlet account, John Smith also witnessed it; see his deposition, 21 Mar. 1711 (TCD, Ms 883/2: 274).

34 C. L'Estrange Ewen, *Witchcraft and Demonism*: 91, 92.

35 Tisdall, 'Account of the Trial': 49: 'The afflicted during one of her fits, was observed by several persons to slide off the bed in an unaccountable manner, and to be laid gently on the ground, as if supported and drawn invisibly. Upon her recovery, she told them the several persons who had drawn her in that manner, with an intention, as they told her, of bearing her out of the window, when open; but that, reflecting at the time, and calling upon God in her mind, they let her drop on the floor.'

36 Andrew Cambers, 'Demonic Possession, Literacy and "Superstition" in Early Modern England', in *Past and Present*, 202/1 (2009): 10.

37 Ordnance Survey Ireland, 6in coloured map of Ireland, 1829–41; *OSMI*, x, 28, 32, 68.

38 Straw and hay were kept in stacks in Hag-yards; also known as Haggards or Haggarts: *Dictionaries of the Scots Language*, dsl.ac.uk [last accessed May 2023].

39 James Haltridge gave a deposition to Mayor Clements on 24 March, during which he described events which occurred in previous days. It is thus to be presumed that he returned to Ulster at this time. See deposition of James Haltridge, 'of Island Magee, GENT', 24 Mar. 1711 (TCD, Samuel Molyneux Papers, Ms 883/2: 282–3).

40 The pamphlet account erroneously states that Sunday was 24 March, when internal evidence suggests that it was 25 March.

Chapter 8

1 'Jesus saith unto him, I am the way, the truth, and the life: no man cometh to the father, but by me.'

2 'And God saw that the wickedness of man was great in the earth, and that every imagination of the thoughts of his heart was only evil continually.'

3 *Records of the General Synod of Ulster, 1691–1820* (3 vols, Belfast, 1890), i, 190; 'Funeral Register of the First Presbyterian Church of Belfast, 1712–36', Jean Agnew (ed.) (Belfast, 1995): 20, 46–7.

4 Peter Elmer, *Witchcraft, Witch-Hunting, and Politics in Early Modern England* (Oxford, 2016): 294.

5 The third chapter describes God's speech to Moses, commanding him to confront the Egyptian Pharaoh in order to set the Jewish people free. It includes a description of the burning bush, which Mary Dunbar probably alludes to because it reflects her own struggle, in that she is burnt by the devilry of witches but not consumed by them. Moses in the thirteenth chapter informs his people that the first born belongs to and is consecrated by God, which Dunbar may be alluding to because she is the first born and thus consecrated to the Lord.

6 Anon., *A Tryal of Witches at the Assizes Held at Bury St Edmunds for the County of Suffolk; on the Tenth Day of March, 1664* ... (London, 1682): 14, 12.

7   *OSMI*, xiv: 21; County Antrim Grand Jury Presentments, Assizes, Carrickfergus, 27 Aug. 1712 (PRONI, ANT/4/1/1).

8   Garnham, *Courts, Crime and the Criminal Law*: 108.

9   County Antrim Grand Jury Presentments, Quarter Sessions, Carrickfergus, 12 Jul. 1716 (PRONI, ANT/4/1/1).

10   See: Garnham, *Courts, Crime and the Criminal Law*: 87–90.

11   *Dublin Intelligence*, 17 Feb. 1711.

12   Anon., *The Report of the Judges of the Assize for North-East Circuit of Ulster ... Depositions Annexe'd; and the Representation of the Grand Jury of the County of Antrim* (Dublin, 1716): 31–2.

13   'Grand Juries ... [are] generally composed of persons of the first rank, and best credit in their country': Richard Ashton, *Charge Given to the Grand Juries of the County of the City of Dublin ... Saturday the 3rd Day of December, 1763* (Dublin, 1763), sig. A3. See also: Garnham, *Courts, Crime and Criminal Law*, chapter 7.

14   The following is a list of the grand jury who gathered together on 23 April 1712, of which the first ten were present at the next session of the Assizes, held in late summer: Robert Green Esq., Paule Warring, Frank Mankin, Edw[ar]d Hall, Bryan O'Neill, Henry Mulhallen, Cornelius O'Cahane, Fortescue Dogherty, Rodger McCormicke, Edmund W[illiam]son', William Carter, Brent Spencer Esq., Arthur Mathews, Alex[ander] Acton, Val[entine] Jones, Ed[war]d Obrey, Allex[ander] Stewart; see County Antrim Grand Jury Presentments, Assizes, Carrickfergus, 23 Apr., 27 Aug. 1712 (PRONI, ANT/4/1/1). Robert Whan has suggested that most of these men were communicants of the Church of Ireland. This was not because of restrictions contained in the 1704 Test Act (which did not exclude Presbyterians from grand juries), but due to the fact they had been empanelled by high Tory Sheriffs. It is therefore possible that the grand jury of the previous year, 1711, may have contained more Presbyterians, as it had been empanelled by a Whig, Andrew Clements. See Whan, *Presbyterians in Ulster*: 220–1, 143.

15   'High Sheriffs of the County of Antrim', in *Ulster Journal of Archaeology*, 11/2 (1905): 80; Whan, *Presbyterians in Ulster*: 216–8.

16   Tisdall, 'Account of the Trial': 47.

17   Garnham, *Courts, Crime and the Criminal Law*: 244.

18   Tisdall, 'Account of the Trial': 47.

19   Ibid., 48.

20   Benjamin Bankhurst, 'The Politics of Dissenting Demography in Ireland, 1690–1735', in Nigel Aston, Benjamin Bankhurst (eds.), *Negotiating Toleration: Dissent and the Hanoverian Succession, 1714–1760* (Oxford, 2019): 171. For more on Tisdall: Hayton, *Ruling Ireland*: 202–3; Irvin Ehrenpreis, *Swift, the Man, his Age and his Works: volume two, Dr Swift* (London, 1967), ii, 120–30; Neal Garnham, *The Militia in Eighteenth-Century Ireland: In Defence of the Protestant Interest* (Woodbridge, 2012): 22, 26. See also chapter 9 below.

21   Garnham, *Courts, Crime and the Criminal Law*: 246.

22   Ibid., 49.

23   Tisdall, 'Account of the Trial': 47.

24 Ibid.
25 The pamphlet account lists these people as: 'John Smith, John Blair, James Blythe, the Rev. Mr W[illia]m Ogilvy, Rev. Mr [William] Skeffington, Mr W[illia]m Fenton, Mr W[illia]m Hately, Mr Cha[rle]s Lennon, John Wilson, Hugh Wilson, Mr Hugh Donaldson, James Hill, Mr James Haltridge, Mrs Haltridge, the Rev. Mr Patrick Adair, the Rev. Mr James Cobham, Patrick Ferguson, James Edmonston, Mr Jameson.'
26 Tisdall, 'Account of the Trial': 47.
27 Ibid., 48–9.
28 Tisdall, 'Account of the Trial': 49.
29 Ibid., 48.
30 Tisdall, 'Account of the Trial': 49.
31 Ibid., 49. Tisdall was probably referring to Janet Main.
32 Tisdall, 'Account of the Trial': 49.
33 Samuel to Thomas Molyneux, 14 May 1711 (TCD, Ms 889, ff 31r–31v).
34 Tisdall, 'Account of the Trial': 49.
35 Tisdall, 'Account of the Trial': 51: 'Neither do I see why a real witch may not have permission to personate a real saint, as well as the Devil has been permitted to personate an angel of light; or why a person in contract with the devil may not be guilty of this worse hypocrisy, which gives her apostacy a deeper dye; if, as a witch, she was deprived of her power of praying, and receiving the sacrament visibly, she must be deprived of this power either by the Devil or by God himself. It cannot be supposed that the Devil would hinder her from the basest and vilest acts of hypocrisy, or that God would interpose miraculously to deprive this wretch of her natural faculties, any more than he doth other profligate sinners who receive unworthily, and eat and drink their own damnation'.
36 Ibid., 50.
37 F.E. Ball, *The Judges in Ireland, 1221–1921* (New York, 2 vols, 1927): ii, 23, 66.
38 Tisdall, 'Account of the Trial': 50–1.
39 Anon., *The Tryal of Richard Hathaway*: 14, 22, 24, 13, 19, 24–7.
40 Tisdall, 'Account of the Trial': 50.
41 Ball, *Judges in Ireland*, ii, 37, 65.
42 Tisdall, 'Account of the Trial': 51.
43 *The Dublin Penny Journal*, 47/1 (18 May 1833). This story was first related in McSkimin, *History of Carrickfergus, 1823*: 74–5.

Chapter 9

1 Tisdall, 'Account of the Trial': 50–1.
2 Wendel D. Craker, 'Spectral Evidence, Non-Spectral Acts of Witchcraft, and Confession at Salem in 1692', in *The Historical Journal*, 40/2 (1997): 331–58 (quote at 349); Paul Boyer, Stephen Nissenbaum, *Salem Possessed: The Social Origins of Witchcraft* (London, 1974): 18.

3   List of Burgesses, 1706 (PRONI, List of Burgees and Freemen of Carrickfergus, D162/18); Ehrenpreis, *Swift, the Man, his Age and his Works*, ii: 134.

4   Hayton, *Ruling Ireland, 1685–1742*: 203.

5   For more on Tisdall: David Hayton, 'Presbyterians and the Confessional State: The Sacramental Test as an Issue in Irish Politics, 1704–1780', in *Bulletin of the Presbyterian Historical Society of Ireland*, 26 (1997): 16–8; Ehrenpreis, *Swift, the Man, his Age and his Works*, ii: 120–30, 134.

6   For a classic discussion of the development and passage through parliament of this landmark Penal Law: J.G. Simms, 'The Making of a Penal Law (2 Anne, c. 6)', in *Irish Historical Studies*, 12/46 (1961): 105–18.

7   For more on consequences of the Irish Test Act: Hayton, *Ruling Ireland*: 196–203; Whan, *Presbyterians in Ulster*: 216–9, 223–5; Garnham, *Militia*: 20.

8   For example, Chief Justice, Sir Richard Cox was 'pro-Hanoverian but fiercely anti-Whig': David Hayton, 'The Crisis in Ireland and the Disintegration of Queen Anne's Last Ministry', in *Irish Historical Studies*, 22/87 (1981): 206.

9   Robert Howard, *A Sermon Preached in Christ-Church, Dublin ... October 23d, 1722 ...* (Dublin, 1722): 25.

10 William Tisdall, *A Sample of True-Blew Presbyterian Loyalty ...* (Dublin, 1709): 3–4; idem., *The Conduct of the Dissenters of Ireland, with Respect both to Church and State ...* (Dublin, 1712): 32–3; McSkimin, *History of Carrickfergus, 1823*: 75–6. For a similar royal address containing Tory overtones and delivered to Queen Anne in 1712, see *Post Boy, London*, 2–4 Oct. 1712.

11 McSkimin, *History of Carrickfergus, 1823*: 77. This could be the same Edward Mathews who was born in England in 1681, educated at Trinity College, Dublin, held various positions in the Diocese of Down and Connor, and died in January 1755: Leslie, *Clergy of Connor*: 490.

12 Matthew French, *Of Submission to the Supreme and Subordinate Magistrates. A Sermons Preach'd at the Assizes Held at Carrickfergus for the County of Antrim, the 23rd of April, 1712 ...* (Dublin, 1712); Hayton, *Ruling Ireland*: 202–3.

13 Edward Mathews, *The Divine Original of Civil Government: a Sermon Preached at the Assizes Held at Carrickfergus, for the county of Antrim, the 17th of July 1713* (Dublin, 1714): 11–2, 14–6, 26; Hayton, *Ruling Ireland*: 202–3; E.M. Johnston-Liik, *History of the Irish Parliament, 1692–1800: Commons, Constituencies and Statutes* (6 vols, Belfast 2002), iv, 18.

14 *The Journals of the House of Commons for the Kingdom of Ireland ...* (Dublin, 19 vols, 1796–1800), iii, appendix, vii-ix; *London Gazette*, 27 Apr.–1 May 1714.

15 McSkimin, *History of Carrickfergus, 1823*: 77.

16 This address was reproduced verbatim in: *Belfast News Letter*, 30 Nov.–4 Dec. 1792.

17 Ball, *Judges in Ireland*, ii, 17, 23, 27, 51–2, 65–6, 93, 106.

18 Bishop Francis Hutchinson to Sir Hans Sloane, 3 Apr. 1712 (British Library, Sloane MS 4043, f. 38); Hutchinson, *Historical Essay*: 129–35.

Chapter 10

1   Tisdall, 'Account of the Trial': 47.
2   *The Islandmagee Witches*: 33; *Dublin Intelligence*, 11 Aug. 1711.
3   *Dublin Intelligence*, 11 Aug. 1711; Ball, *Judges in Ireland 1221–1921*: ii, 29, 56–7, 84, 87, 146–47; Johnston-Liik, *History of the Irish Parliament*, v, 89–91.
4   *Dublin Intelligence,* 24 Apr. 1711.
5   Almond, *Demonic Possession:* 42
6   Robert Walinski-Kiehl, 'Males, "Masculine Honour," and Witch Hunting in Seventeenth-Century Germany', in *Men and Masculinities*, 6/3 (2004): 265.
7   Malcolm Gaskill, 'Masculinity and Witchcraft in Seventeenth-Century England', in Alison Rowlands (ed.), *Witchcraft and Masculinities in Early Modern Europe* (Basingstoke, 2009): 182.
8   'Jolly Bachelors' is a reference to an English ballad, *The Thankful Country Lass*, or, *The Jolly Batchelor Kindly Entertained* (London, 1684–1700?), which was often sung to the tune of 'Aye, Marry, and Thank You Too': *English Broadside Ballad Archive* (ebba. english.ucsb.edu/ballad/22217/citation) [last accessed 15 Feb. 2024].

Chapter 11

1   Andrew Sneddon, John Fulton, 'Witchcraft, the Press, and Crime in Ireland, 1822–1922', in *Historical Journal*, 62/3 (2019): 754.
2   *Belfast News Letter*, 9 June 1870.
3   Sneddon, Fulton, 'Witchcraft, the Press, and Crime': 757–8
4   *Anglo-Celt*, 9 Jan. 1851.
5   *Nenagh Guardian,* 9 Oct. 1895; Sneddon, Fulton, 'Witchcraft, the Press, and Crime': 759.
6   *OSMI*, x: 40.
7   Akenson, *Two Revolutions*: 88–9, 135–7, 142–3.
8   *OSMI*, x: 62–3, 67; Jeanne Cooper Foster, *Ulster Folklore* (Belfast, 1951): 90; Akenson, *Two Revolutions*: 54–5, 135–6, 143. For witch-stones: Ralph Merrifield, *The Archaeology of Ritual and Magic* (London, 1987): 161–2; J.G. Dent, 'The Witch-stone in Ulster and England', in *Ulster Folklife,* 10 (1964): 46–8.
9   *Ulster Folk and Transport Museum* (UFTM), Collection Number 186.1972, 'Witch-stone originally hung in a byre in Islandmagee', E.N. (donator), 1972; UFTM, Collection Number 563.1972, 'Witch-stone from Gransha, Islandmagee', A.W.J. (donator), 1972.
10 UFTM, 63/Q2b/0056, E.F., 'Completed folklore questionnaire on Witch-stones, Islandmagee', 1963.
11 UFTM 63/Q2b/0014, E.L.M., 'Completed folklore questionnaire on Witch-stones, Islandmagee', 1963.
12 *Belfast News Letter*, 18 Sept. 1876; Sneddon, 'Witchcraft Belief, Representation and Memory': 255–7.

13 Donaldson, *History of Islandmagee*: 48; *Ordnance Survey of Northern Ireland* (OSNI) Historical Maps, First Edition (1832–46), PRONI historical map viewer, www. nidirect.gov.uk/services/search-proni-historical-maps-viewer [last accessed 13 March 2024].

14 Donaldson, *History of Islandmagee*: 48.

15 'Family Footsteps', BBC1 NI/ Waddell Media. Series 2, episode 3. First broadcast 2 Nov. 2019.

16 Sneddon, *Representing Magic*: 26–45 (quotation at 38).

17 Of the twenty-six newspaper articles detailing the Islandmagee witch trials written between the mid-nineteenth and late twentieth century, most were published in the north of Ireland in newspapers such as the *Northern Whig*, *Ballymena Observer*, and *Larne Times*. The following is based on: Sneddon, 'Witchcraft Representation and Memory in Modern Ireland'; idem., *Representing Magic*: 47–51.

18 *Larne Times*, 23 July 1910.

19 M.T. Pender, 'The Irish Rapparees or the Jackets Green: A Tale of the Brave Days of Old', *Dundalk Democrat*, 27 Dec. 1913. For Pender's obituary: *Irish Independent*, 19 Mar. 1920.

20 Olga Fielden, *Witches in Eden*, in Patricia O'Connor (ed.), *Four New One-Act Plays* (Belfast, 1948): 7–25. For Fielden: Naomi Doak, 'Ulster Protestant Women Authors: Olga Fielden's Island Story', in *Irish Studies Review*, 15/1 (2007): 37.

21 *Ballymena Observer*, 5 Nov. 1948.

22 *Larne Times*, 1 Mar. 1951.

23 *Northern Whig*, 8 Mar. 1951.

24 *Belfast Telegraph*, 2 Feb. 1975.

25 Fielden, 'Witches in Eden', (quotation at 10); Sneddon, *Representing Magic*: 54–9.

26 See: Adrian Rice, 'Margaret Mitchell', in *The Mason's Tongue* (Belfast, 1999); Martina Devlin, *The House Where It Happened* (Dublin, 2014, repr. 2015); Sarah Sheil, 'The Revelry of Janet & Patrick Sellor', ink drawing on paper (2016).

Further Reading

Reference Works

Dictionary of Irish Biography, Irish Royal Academy, www.dib.ie/index.php/about.

Oxford Dictionary of National Biography (online ed.), Oxford University Press, www.oxforddnb.com.

Richard M. Golden (ed.), *Encyclopedia of Witchcraft: The Western Tradition* (4 vols, Santa Barbara, 2006).

Chapter 1

For an excellent summary of political, economic, religious, and social conditions in eighteenth-century Ireland, see: S.J. Connolly, *Divided Kingdom, Ireland 1630–1800* (Oxford, 2008). A number of good overviews of Ulster (including dedicated studies of Belfast) in this period have also been produced, see: Raymond Gillespie, *Early Belfast: The Origins and Growth of an Ulster Town to 1750* (Belfast, 2007), chapter 5; Raymond Gillespie, 'Making Belfast, 1600–1750', in S.J. Connolly (ed.), *Belfast 400: People, Place and History* (Liverpool, 2012): 123–61; A.T.Q. Stewart, *The Narrow Ground: Roots of Conflict in Ulster* (2nd ed., 1989), part 2; Jonathan Bardon, *A History of Ulster* (Belfast, 2nd ed., 2005), chapter 6; David Kennedy, 'The Early Eighteenth Century', in J.C. Beckett and R.E. Glascock (eds), *Belfast: The Origin and Growth of an Industrial City* (Belfast, 1967): 39–54; W.A. Maguire, *Belfast* (Keele, 1993), chapter 1; Jean Agnew, *Belfast Merchant Families in the Seventeenth-Century* (Dublin, 1996), chapters 1–4; D.W. Hayton, *Ruling Ireland, 1685–1742: Politics, Politicians and Parties* (Suffolk, 2004), especially chapters 2, 4, 5. The religious culture of Presbyterian women, along with domestic service in Ireland in general, is discussed in Mary O'Dowd, *A History of Women in Ireland, 1500–1800* (Harlow, 2005): 134–8. For a review of recent literature on Protestant Dissent in Ireland, in particular Ulster Presbyterianism, see 'Further Reading' section for chapters 2 and 3. Of particular use in this chapter were contributions by Robert Armstrong, Benjamin Bankhurst, Lauren Bell and Robert Whan, which explore the ecclesiastical, social, and cultural dimensions of Ulster Presbyterianism.

For Islandmagee, Dixon Donaldson, *History of Islandmagee* (Islandmagee, 1927, repr. 2002) and Donald Harmon Akenson, *Between Two Revolutions: Islandmagee County Antrim, 1798–1920* (Ontario, 1979). For earlier treatments of the Islandmagee witchcraft trial, see preface for first edition and chapter 11. For belief in witchcraft, see Further Reading for chapter 4.

For accessible studies of ghosts in British culture, art and literature: Roger Clarke, *A Natural History Ghosts: 500 Years of Hunting for Proof* (London, 2012), and Susan Owens, *The Ghost: A Cultural History* (London, 2017, repr. 2019). For a readable study that explores how poltergeist phenomena have been almost constantly reinterpreted during the last 1,500 years: P.G. Maxwell-Stuart, *Poltergeists: A History of Violent Ghostly Phenomena* (Stroud, 2011). For more academic studies of how ghost beliefs and stories were interwoven with, and often reflected, the political, social, religious, and gender concerns of their day: Keith Thomas, *Religion and the Decline of Magic: Studies in Popular Beliefs in Sixteenth- and Seventeenth-Century England* (London, 1971, repr. 1978): 587–601; Darren Oldridge, *The Supernatural in Tudor and Stuart England* (London: Routledge, 2016), chapter 6; Peter Marshall, *Mother Leakey & the Bishop: A Ghost Story* (Oxford, 2007, repr. 2008): 1–7, 42–52; Sasha Handley, *Visions of an Unseen World: Ghost Beliefs and Ghost Stories in Eighteenth-Century England* (London, 2007); Laura Gowing, 'The Haunting of Susan Lay: Servants and Mistresses in Seventeenth-Century England', in *Gender & History*, 14/2 (2002): 183–201; Jo Bath, and John Newton, '"Sensible Proof of Spirits": Ghost Belief during the Later Seventeenth Century', in *Folklore*, 117/1 (2006): 1–14. Irish ghosts are yet to receive the same level of attention and most work has been carried out on the modern period: Raymond Gillespie, *Devoted People: Belief and Religion in Early Modern Ireland* (Manchester, 1997), 110–4; Clodagh Tait, 'Worry Work: The Supernatural Labours of Living and Dead Mothers in Irish Folklore', in *Past & Present*, 246/15 (2020): 217–38; idem., 'Phantoms in and of the Archive: Mary Cudmore's Encounters with a Ghost in Cork in 1688 and 1689', in *The Historical Journal*, published online (2024): 1–23; Shane McCorristine, 'Science and Spiritualism in an Irish Context: The Psychical Research Networks of William Fletcher Barrett', in *Aries – Journal for the Study of Western Esotericism*, 22 (2022): 89–113; Anne O'Connor, 'Beyond Cradle and Grave: Irish Folklore About the Spirits of Unbaptized Infants and the Spirits of Women who Murdered Babies', in Elaine Farrell (ed.), *'She Said she was in the Family Way': Pregnancy and Infancy in Modern Ireland* (London, 2012): 223–38.

For studies of Satan, demons, and Hell in the early modern period: Darren Oldridge, *The Devil in Early Modern England* (2000); Thomas, *Religion and the Decline of Magic*; Phillip C. Almond, *Heaven and Hell in Enlightenment England* (Cambridge, 1994, repr. 2008); idem., *The Devil: A New Biography* (Ithaca, 2014), chapters 5–7; Michelle D. Brock, Richard Raiswell, David R. Winter (eds), *Knowing Demons, Knowing Spirits in the Early Modern Period* (London, 2018); Nathan Johnstone, *The Devil and Demonism in Early Modern England* (Cambridge, 2006); D.P. Walker, *The Decline of Hell: Seventeenth-Century Discussions of Eternal Torment* (London, 1964); Joyce Miller, 'Beliefs, Religions, Fears and Neuroses', in

Elizabeth Foyster and Christopher A. Whatley (eds), *A History of Everyday Life in Scotland, 1600 to 1800* (Edinburgh, 2010): 243–8; idem., *Magic and Witchcraft in Scotland* (Musselburgh, 2004): 86–9; idem., 'Men in Black: Appearances of the Devil in Early Modern Scottish Witchcraft Discourse', in Julian Goodare, Lauren Martin and Joyce Miller (eds), *Witchcraft and Belief in Early Modern Scotland* (Basingstoke, 2008): 144–65.

The increasingly expansive literature of demonic possession is covered in the next section, but for a useful definition of demonic obsession, see P.G. Maxwell-Stuart, *Witch-Hunters* (Stroud, 2006): 103–4, and Barbara Rosen, *Witchcraft in England, 1558–1618* (Massachusetts, 1969, repr. 1991): 227; Brian P. Levack, *The Devil Within: Possession & Exorcism in the Christian West* (London, 2013): 16–7.

Chapter 2

For general treatments of demonic possession and exorcism, on which I have drawn heavily, Levack, *Devil Within*; Francis Young, *A History of Anglican Exorcism: Deliverance and Demonology in Church Ritual* (London, 2018), chapters 4–5; Philip C. Almond, *The Devil: A New Biography* (Ithaca, 2014), chapter 7; idem., *Demonic Possession and Exorcism in Early Modern England: Contemporary Texts and their Cultural Contexts* (Cambridge, 2004); Thomas, *Religion and the Decline of Magic*: 477–92; James Sharpe, *Instruments of Darkness: Witchcraft in Early Modern England* (Philadelphia, 1996), chapter 8; Kathleen R. Sands, *Demon Possession in Elizabethan England* (London, 2004). For demonic possession and gender, see Sarah Ferber, 'Possession and the Sexes', in Alison Rowlands (ed.), *Witchcraft and Masculinities in Early Modern Europe* (Basingstoke, 2009): 214–38.

For notable witchcraft trials involving demonic possession, see: James Sharpe, *The Bewitching of Anne Gunter: A Horrible and True Story of Football, Witchcraft, Murder and the King of England* (London, 1999); Ivan Bunn, Gilbert Geis, *A Trial of Witches: A Seventeenth-Century Witchcraft Prosecution* (London, 1997); Phillip C. Almond, *Witches of Warboys: An Extraordinary Story of Sorcery, Sadism and Satanic Possession* (London, 2008). For the trial of Jane Wenham see: P.J. Guskin, 'The Context of Witchcraft: The Case of Jane Wenham (1712)', in *Eighteenth-Century Studies*, 15/1 (1981): 48–71, Mark Knights, *The Devil in Disguise: Deception, Delusion and Fanaticism in the English Early Enlightenment* (Oxford, 2011), chapter 6; and Ian Bostridge, *Witchcraft and its Transformations* (Oxford, 1997): 132–8, 143–4. Brian Levack discusses the late onset of demonic possession in Scotland and places it within the British Calvinist network, *Witch-Hunting in Scotland: Law, Politics and Religion* (Abingdon, 2008), chapter 7. For demonic possession, exorcism and witchcraft in Ireland: Mary McAuliffe, 'Gender, History and Witchcraft in Early Modern Ireland: a Re-Reading of the Florence Newton Trial', in Maryann Gialenella Valiulis (ed.), *Gender and Power in Irish History* (Dublin, 2009): 39–58; Andrew Sneddon, 'Medicine, Belief, Witchcraft and Demonic Possession in late Seventeenth-Century Ulster', in *Medical Humanities*, 42/2 (2016): 1–6; idem., *Witchcraft and Magic in Ireland*, chapters 4–5; idem., 'Select Document: Florence Newton's Trial for Witchcraft, Cork, 1661: Sir William Aston's Transcript', in *Irish Historical Studies*, 43/169 (2019): 298–319.

For a discussion of how witchcraft writers dealt with possession, see Stuart Clark, *Thinking with Demons: The Idea of Witchcraft in Early Modern Europe* (Oxford, 1997), chapters 26–28, and Clive Holmes, 'Witchcraft and Possession at the Accession of James I: The Publication of Samuel Harsnett's A Declaration of Egregious Popish Impostures', in John Newton and Jo Bath, *Witchcraft and the Act of 1604* (Leiden, 2008): 69–90. For demonic possession and adolescence, see James Sharpe, 'Disruption in the Well-Ordered Household: Age, Authority and Possessed Young People', in Paul Griffiths, Adam Fox and Steve Hindle (eds), *The Experience of Authority in Early Modern England* (London, 1996): 187–212. Demonic possession on the Continent is covered in a number of works, see: Daniel Walker, *Unclean Spirits: Possession and Exorcism in France and England in the late Sixteenth and early Seventeenth Centuries* (Philadelphia, 1981); Michelle Marshman, 'Exorcism as Empowerment: A New Idiom', in *The Journal of Religious History*, 23/3 (1999): 265–81; Sarah Ferber, *Demonic Possession and Exorcism in Early Modern France* (Abingdon, 2004); Francis Young, *A History of Exorcism in Catholic Christianity* (London, 2016); Michel de Certeau, *The Possession at Loudun* (1970, trans. English, 2000); C. Erik Midelfort, *Exorcism and Enlightenment: Johann Joseph Gassner and the Demons of Eighteenth-Century Germany* (New Haven, Conn: 2005).

The Salem witch-hunt has a large historiography. A good starting point would be: Stacy Schiff, *The Witches Salem, 1692: A History* (London, 2015); or, John Putnam Demos, *Entertaining Satan, Witchcraft and the Culture of Early Modern New England* (Oxford, 1982). For an exploration of the social tensions and conflict underpinning the Salem trials, see: Paul Boyer and Stephen Nissenbaum, *Salem Possessed: The Social Origins of Witchcraft* (Cambridge, Massachusetts, 1974). For an examination of the relationship between Salem and political and economic crisis, see: Richard Godbeer, *The Devil's Dominion, Magic and Religion in Early New England* (Cambridge, 1992). The gender aspect of Salem is examined in Carol F. Karlsen, *The Devil in a Shape of a Woman: Witchcraft in Colonial New England* (New York, 1989). Poppets are discussed in Godbeer, *The Devil's Dominion*: 39.

Little research has been done on the small group of people who made up the Presbyterian gentry in Ireland in the early eighteenth century, but the best study to date is: Robert Whan, 'Presbyterians in Ulster, 1680–1730: A Social and Political Study' (unpublished PhD thesis, Queen's University, Belfast, 2009), chapter 2. The thesis was subsequently published as: Robert Whan, *The Presbyterians of Ulster, 1680–1730* (Woodbridge, 2013).

Chapter 3

For reading on demonic possession see Further Reading section for chapter 2, especially Brian Levack's work on Scotland. The best description of the role of JPs in the early modern Irish criminal justice system is in Neal Garnham, *The Courts, Crime and the Criminal Law in Ireland, 1692–1760* (Dublin, 1996): 33–4. Presbyterianism in their coverage can be found in: Benjamin Bankhurst, 'The Politics of Dissenting Demography in Ireland, 1690–1735', in Nigel Aston, Benjamin Bankhurst (eds.), *Negotiating Toleration: Dissent and the Hanoverian Succession, 1714–1760* (Oxford, 2019): 168–90; Toby Barnard, 'Enforcing the Reformation in Ireland, 1660–1704', in Elizabethanne Boran and Crawford Gribben (eds),

Enforcing Reformation in Ireland and Scotland, 1550–1700 (Manchester, 2006): 202–27; Phil Kilroy, *Protestant Dissent and Controversy, 1660–1714* (Cork, 1994); S.J. Connolly, *Religion, Law and Power: The Making of Protestant Ireland* (Oxford, 1992), chapter 5; idem., *Divided Kingdom*, chapters 5 and 7; Kevin Herlihy (ed.), *Propagating the Word of Irish Dissent 1650–1800* (Dublin, 1998); idem., *The Politics of Irish Dissent, 1650–1800* (Dublin, 1997); idem., *The Religion of Irish Dissent, 1650–1800* (Dublin, 1997). For a classic study of how the Church and state in England dealt with the problem of dissent, see J.C. Beckett, *Protestant Dissent in Ireland, 1687–1780* (1948, repr., London, 2008). For a study that re-maps and recontextualises the contours and complexities of Scottish migration to Ulster in the mid-1690s: Lauren Bell, 'The Great Scottish Migration to Ulster in the 1690s' (Unpublished PhD thesis, Ulster University, 2022). For readable overviews of Presbyterianism in Ireland and Ulster in the late seventeenth and early eighteenth centuries, see Raymond Gillespie, 'The Presbyterian Revolution in Ulster', in W.J. Sheils and Diane Wood (eds), *The Churches and the Irish: Studies in Church History*, 25 (Oxford, 1989): 159–70; Whan, 'Presbyterians in Ulster, 1680-1730'; Robert Armstrong, 'Of Stories and Sermons: Nationality and Spirituality in the later Seventeenth-Century', in Tadhg Ó hAnnracháin, Robert Armstrong (eds), *Community in Early Modern Ireland* (Dublin, 2006): 215–31.

For pioneering research on sexuality, gender, and family in eighteenth- and nineteenth-century Presbyterian Ulster see the work of Leanne Calvert, including: Leanne Calvert, '"From a Woman's Point of View": the Presbyterian Archive as a Source for Women's and Gender History in Eighteenth- and Nineteenth-century Ireland', in *Irish Historical Studies*, 46/170 (2022): 301–18; idem., '"To Recover his Reputation Among the People of God": Sex, Religion and the Double Standard in Presbyterian Ireland, c.1700–1838', in *Gender & History*, 35/3 (2022): 898–915; idem., '"Her Husband Went Away Some Time Agoe": Marriage Breakdown in Presbyterian Ulster, c.1690–1830', in *Women's History*, 2/15 (2020): 6–13; idem., '"He Came to her Bed Pretending Courtship": Sex, Courtship and the Making of Marriage in Ulster, 1750-1844', in *Irish Historical Studies*, 42/162 (2018): 244–64. For the clergy and witch-hunting in Scotland, see: Julian Goodare, 'Witch-Hunting and the Scottish State', in Julian Goodare (ed.), *The Scottish Witch-Hunt in Context* (Manchester, 2002): 139; Owen Davies, 'Decriminalising the Witch: The Origin and Response to the 1736 Witchcraft Act', in Bath and Newton, *Witchcraft and the Act of 1604*: 209–13; and P.G. Maxwell-Stuart, 'Witchcraft and Magic in Eighteenth-century Scotland', in Owen Davies and Willem De Blecourt, *Beyond the Witch Trials: Witchcraft and Magic in Enlightenment Europe* (Manchester, 2004): 81–100.

Chapter 4

The literature of early modern witchcraft is vast, and the following discussion is meant as a guide to important works on which this chapter has drawn. For general introductions to European witchcraft: Owen Davies (ed.), *The Oxford Illustrated History of Witchcraft and Magic* (Oxford, 2017); Marion Gibson, *Witchcraft: The Basics* (Abingdon, 2018); Malcolm Gaskill, *A Very Short Introduction to Witchcraft* (Oxford, 2010); Darren Oldridge (ed.),

The Witchcraft Reader (Abingdon, 2nd ed., 2008). For more in-depth and detailed, academic surveys of European witch-hunting: Jonathan Barry and Owen Davies (eds), *Witchcraft Historiography* (Basingstoke, 2007); Brian Levack (ed.), *The Oxford Handbook of Witchcraft in Early Modern Europe and Colonial America* (Oxford, 2013); idem., *The Witch-hunt in Early Modern Europe* (Edinburgh, 3rd ed., 2006); Julian Goodare, *The European Witch-hunt* (Abingdon, 2016); Ronald Hutton, *The Witch: The History of Fear, From Ancient Times to the Present* (London, 2017), chapter 7; Wolfgang Behringer, *Witches and Witch-hunts: a Global History* (Cambridge, 2004), chapter 4; Robin Briggs, *Witches and Neighbours: the Social and Cultural Context of Witchcraft* (Oxford, 2nd ed., 2002), chapters 4–6, 8; Bengt Ankarloo and Gustav Henningsen (eds), *Early Modern European Witchcraft: Centres and Peripheries* (Oxford, 1990).

The best study for the intellectual foundations of early modern witchcraft belief is Stuart Clark, *Thinking with Demons*. For a more readable account of demonological texts written in support of witch-hunting: James Sharpe, 'The Demonologists', in *Oxford Illustrated History of Witchcraft*: 65–96. For works that focus on demons, scepticism and demonology: Walter Stephens, 'The Sceptical Tradition', in *Oxford Handbook of Witchcraft*: 101–21; Brock, Raiswell, Winter, *Knowing Demons, Knowing Spirits in the Early Modern Period* (London, 2018); Jan Machielsen (ed), *The Science of Demons: Early Modern Authors Facing Witchcraft and the Devil* (Abingdon, 2020); Philip C. Almond, *England's First Demonologist: Reginald Scot and 'The Discoverie of Witchcraft'* (London, 2014). For demonology and the rise of the cumulative concept of malefic, demonic belief in the later Middle Ages: Johannes Dillinger (ed), *The Routledge History of Witchcraft* (Abingdon, 2020), chapters 4–5. For demonology and its relationship with witch-hunting in a European context: Julian Goodare, Rita Voltmer, and Liv Helene Willumsen (eds), *Demonology and Witch-Hunting in Early Modern Europe* (Abingdon, 2020).

For a discussion of the division of witchcraft culture into popular and elite traditions, see: Sharpe, *Instruments of Darkness*, chapters 1–2; Barry Reay, *Popular Culture in England, 1550–1750* (London, 1998): 115–9. This issue is placed within the context of a detailed discussion of the Lancaster witch trial of 1612, in: Phillip C. Almond, *The Lancashire Witches: A Chronicle of Sorcery and Death on Pendle Hill* (London, 2012), chapters 1, 3 and 5. Building on arguments first raised in *Instruments of Darkness*, James Sharpe has suggested that popular witchcraft pamphlets in England increasingly incorporated elements of elite, demonic witchcraft during the early modern period: 'English Witchcraft Pamphlets and the Popular Demonic', in *Demonology and Witch-hunting in Early Modern Europe*: 127–146. Based on an examination of sixty-six popular witch trial pamphlets (excluding possession cases), Charlotte-Rose Millar has argued for the centrality of the Devil (often in the form of a familiar spirit) in English popular witchcraft belief and highlighted the prominence of illicit sexual activity and Sabbat-type group meetings: *Witchcraft, the Devil, and Emotions in Early Modern England* (Abingdon, 2017). For more on familiar spirits in English witchcraft, see Sharpe, *Instruments of Darkness*: 71–4, 137, 283. Some historians have argued that the Devil's central presence in Scottish witchcraft trials was due to the fact that the Satanic formed an inherent part of peasant witch beliefs, while others suggest it was more likely to have been 'read' into evidence provided by victims, accusers and suspected witches by zealous interrogators: Stuart MacDonald, 'Enemies of God Re-visited: Recent Publications on Scottish Witchcraft', in *Scottish Economic and Social History*, 23/2 (2003): 65–84.

For a short, textbook introduction to English witchcraft, see: James Sharpe, *Witchcraft in Early Modern England* (Edinburgh, 2nd ed., 2019). For a short overview of the vast historiography of English witchcraft, see William Monter, 'Re-contextualizing British Witchcraft', in *Journal of Interdisciplinary History*, 35/1 (2004): 105–11. For the social tensions/charity-refused model of witchcraft, see Thomas, *Religion and the Decline of Magic*, chapter 17, and Alan Macfarlane, *Witchcraft in Tudor and Stuart England: a Regional and Comparative Study* (London, 1970). For research which problematises this model, suggesting that it was just one of the many contexts involving interpersonal conflict in which witchcraft accusation arose: Malcolm Gaskill, *Crime and Mentalities in Early Modern England* (Cambridge, 2002), chapters 1–2; idem., 'The Devil in the Shape of a Man: Witchcraft, Conflict and Belief in Jacobean England', in *Historical Research*, 71 (1998): 142–71; idem., 'Masculinity and Witchcraft in Seventeenth-century England', in Rowlands, *Witchcraft and Masculinities*; Jonathan Barry, Marianne Hester and Gareth Roberts (eds), *Witchcraft in Early Modern Europe: Studies in Culture and Belief* (Cambridge, 1996), chapters 1, 6, 9, 10. For the witch-hunts conducted by Matthew Hopkins and John Stearne in East Anglia during the English civil war in the 1640s: Scott Eaton, *John Stearne's Confirmation and Discovery of Witchcraft Text, Context and Afterlife* (Abingdon, 2020); Malcom Gaskill, *Witchfinders: a Seventeenth-Century English Tragedy* (London, 2006); James Sharpe, 'The Devil in East Anglia: the Matthew Hopkins Trials Reconsidered', in *Witchcraft in Early Modern Europe*: 237–54.

The problems of proving the crime of witchcraft are covered in: Malcolm Gaskill, 'Witchcraft and Evidence in Early-Modern England', in *Past and Present*, 198/1 (2008): 33–70. The best textbook on the early modern English legal system remains James Sharpe, *Crime in Early Modern England, 1550–1750* (2nd ed., 1998). For crime and the law in early modern Ireland, see Further Reading Section for chapter 8. For judicial scepticism: Knights, *Devil in Disguise*: chapter 6; Sharpe, *Instruments of Darkness*, chapter 9; Brian P. Levack, 'The Decline and End of Scottish Witch-Hunting', in Julian Goodare (ed.), *Scottish Witch-Hunts in Context* (Manchester, 2002): 166–81; idem., *Witch-Hunt in Early Modern Europe*: 253–64; Owen Davies, 'Decriminalising the Witch: the Origin and Response to the 1736 Witchcraft Act', in Jo Bath and John Newton (eds), *Witchcraft and the Act of 1604* (Leiden, 2008): 207–32; and Michael Hunter, *The Decline of Magic: Britain in the Enlightenment* (Padstow, 2020). For the role of politics in English witch trials, see Annabel Gregory, 'Witchcraft, Politics and "Good Neighbourhood" in Early Seventeenth-Century Rye', in *Past and Present*, 133/1 (1991): 31–66; idem., *Rye Spirits: Faith, Faction and Fairies in a Seventeenth Century English Town* (London, 2013). Peter Elmer has argued that the practice of witch-hunting, along with the idea of witchcraft itself, was shaped by England's ever changing, often tumultuous, political and religious landscape: *Witchcraft, Witch-Hunting, and Politics in Early Modern England* (Oxford, 2016): chapter 3 deals with the Hopkins trials. He has also suggested that witchcraft accusations were more likely to arise and be taken seriously by authorities at times of political crisis: Peter Elmer, 'Towards a Politics of Witchcraft in Early Modern England', in Stuart Clark (ed.), *Languages of Witchcraft: Narrative, Ideology and Meaning in Early Modern Culture* (Hampshire, 2001): 101–18.

For a good introduction to witchcraft in Scotland for the interested, general reader, see: Miller, *Magic and Witchcraft in Scotland*, and P.G. Maxwell-Stuart, *The Great Scottish Witch-Hunt* (Stroud, 2008). The work of Christina Larner remains the cornerstone of academic research into the subject: *Enemies of God: The Witch-hunt in Scotland* (Baltimore, MD, 1981), and idem., *Witchcraft and Religion: the Politics of Popular Belief* (Oxford, 1984). For how historians have built on Larner's legacy and reinterpreted her findings: MacDonald, 'Enemies of God Re-visited'. For an easy-to-read overview of Scottish witchcraft see, Brian P. Levack, *Witch-hunting in Scotland: Law, Politics and Religion* (Abingdon, 2008). Three collections of essays have also been fundamental to our current understanding of the subject: Goodare, *Scottish Witch-Hunts in Context*; idem., *Scottish Witches and Witch-Hunters* (Basingstoke, 2013); Goodare, Martin and Miller, *Witchcraft and Belief in Early Modern Scotland*. For witchcraft in Scotland in the later seventeenth and early eighteenth centuries: Lizanne Henderson, *Witchcraft and Folk Belief in the Age of Enlightenment: Scotland, 1670–1740* (Basingstoke, 2016). A database containing details of every recorded witchcraft trial in early modern Scotland has been constructed and is available free online: *The Survey of Scottish Witchcraft, 1563–1736*, witches.hca.ed.ac.uk. This data has been recently transferred to a more user-friendly interactive map: witches.is.ed.ac.uk.

For witchcraft in Gaelic-speaking regions of the British Isles and Ireland: Ronald Hutton, 'Witch-hunting in Celtic Societies', in *Past and Present*, 212/1 (2011): 43–71. An updated version of this article can be found in Hutton's *The Witch,* chapter 9. For a focused study of the Northern Highlands that builds on Hutton's argument concerning the lack of witch-hunting in Northern Scotland: Thomas Brochard, 'Scottish Witchcraft in a Regional and Northern European Context: The Northern Highlands, 1563–1660', in *Magic, Ritual, and Witchcraft*, 10/1 (2015): 41–74. For the Isle of Man, see James Sharpe 'Witchcraft in the Early Modern Isle of Man', in *Cultural and Social History*, 4/1 (2007): 9–20, and Ronald Hutton, 'The Changing Faces of Manx Witchcraft', in *Cultural and Social History*, 7/2 (2010): 153–69. The best studies of witchcraft and magic in early modern Wales are by Richard Suggett: 'Witchcraft Dynamics in Early Modern Wales', in Michael Roberts and Simone Clarke (eds), *Women and Gender in Early Modern Wales* (Cardiff, 2000), and *A History of Magic and Witchcraft in Wales* (Stroud, 2008): 84, 45–6, 99–100. See also Sally Parkin, 'Witchcraft, Women's Honour and Customary Law in Early Modern Wales', in *Social History*, 31/3 (2006): 295–318, and Lisa Mari Tallis, 'The Conjuror, the Fairy, the Devil and the Preacher: Witchcraft, Popular Magic and Religion in Wales 1700–1905' (Unpublished PhD thesis, University of Wales, Swansea, 2007).

The discussion of Irish witchcraft in this chapter is largely based on books and articles I have published during the last decade or so: Andrew Sneddon, 'Witchcraft Belief and Trials in Early Modern Ireland', in *Irish Economic and Social History,* 39 (2012): 1–25; idem., 'Medicine, Belief, Witchcraft and Demonic Possession in Late Seventeenth-Century Ulster': 81–6; idem., *Witchcraft and Magic in Ireland*; idem., 'Florence Newton's Trial for Witchcraft, Cork, 1661: Sir William Aston's Transcript'. This book has also drawn on the work of Ronald Hutton detailed above. For a pioneering article which tackled the question as to why Ireland escaped the worst excesses of the European witch-hunting: E.C. Lapoint, in 'Irish immunity to Witch-hunting, 1534–1711', in *Eire-Ireland*, 37 (1992): 76–92. Lapoint argues that the low prosecution rates in Ireland were because the mass of the population, the Catholic, Gaelic-Irish, refused to lodge witchcraft accusations with what were in essence English legal structures. Lapoint also argued that this community shared their malefic, demonic witchcraft beliefs with most parts of Britain and continental

Europe. Raymond Gillespie in 'Women and Crime in Seventeenth-Century Ireland', in Margaret MacCurtain and Mary O' Dowd (eds), *Women in Early Modern Ireland* (Edinburgh, 1991), argued that everyone in Ireland at that time believed in the same type of witches, whether Catholic or Protestant, but suggested there were no trials because the gender, social, and economic tensions that led to witchcraft accusations in England (outlined in the Macfarlane-Thomas charity refused model) were absent in Ireland. Gillespie in 'Ireland', in Golden, *Encyclopaedia of Witchcraft*, ii, 567–8, reiterates this argument, adding, as a caveat to Lapoint's thesis, that the Gaelic-Irish did indeed use English courts to settle disputes and some criminal matters.

Gillespie's *Devoted People: Belief and Religion in Early Modern Ireland* (Manchester, 1997), on the other hand, examines magic, witchcraft and supernatural belief in general from a holistic, non-denominational, religious perspective. S.J. Connolly's *Priests and People in Pre-famine Ireland, 1780–1845* (1982, repr. Dublin, 2001), chapter 3, is concerned with the nineteenth century but contains descriptions of Gaelic-Irish witchcraft and magical belief typical of the early modern period. Richard Jenkins, 'Witches and Fairies: Supernatural Aggression and Deviance among the Irish Peasantry', in *Ulster Folklife*, 23 (1977): 33–56, was one of the first articles to use folklore to explore Irish witchcraft and magic. See also, G. W. Saunderson, 'Butterwitches and Cow doctors', in *Ulster Folklife*, 7 (1961): 72–4, and J.G. Dent, 'The Witch-stone in Ulster and England', in *Ulster Folklife*, 10 (1964): 46–8. For literature and print in Irish written between the sixteenth and eighteenth centuries: Jane Ohlmeyer (ed), *The Cambridge History of Ireland, Volume II 1550–1730* (Cambridge, 2018, repr. 2020), chapters 16, 17; and Vincent Morley, *The Popular Mind in Eighteenth-Century Ireland* (Cork, 2017).

For an overview of gender and witchcraft, especially for those coming to it for the first time, see Oldridge, *Witchcraft Reader*, part seven; Raisa Maria Toivo, 'Witchcraft and Gender', in *Routledge History of Witchcraft*: 219–32; Garthine Walker, 'Witchcraft and History', in *Women's History Review*, 7/3 (1998): 425–32. The argument that women who failed to accept the standards of behaviour and deportment were more susceptible to charges of witchcraft can be found in: Karen Jones and Michael Zell, '"The Divels Speciall Instruments": Women and Witchcraft before the "Great Witch-Hunt"', in *Social History*, 30/1 (2005): 45–63, and Frances Timbers, 'Witches' Sect or Prayer meeting?: Matthew Hopkins Revisited', in *Women's History Review*, 17/1 (2008): 21–37. For a historicist view of prosecution which suggests that each witchcraft accusation/trial was different and therefore the extent to which gender issues drove it varied from case to case: Alison Rowlands, 'Witchcraft and Old Women in Early Modern Germany', in *Past and Present*, 173/1 (2001): 79–85. For witch trials and the 'witch family': Alison Rowlands, 'Gender, Ungodly Parents, and a "Witch Family" in Seventeenth-Century Germany', in *Past and Present*, 232/1 (2016): 45–86; Lauren Martin, 'Witchcraft and Family: What can Witchcraft Documents tells us about Early Modern Scottish Family Life?', in *Scottish Tradition*, 27 (2002): 7–17; Gustav Henningsen, *The Witches Advocate: Basque Witchcraft and the Spanish Inquisition, 1609–1614* (Reno, 1980): 197; Kateryna Dysa, 'A Family Matter: The Case of a Witch Family in an Eighteenth-Century Volhynian Town', in *Russian History*, 40 (2013): 352–63; and Deborah Willis, 'The Witch Family in Elizabethan and Jacobean Print Culture', in *Journal of Early Modern Cultural Studies*, 13/1 (2013), 4–31. For children and witch trials: Liv Helene Willumsen, 'Children Accused of Witchcraft in Seventeenth-Century Finnmark', in *Scandinavian Journal of History*,

38/1 (2013): 18–41; Goodare, *European Witch-hunt*: 152, 292–5; Lyndal Roper, *Witch-Craze* (Bodmin, 2004), chapters 8–9; Almond, *Lancashire Witches*: 57–61, 69–70, 132–6; Nicole J. Bettlé, 'Child-Witches', in *Routledge History of Witchcraft*: 233–43.

The most straightforward discussion of angel belief in early modern Europe (including Ireland) can be found in: Peter Marshall and Alexandra Walsham (eds), *Angels in the Early Modern World* (Cambridge, 2006). The best guide to the 'moral universe' in Ireland is in Gillespie's *Devoted People*. No study has as yet been produced of the French Prophets in Ireland, but for their activities in England: Lionel Laborie, *Enlightening Enthusiasm: Prophecy and Religious Experience in Early Eighteenth-century England* (Manchester, 2015); Clarke Garrett, *Spirit Possession and Popular Religion: from the Camisards to the Shakers* (Baltimore, 1997); Hillel Schwartz, *Knaves, Fools, Madmen and that Subtile Effluvium: a Study of the Opposition to the French Prophets in England, 1706–1710* (Gainesville, 1978); and idem., *The French Prophets: the History of a Millenarian Group in Eighteenth-Century England* (University of California Press, 1980). For readable, scholarly books on fairy belief in Britain and Ireland: Angela Bourke, *The Burning of Bridget Cleary* (London, 1999), chapter 2; Simon Young and Ceri Houlbrook (eds), *Magical Folk: British and Irish Fairies, 500 AD to the Present* (London, 2018); Richard Sugg, *Fairies: A Dangerous History* (London, 2018); Lizanne Henderson, Edward J. Cowan, *Scottish Fairy Belief* (East Linton, 2001, repr. 2004); and Peter Narváez (ed), *The Good People: New Fairylore Essays* (New York, 1991).

Chapter 5

For county gaols in England see Sharpe, *Crime in Early Modern England*: 46–7. For an overview of law enforcement in Ireland, see the work of Dr Neal Garnham in the further reading section for chapter 8; while a good introduction to the army in eighteenth-century Ireland can be found in: Thomas Bartlett, 'Army and Society in Eighteenth-Century Ireland', in W.A. Maguire (ed.), *Kings in Conflict: The Revolutionary War in Ireland and its Aftermath, 1689–1750* (Belfast, 1990): 173–84. For a readable overview of the Irish economy in the eighteenth century, see David Dickson, *New Foundations: Ireland, 1660–1800* (Dublin, 2nd ed., 2004), chapter 4. For descriptions of famine-prone, early eighteenth-century Ireland, see: James Kelly, 'Harvests and Hardship: Famine and scarcity in Ireland in the late 1720s', in *Studia Hibernica*, xxvi (1991–92): 65–105. For a study which ponders how the Irish Protestant Ascendancy reacted to widespread poverty and economic downturn, see: Patrick Kelly, 'The Politics of Political Economy in mid Eighteenth-Century Ireland', in S.J. Connolly (ed.), *Political Ideas in Eighteenth-Century Ireland* (Dublin, 2000): 105–29. For a collection of essays dealing with the political, social and cultural aspects of early modern Irish towns in a comparative light, see: Peter Borsay and Lindsay Proudfoot (eds), *Provincial Towns in Early Modern England and Ireland: Change, Convergence, and Divergence* (Oxford, 2002). The best local history of Carrickfergus remains Samuel McSkimin's *The History and Antiquities of the County of the Town of Carrickfergus in Four Parts* ... (Belfast, 1st ed., 1811).

For families who fought for their loved ones in the face of witchcraft accusations: Malcolm Gaskill, *Crime and Mentalities in Early Modern England* (Cambridge, 2000): 51–2, and Robin Briggs, *Witches & Neighbours: The Social and Cultural Context of European Witchcraft* (Oxford, 2nd ed., 2002): 197.

Chapter 6

For an erudite and nuanced discussion of the problem of the imposition of historians' view of reality onto supernatural events that occurred in the past, see Malcolm Gaskill, 'The Pursuit of Reality: Recent Research in the History of Witchcraft', in *Historical Journal*, 51/4 (2008): 1083–6. The problem with retrospective diagnoses of early modern disease is discussed in John Thielmann, 'Disease or Disability? The Conceptual Relationship in Medieval and Early Modern England', in Wendy J. Turner and Tory Vandeventer Pearman (eds), *The Treatment of Disabled Persons in Medieval Europe* ... (Lewiston, New York, 2010): 200–1, and Jon Arrizabalaga, 'Problematizing Retrospective Diagnosis in the History of Disease', in *Ascelpio*, 54 (2002): 55–67. Brian Levack tackles this problem in relation to possession cases in Levack, *Devil Within*: 26–9, 129–38.

For further reading on demonic possession, see chapter 2: the works of Phillip Almond, Brian Levack and James Sharpe have proven especially useful when writing this chapter. For research that applies modern diagnostic models in nuanced and interesting ways to more fully understand the symptoms of victims in early modern demonic possession and witchcraft cases: Andrew Pickering, 'Great News from the West of England: Witchcraft and Strange Vomiting in a Somerset Village', in *Magic, Ritual, and Witchcraft*, 13/1 (2018): 71–97; Kirsten C. Uszkalo, *Bewitched and Bedevilled: A Cognitive Approach to Embodiment in Early English Possession* (New York, 2015); Edward Bever, *The Realities of Witchcraft and Popular Magic in Early Modern Europe: Culture, Cognition, and Everyday Life* (London, 2008). See also: Almond, *Demonic Possession*: 33 (eating disorders); Sands, *Demon Possession in Elizabethan England*: 76, 155–6, 203 (pica, various mental health issues, including 'psychic epidemics', and diabetes); and Linda R. Caporael, 'Ergotism: The Satan loosed in Salem?', in *Science*, New Series, 192/4234 (1976): 21–6 (ergot poising). For how the medical diagnoses of seventeenth-century English physicians involved in possession cases were manipulated and influenced by family members and local communities, see Judith Bonzol, 'The Medical Diagnosis of Demonic Possession in an Early Modern community', in *Parergon*, 26/1 (2009): 115–40. For a discussion of contemporary medical explanations of symptoms of possession, see: Levack, *Devil Within*: 115–29; Almond, *Demonic Possession*: 2–7; and Ronald C. Sawyer, 'Strangely Handled in All Her Lyms: Witchcraft and Healing in Jacobean England', in *Social History*, 22/3 (1989): 461–85. The latter study in particular provides an overview of which illnesses were most likely to be attributed to witchcraft. For an article which places post-1660 medical debates concerning witchcraft in the context of wider scientific debates, see: Garfield Tourney, 'The Physician and Witchcraft in Restoration England', in *Medical History*, 16/2 (1972): 143–55; while Peter Elmer discusses how non-conformist physicians dealt with possession cases in the period 1660–1700 in 'Medicine, Witchcraft and the Politics of Healing in Late-Seventeenth-Century England', in Ole Peter Grell and Andrew Cunnigham (eds), *Medicine and Religion in Enlightenment Europe* (Aldershot, 2007): 237–40. James Sharpe, in *Instruments of Darkness*: 10–1, 271, suggests that Church of England physicians in the same period were backing away from supernatural diagnoses in bewitchment and possession cases by the latter half of the seventeenth century.

There are numerous works which suggest that demoniacs were able to counterfeit their symptoms by reading published accounts of other possession cases, see: Levack, *Devil Within*: 23–6; idem., *Witch-Hunting in Scotland*: 115–28; Maxwell-Stuart, 'Witchcraft and Magic in Eighteenth-Century Scotland': 84–5; Sharpe, *Anne Gunter*: 7–8, 62–3. For a discussion of famous impostures, and in particular the theatricality of possession, see Almond, *Demonic Possession*: 15, 38–41; Levack, *Devil Within*: 141–68. P.G. Maxwell-Stuart in chapter 4 of *Witch-Hunters* focuses on the Patrick Morton case of 1704 in a detailed and refreshing way. For works which suggest possession was a way for otherwise marginalised demoniacs to attract attention or escape the social and cultural bonds of a strict upbringing, see Almond, *Demonic Possession*: 14–5, 22–6; Sharpe, 'Disruption and Possessed Young People': 118–9; Levack, *Witch-hunt in early modern Europe*: 139–40.

Malcolm Gaskill examines how the stereotyping of witches influenced judicial procedure in *Crime and Mentalities*: 37–40, 46–9, while authors who argue that women who failed to meet male standards were more susceptible to witchcraft accusation are discussed in the further reading section for chapter 4. The importance of reputation in relation to witchcraft accusations and trials has been noted by Sharpe, *Witchcraft in Early Modern England*: 45; Gaskill, *Crime and Mentalities*: 57–8; and Rowlands, 'Witchcraft and Old Women in Early Modern Germany'.

The study of disability in early witchcraft and popular magic is in its infancy, but see: Scott Eaton, 'Witchcraft and Deformity in early modern English literature', in *The Seventeenth Century*, 35/6 (2020): 815–28; and Andrew Sneddon, *Disability and Magic in Early Modern Britain and America* (forthcoming, Cambridge University Press). The study of disability in the early modern period is still weighted towards literary rather than historical studies but the following work is highly recommended: Douglas C. Baynton, 'Disability: A Useful Category of Historical Analysis', in *Disability Studies Quarterly*, 17/2 (1997): 81–7; Alison P. Hobgood and Davis Houston Wood (eds), *Recovering Disability in Early Modern England* (Columbus, 2013); David M. Turner, *Disability in Eighteenth-Century England: Imagining Physical Impairment* (Abingdon, 2012); Catherine J. Kudlick, 'Disability History: Why We Need Another "Other"', in *The American Historical Review*, 108/3 (2003): 763–93; David M. Turner, Kevin Stagg (eds), *Social Histories of Disability and Deformity* (Abingdon, 2006).

For an overview of the medical profession and practice in seventeenth- and eighteenth-century Ireland, see Fiona Clark and James Kelly (eds), *Ireland and Medicine in the Seventeenth and Eighteenth-Centuries* (Farnham, 2010), especially the introduction by the editors and articles by Toby Barnard, James Kelly and Laurence Brockliss. See also: John Cunningham (ed), *Early Modern Ireland and the World of Medicine: Practitioners, Collectors and Contexts* (Manchester, 2019); James Kelly, 'The Emergence of Scientific and Institutional Medical Practice in Ireland, 1650–1800', in Greta Jones, Elizabeth Malcolm (eds), *Medicine, Disease and the State in Ireland* (Cork, 1999): 21–39; idem., 'Bleeding, Vomiting and Purging:

The Medical Response to Ill-Health in Eighteenth-Century Ireland', in Catherine Cox and Maria Luddy (eds), *Cultures of Care in Irish Medical History, 1750–1970* (Basingstoke, 2010): 13–36; and Barnard, *A New Anatomy of Ireland*: 129–42. For an overview of the Presbyterian medical profession in Ulster, see: Whan, 'Presbyterians in Ulster': 188–21, while Roman Catholic physicians in Dublin are detailed in Patrick Fagan, *Catholics in a Protestant Country: The Papist Constituency in Eighteenth-Century Dublin* (Dublin, 1998): 77–100. The best overview of the first charitable hospitals in Ireland can be found in Laurence M. Geary, *Medicine and Charity in Ireland, 1718–1851* (Dublin, 2004), chapter 1.

For an exceptional study of the life of a gentry-woman in mid-eighteenth-century Ireland, see: S.J. Connolly, 'A Woman's Life in Mid-Eighteenth-Century Ireland: The Case of Letitia Bushe', in *Historical Journal*, 43/2 (2000): 433–51. This author has also suggested relationships between children and parents in Ireland in our period were warmer than once thought, see: 'Family, Love and Marriage: Some Evidence from the Early Eighteenth-Century', in Margaret MacCurtain and Mary O'Dowd (eds), *Women in Early Modern Ireland* (Edinburgh, 1991): 276–8, 284–8. For a reappraisal of the family in early modern England, see Helen Barry and Elizabeth Foyster (eds), *The Family in Early Modern England* (Cambridge, 2007), especially chapters 1 and 9.

Chapter 7

Some recent work has subsumed cunning-folk and ritual magicians into the larger category of 'service magician' by categorising practitioners according to their function (the services they provided) rather than their methodologies (how they did it) or education levels: for example, Tabitha Stanmore, 'Magic as a Useful Category of Historical Analysis', in *History*, 106/370 (2021): 204–20. 'Service magician' is a term coined by Ronald Hutton to describe magical practitioners across time, continents, and countries who provide a useful magical service for others for a fee, whether this was payment in kind, money, or favours redeemable at a future date. This includes cunning-folk, 'medicine' men or women, or witch-doctors: Hutton, *The Witch*: xi. I have used cunning-folk in this book and maintained the distinction between them and ritual magicians as they differed not only in terms of learning and methodology but also in social position. This in its turn determined the fees they could charge, which had a bearing on where they lived, where and how they worked, the social circles they moved in, and the type of client they could attract.

For an excellent overview of popular magic in the early modern period: Owen Davies, 'The World of Popular Magic', in *Oxford Illustrated History of Witchcraft*: 167–94. For cunning-folk and the countermeasures taken against witches and witchcraft in early modern England, see: Sharpe, *Instruments of Darkness*: 66–70, 86–7, 155–62; and Macfarlane, *Witchcraft in Tudor and Stuart England*, chapter 8. The best overview of cunning-folk and popular magic is: Owen Davies, *Popular Magic in English History* (London, 2003, repr. 2007); and idem., *Witchcraft, Magic and Culture, 1736–1951*, chapter 6. For the later eighteenth century, see: Stephanie Elizabeth Churms, *Romanticism and Popular Magic: Poetry and Cultures of the Occult in the 1790s* (Cham, 2019). These books are best read in conjunction with the pioneering work of Keith Thomas in *Religion and the Decline of Magic*, chapters 7 and 8. Emma Wilby in *Cunning Folk and Familiar Spirits: Shamanistic Visionary Traditions in Early Modern British Witchcraft and Magic* (Eastbourne, 2005, repr, 2010), examines the use of 'fairy familiars' by cunning-folk and suggests that this represents the folkloric root of the witch's familiar. For a critique of Wilby's thesis: Henderson, *Witchcraft and Folk Belief*: 122, and Malcom Gaskill, 'The Pursuit of Reality: Recent Research into the History of Witchcraft': 1083–5.

For popular magic and cunning-folk in early modern and modern Ireland: Sneddon, *Witchcraft and Magic in Ireland*, chapters 3 and 7; idem., *Representing Magic;* idem., 'Popular Religion in Ireland, 1822–1922', in Gladys Ganiel, Andrew Holmes (eds), *Oxford Handbook of Religion in Modern Ireland* (Oxford University Press, 2024); idem., 'Fortune Telling in Enlightenment Ireland, 1691–1840', in Michael Lynn (ed.), *Magic, Witchcraft and Ghosts in the Enlightenment* (Routledge, 2022); and Andrew Sneddon, John Fulton, 'Witchcraft, the Press and Crime in Ireland, 1822–1922', in *The Historical Journal*, 62/3 (2019): 741–64.

For charms and charming (magical healing) in Ireland: Leanne Calvert, 'Curing a Woman in Childbed: Charms and Magical Healing in Eighteenth-century Templepatrick, County Antrim', in Salvador Ryan (ed.), *Birth and the Irish: an Miscellany* (Dublin, 2021): 73–6; Andrew Sneddon, 'Gender, Folklore and Magical Healing in Ireland, 1852–1922', in Jyoti Atwal, Ciara Breathnach, Sarah-Ann Buckley (eds), *Gender and History: Ireland 1852–1922* (Abingdon, 2023): 104–16; Nicholas Wolf, 'Orthaí and Orthodoxy: Healing Charms in Irish Popular Religion', in Michael De Nie, Sean Farrell (eds.), *Power and Popular Culture in Modern Ireland: Essays in Honour of James S. Donnelly* (Dublin, 2010): 125–44; Ronnie Moore and Stuart McClean (eds.), *Folk Healing and Health Care Practices in Britain and Ireland: Stethoscopes, Wands and Crystals* (Oxford, 2010), especially chapters by Ronnie Moore and Catherine Cox; Meredith B. Linn, 'Irish Immigrant Healing Magic in Nineteenth-Century New York City', in *Historical Archaeology*, 48/3 (2014): 144–65; Barbara Hillers, Ciarán Ó Gealbháin, Ilona Tuomi and John Carey (eds.), *Charms, Charmers and Charming in Ireland: From the Medieval to the Modern* (Melksham, 2019); Ronan Foley, 'Indigenous Narratives of Health: (Re)Placing Folk-Medicine within Irish Health Histories', in *Journal of Medical Humanities*, 18 (2015): 5–18. For a discussion of the Cailleach and its place in Irish folk tradition: Gearóid, Ó Crualaoich, *The Book of the Cailleach: Stories of the Wise-Woman Healer* (Cork, 2003, repr. 2015); and Shane Lehane, 'The Cailleach and the Cosmic Hare', in *Charms, Charmers and Charming in Ireland:* 189–204. For magic and supernatural belief in nineteenth- and twentieth-century Northern Ireland and the Republic of Ireland: Richard Jenkins, *Black Magic and Bogeymen: Fear, Rumour and Popular Belief in the North of Ireland, 1972–4* (Cork, 2014); idem., 'The Transformations of Biddy Early: from Local Reports of Magical Healing to Globalised New Age Fantasy', in *Folklore*, 118/2 (2007): 162–82; Ciaran McDonough, 'Folk Belief and Landscape in Connacht: Accounts from the Ordnance Survey letters', in *Folk Life*, 57/1 (2019): 56–69; Anthony D. Buckley, 'Unofficial Healing in Ulster', in *Ulster Folklife*, 26 (1980): 15–34.

To confuse matters, 'charmer' in early modern Scotland is often used to refer not to magical healers but to cunning-folk. For guidance on how to differentiate between the two: Owen Davies, 'A Comparative Perspective on Scottish Cunning-Folk', in *Witchcraft and Belief in*

Early Modern Scotland: 185–205. However, for a study that conflates cunning-folk with magical healing: Joyce Millar, 'Devices and Directions: Folk Healing Aspects of Witchcraft Practice in Seventeenth-Century Scotland', in *Scottish Witch-Hunt in Context*: 92–105. For charmers in late seventeenth- and early eighteenth-century Scotland, see: Henderson, *Witchcraft and Folk Belief*: 107–16, 121–3 (for magical healers, see 116–21). For charms and charming and its relationship to witch trials and fairy belief: Henderson, Cowan, *Scottish Fairy Belief*: 78, 87–8, 96–100, 127–31. For the material culture of charms: Hugh Cheape, 'From Natural to Supernatural: The Material Culture of Charms and Amulets', in Lizanne Henderson (ed.), *Fantastical Imaginations: The Supernatural in Scottish History and Culture* (Edinburgh, 2009): 70–90.

For a classic study of popular magic in continental Europe, see: Robin Briggs, 'Circling the Devil: Witch-Doctors and Magical Healers in Early Modern Lorraine', in Stuart Clark (ed.), *Languages of Witchcraft: Narrative, Ideology and Meaning in Early Modern Culture* (Basingstoke, 2001): 101–88; and idem., *Witches and Neighbours*, chapter 5. For a more international approach: Jonathan Roper (ed.), *Charms, Charmers, and Charming: International Research on Verbal Magic* (Basingstoke, 2009). Cunning-folk also operated in seventeenth-century New England where they specialised in fortune-telling, folk medicine and counter-magic: Godbeer, *The Devil's Dominion: Magic and Religion in Early Modern New England*: 7, 24, 30–47.

For shape-shifting witches, see Hutton, *The Witch*: 277, 268–9; Briggs, *Witches and Neighbours*: 91; Davies, *Witchcraft, Magic and Culture*: 189–90; and Almond, *Lancashire Witches*: 77–9, 111–3, 119. The Church of Ireland's response to Presbyterian education can be found in chapter 5 of J.C. Beckett, *Protestant Dissent in Ireland, 1697–1780* (1948, repr. London, 2008); Whan, 'Presbyterians': chapter 1, part 2; and Ian McBride, 'Presbyterianism in the Penal Era': 15. For linen production in Ulster, see Connolly, *Divided Kingdom*: 351–8, and Bardon, *Ulster*: 179–82. For Swift's time in Kilroot, see Irvin Ehrenpreis, *Swift, the Man, His Works, and the Age*, i, chapter 6; and Louis A. Landa, *Swift and the Church of Ireland* (Oxford, 1954): 8–24.

Chapter 8

This chapter draws extensively on the work of Dr Neal Garnham: Neal Garnham, 'How Violent was Eighteenth-Century Ireland?', in *Irish Historical Studies*, 30/119 (1997): 377–92; idem., *The Militia in Eighteenth-Century Ireland: In Defence of the Protestant Interest* (Woodbridge, 2012); idem., 'The Criminal Law 1692–1760: England and Ireland Compared', in S.J. Connolly (ed.), *Kingdoms United? Great Britain and Ireland since 1500* (Dublin, 1999): 215–24; idem., *The Courts, Crime and the Criminal Law in Ireland 1692–1760* (Dublin, 1996); idem., 'Local Elite Creation in Early Hanoverian Ireland: The Case of the County Grand Juries', in *Historical Journal*, 42/3 (1999): 623–43. See also: Andrea Knox, 'Female Criminality and Subversion in Early Modern Ireland', in *Journal of Criminal Justice History*, 17 (2000).

Chapter 9

For the early phase of the English Enlightenment: Knights, *Devil in Disguise,* and Roy Porter, *Enlightenment: Britain and the Creation of the Modern World* (London, 2000), chapters 1–11. For the idea that the enlightenment manifested in a naturalisation of outlook that removed the cultural and intellectual context in which educated belief in witchcraft thrived: Sharpe, *Instruments of Darkness,* chapter 11. For work that separates the decline in belief from trials in both chronological and causal terms, and suggests that witchcraft belief was marginalised within educated culture for political reasons during the Whig and Tory 'Rage of Party' of Queen Anne's reign (1702–14): Ian Bostridge, *Witchcraft and its Transformations* (Oxford, 1997), chapters 5–7; and idem., 'Witchcraft Repealed', in Brian Levack (ed.), *New Perspectives on Witchcraft, Magic and Demonology: Witchcraft in the British Isles and New England* (New York, 2001): 341–66. Peter Elmer took this position further by arguing that political partisanship became institutionalised in England in the 1680s and peaked during the 'Rage of Party', ensuring support for witchcraft dwindled and the few trials that were held became highly politicised and increasingly associated with those excluded from mainstream politics. This development reached maturity in the early years of the Whig and Hanoverian Ascendancy (after 1715) when witchcraft became completely marginalised within mainstream elite culture and was now widely seen as fanatical, enthusiastic, and ideologically redundant: Peter Elmer, *Witchcraft, Witch-Hunting, and Politics in Early Modern England,* chapters 6–7. For the party politicisation of witchcraft during the Jane Wenham Trial of 1712, see Knights, *Devil in Disguise*: 213–7, 220–40. The best overview of the case, and the pamphlet debate that followed, remains Guskin, 'Jane Wenham': 48–7. In my book, *Witchcraft and Whigs: the Life of Bishop Francis Hutchinson* (Manchester, 2008), chapter 5, I suggest that educated scepticism towards witchcraft in early eighteenth-century England had been overestimated and that leading Whigs, such as Bishop Francis Hutchinson, turned away from it not only because it clashed with their Whiggish cultural and social ideology but because they had witnessed at first hand the human cost of trials. Michael Hunter takes a different view by suggesting that the half-hearted scepticism displayed towards witchcraft in the early eighteenth century by moderate, educated elites such as Bishop Hutchinson was not party political in orientation, but a consequence of the fact that outright disbelief in witchcraft had in previous decades become associated with radicalism and 'free-thinking': 'The Decline of Magic: Challenge and Response in Early Enlightenment England', in *The Historical Journal,* 55/2 (2012): 399–425; idem., *Decline of Magic.*

For decline in educated belief in Scotland and Europe: Edward Bever, 'Witchcraft Prosecutions and the Decline of Magic', in *Journal of Interdisciplinary History,* 40/2 (2009): 263–93; Brian P. Levack, 'The Decline and End of Witchcraft Prosecutions', in *Oxford Handbook of Witchcraft*: 429–46; Michael Wasser, 'The Mechanical World-View and the Decline of Witch Belief in Scotland', in *Witchcraft and Belief in Early Modern Scotland*: 206–26; Henderson, *Witchcraft and Folk Belief in Scotland*: 188–9, 327; Maxwell-Stuart, 'Witchcraft and Magic in Scotland': 81–95. For decline in belief in Ireland: Sneddon, *Witchcraft in Ireland,* chapters 2, 6–7. For the argument that both Catholic and Protestant dissenters were reluctant in England to reject traditional demonological beliefs: Francis Young, *English Catholics and the Supernatural, 1553–1829* (Farnham, 2013), chapter 5; Owen

Davies, 'Methodism, the Clergy, and Popular Belief in Witchcraft and Magic', in *History*, 82 (1997): 252–65. For more on continuation of belief among the mass of the population, see further reading for chapter 10.

A discussion of the effects of myths and memory on Presbyterians' sense of community in this period, see: Ian McBride, 'Ulster Presbyterianism and the Confessional state 1688–1733', in D. George Boyle, Robert Eccleshall and Vincent Geoghegan (eds), *Political Discourse in Seventeenth and Eighteenth-Century Ireland* (Basingstoke, 2001): 169–92. For the Tory, High Church of Ireland backlash against Presbyterianism, especially during the reign of Queen Anne: David Hayton, 'The Development and Limitations of Protestant Ascendancy: the Church of Ireland Laity in Public Life, 1660–1740', in Raymond Gillespie and W.G. Nealy (eds), *The Laity and the Church of Ireland, 1000–2000: all Sorts and Conditions* (Dublin, 2002): 118–21; idem., 'Presbyterians and the Confessional State: The Sacramental Test as an Issue in Irish Politics, 1704–80', in *Bulletin of the Presbyterian Historical Society of Ireland*, 26 (1997): 11–31; idem., *Ruling Ireland*, chapter 4; Ian McBride, 'Presbyterians in the Penal Era', in *Bulletin of the Presbyterian Historical Society of Ireland*, 27 (1998–2000): 14–28; Armstrong, 'Of Stories and Sermons': 215–31; David Kennedy, 'The Early Eighteenth Century', in J.C. Beckett, R.E. Glasscock (eds), *Belfast: the Origin and Growth of an Industrial City* (London, 1967): 41–5. For party political conflict in Ireland: McBride, *Eighteenth-Century Ireland*: 296–8; Patrick McInally, *Parties, Patriots and Undertakers: Parliamentary Politics in Early Hanoverian England* (Dublin, 1997), chapters 3 and 4; idem., 'The Hanoverian Accession and the Tory Party', in *Parliamentary History*, 14/3 (1996): 263–83; David Hayton, 'Tories and Whigs in County Cork, 1714', in *Journal of the Cork Historical and Archaeological Society* (2nd series), lxxx (1975): 84–8; idem., 'The Crisis in Ireland and the Disintegration of Queen Anne's Last Ministry', in *Irish Historical Studies*, 22/87 (1981): 193–215; J.G. Simms, 'The Irish Parliament of 1713', in G.A. Hayes-McCoy (ed.), *Historical Studies*, iv (London, 1963): 82–92.

Chapter 10

For work that regards male witches as collateral damage in witch hunts directed primarily at women, or as victims guilty by association with female witches: Macfarlane, *Witchcraft in Tudor and Stuart England*: 160; Demos, *Entertaining Satan*: 60–2; Carol Karlsen, *The Devil in the Shape of a Woman: Witchcraft in Colonial New England* (New York, 1987): 47–52; Sharpe, *Instruments of Darkness*: 188. For research that suggests male witches in England and in colonial America were feminised to fit the stereotype of the female witch: Jane Kamensky, 'Talk Like a Man: Speech, Power and Masculinity in Early New England', in *Gender and History*, 8/1 (1996): 35–7; Laura Apps and Andrew Gow, *Male Witches in early modern Europe* (Manchester, 2003): 127–37.

For more recent studies that critique this historiography using more recent work on early modern gender and masculinity: Rowlands, *Witchcraft and Masculinities in Early Modern Europe*, chapters 1, 3, 6, 7; E.J. Kent, 'Masculinity and Male Witches in Old and New England, 1593–1680', in *History Workshop Journal*, 60/1 (2005): 69–92; Rolf Schulte, *Man as Witch: Male Witches in Central Europe* (Basingstoke, 2009); Robert Walinski-Kiehl, 'Males, "Masculine Honour," and Witch Hunting in Seventeenth-Century Germany', in *Men and Masculinities*, 6/3 (2004): 254–71. In her study of German witch trials Laura Kounine warns against the tendency in this work to use gendered binaries of masculinity and femininity to create categories of 'bad' men and 'bad' women to identify individuals most likely to be accused of witchcraft. She argues that gender and what constituted the witch and witchcraft in the early modern period were far more fluid, contested, unstable and reliant on context: Laura Kounine, 'The Gendering of Witchcraft: Defence Strategies of Men and Women in German Witchcraft Trials', in *German History*, 31/3 (2013): 295–317. For recent work that downplays the role of gender in early modern English witchcraft by suggesting that witches in popular representations (for example in popular pamphlets) were not defined by their gender but their association with the devil: Charlotte-Rose Millar, 'Diabolical Men: Reintegrating Male Witches into English Witchcraft', in *The Seventeenth Century*, 36/5 (2021): 693–713.

Chapter 11

For belief in, and practice of, beneficial magic in modern Ireland see Further Reading section for chapter 7. For more on the various ways in witchcraft was represented in modern Irish folklore, from the elderly, supernatural 'hag' figure to the butter-and-milk-stealing witch: Lehane, 'Cailleach and the Cosmic Hare'; McDonough, 'Folk Belief and Landscape in Connacht'; Ó Crualaoich, *Book of the Cailleach*; Críostóir MacCárthaigh, 'The Ship-Sinking Witch: A Maritime Folk Legend from North-West Europe', in *Béaloideas*, 60/61 (1992): 267–86; and Ray Cashman, 'Neighborliness and Decency, Witchcraft and Famine: Reflections on Community from Irish Folklore', in *Journal of American Folklore*, 134/531 (2021): 79–100. For work witchcraft and harmful magic in nineteenth- and twentieth-century Ireland that uses a range of original sources including folklore, church and court records, newspapers, memoir, correspondence, and objects of material culture: Hutton, *The Witch*: 251–2, 256; Sneddon, *Witchcraft and Magic in Ireland*, chapter 6; idem., *Representing Magic*: 10–25; idem., 'Witchcraft Representation and Memory in Modern Ireland'. The latter article deals specifically with continuing belief in nineteenth- and twentieth-century Islandmagee.

For continuing belief in witchcraft and harmful magic in modern Britain, America, and the Isle of Man, including criminal proceedings arising from informal witch accusations: Hutton, 'Changing Faces of Manx Witchcraft'; Suggett, *History of Magic and Witchcraft in Wales*: 128–33, 142–54; Davies, *Witchcraft, Magic and Culture*; idem., *The Supernatural War: Magic, Divination, and Faith* (Oxford, 2018); idem., 'Newspapers and the Popular Belief in Witchcraft and Magic in the Modern Period', in *Journal of British Studies*, 37/2 (1998): 139–65; Thomas Waters, *Cursed Britain: A History of Witchcraft and Black Magic in Modern Times* (New Haven, 2019); idem., 'Belief in Witchcraft in Oxfordshire and Warwickshire, c.1860–1900: the Evidence of the Newspaper Archive', in *Midland History*, 34/1 (2009): 103–5; idem., 'Maleficent Witchcraft in Britain since 1900', in *History Workshop Journal*, 80/1 (2015): 99–122; Henderson, *Witchcraft and Folk Belief*: 312–3. For continuing belief in modern America: Owen Davies, *America Bewitched: the Story of Witchcraft after Salem* (Oxford, 2013). For research on reverse witch trials, when accusers were prosecuted for assaulting a suspected witch, usually after performing an aggressive or violent type of counter spell such as 'scratching' (when the accused were scratched or cut to draw blood): Owen Davies,

'Researching Reverse Witch Trials in Nineteenth- and Early Twentieth-Century England', in Jonathan Barry, Owen Davies, and Cornelie Usborne (eds), *Cultures of Witchcraft in Europe from the Middle Ages to the Present* (Basingstoke, 2018): 215–33. For crimes involving witchcraft (including reverse witch trials) in modern Ireland: Sneddon, Fulton, 'Witchcraft, the Press, and Crime in Ireland, 1822–1922'.

For witchcraft in modern Europe: Owen Davies and Willem de Blécourt (eds), *Beyond the Witch Trials: Witchcraft and Magic in Enlightenment Europe* (Manchester, 2004); Willem De Blécourt, 'On the Continuation of Witchcraft', in Jonathan Barry, Marianne Hester, and Gareth Roberts (eds), *Witchcraft in Early Modern Europe* (Cambridge, 1996): 335–52; Marijke Gijswijt-Hofstra, 'Witchcraft after the Witch Trials', in Marijke Gijswijt-Hofstra and Roy Porter (eds), *Witchcraft and Magic in Europe: Eighteenth and Nineteenth Centuries* (London, 1999): 97–188. For a classic study of the emergence of self-identifying witches and the rise of modern pagan witchcraft, which stands in contrast to the harmful witchcraft studied in this book: Ronald Hutton, *The Triumph of the Moon: A History of Modern Pagan Witchcraft* (Oxford, 1999).

For recent research which challenges how the Salem witch trials have been interpreted and mythologised in modern times: Bernard Rosenthal, *Salem Story: Reading the Witch-Trials of 1692* (Cambridge, 1995); Davies, *America Bewitched*; Marion Gibson, *Witchcraft Myths in American Culture* (Abingdon, 2007). For creative writing and historic witch trials: Marion Gibson, *Rediscovering Renaissance Witchcraft: Witches in Early Modernity and Modernity* (Abingdon, 2018); idem., 'Retelling Salem Stories: Gender Politics and Witches in American Culture', *European Journal of American Culture*, 25/2 (2006): 85–107; Diane Purkiss, *The Witch in History: Early Modern and Twentieth Century Representations* (London, 1996); Jonathan Barry, *Raising Spirits: How a Conjuror's Tale was Transmitted across the Enlightenment* (Basingstoke, 2013). For how historians, journalists, and creative writers reinterpreted and reimagined the case of the Islandmagee witches in the nineteenth and twentieth centuries: Sneddon, 'Witchcraft Representation and Memory in Modern Ireland': 259–63; idem., *Representing Magic*: 26–64 (see 54–9 for a detailed discussion of Olga Fielden's 'Witches in Eden'). For a discussion of how the trials have been commemorated: Andrew Sneddon, 'Social Remembrance, Social Forgetting and Commemoration: The Public History of Witch Trials in Divided Societies with Contested Pasts', in Marion Gibson (ed), *Emplaced Belief: Heritage & Religion Reconsidered* (Berghann, *forthcoming*).

Index